CHEVROLET V8
ENGINE REBUILDING MANUAL

CHILTON'S

Senior Vice President	Ronald A. Hoxter
Publisher & Editor-In-Chief	Kerry A. Freeman, S.A.E.
Executive Editors	Dean F. Morgantini, S.A.E., W. Calvin Settle, Jr., S.A.E.
Managing Editor	Nick D'Andrea
Senior Editors	Jacques Gordon, Michael L. Grady, Ben Greisler, S.A.E., Debra McCall, Kevin M. G. Maher, Richard J. Rivele, S.A.E., Richard T. Smith, Jim Taylor, Ron Webb
Project Managers	Martin J. Gunther, Will Kessler, A.S.E., Richard Schwartz
Production Manager	Andrea Steiger
Product Systems Manager	Robert Maxey
Director of Manufacturing	Mike D'Imperio
Authors	Ron Webb and Rich Rivele

CHILTON BOOK COMPANY

ONE OF THE **DIVERSIFIED PUBLISHING COMPANIES**,
A PART OF **CAPITAL CITIES/ABC, INC.**

Manufactured in USA
© 1996 Chilton Book Company
Chilton Way, Radnor, PA 19089
ISBN 0-8019-8794-6
Library of Congress Catalog Card No. 96-83977
1234567890 5432109876

1471701

ntents

Contents

GLOSSARY

MASTER INDEX

SAFETY NOTICE

Proper service and repair procedures are vital to the safe, reliable operation of all motor vehicles, as well as the personal safety of those performing repairs. This manual outlines procedures for servicing and repairing vehicles using safe, effective methods. The procedures contain many NOTES, CAUTIONS and WARNINGS which should be followed along with standard procedures to eliminate the possibility of personal injury or improper service which could damage the vehicle or compromise its safety.

It is important to note that the repair procedures and techniques, tools and parts for servicing motor vehicles, as well as the skill and experience of the individual performing the work vary widely. It is not possible to anticipate all of the conceivable ways or conditions under which vehicles may be serviced, or to provide cautions as to all of the possible hazards that may result. Standard and accepted safety precautions and equipment should be used when handling toxic or flammable fluids, and safety goggles or other protection should be used during cutting, grinding, chiseling, prying, or any other process that can cause material removal or projectiles.

Some procedures require the use of tools specially designed for a specific purpose. Before substituting another tool or procedure, you must be completely satisfied that neither your personal safety, nor the performance of the vehicle will be endangered.

Although information in this manual is based on industry sources and is complete as possible at the time of publication, the possibility exists that some car manufacturers made later changes which could not be included here. While striving for total accuracy, Chilton Book Company cannot assume responsibility for any errors, changes or omissions that may occur in the compilation of this data.

PART NUMBERS

Part numbers listed in this reference are not recommendation by Chilton for any product by brand name. They are references that can be used with interchange manuals and aftermarket supplier catalogs to locate each brand supplier's discrete part number.

SPECIAL TOOLS

Special tools are recommended by the vehicle manufacturer to perform their specific job. Use has been kept to a minimum, but where absolutely necessary, they are referred to in the text by the part number of the tool manufacturer. These tools can be purchased, under the appropriate part number, from your local dealer or regional distributor, or an equivalent tool can be purchased locally from a tool supplier or parts outlet. Before substituting any tool for the one recommended, read the SAFETY NOTICE at the top of this page.

ACKNOWLEDGMENTS

Portions of the materials contained herein have been reprinted with the permission of General Motors Corporation, Service Technology Group. The Chilton Book Company expresses appreciation to Mardinly Enterprise, Havertown, PA and The Old Car Company, Elverson, PA for their generous assistance in producing this manual.

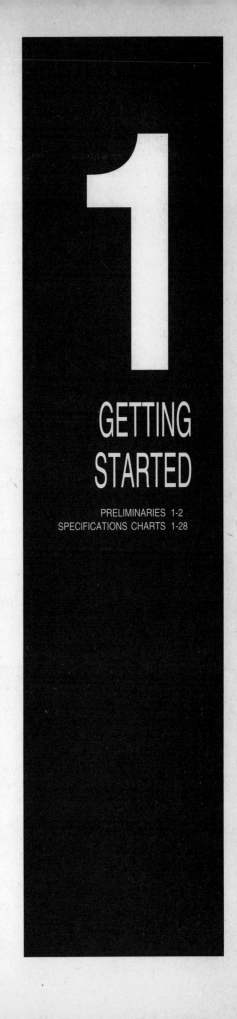

1

GETTING
STARTED

PRELIMINARIES

To Rebuild or Not to Rebuild

That's a good question. The fact that you're looking at this book means that you're seriously considering it. In most cases, people decide to rebuild as a project, not out of necessity. If you are planning the job as a project, you'll probably do a better job than if you are working under the pressure of replacing a non-working engine in a vehicle that you are forced to do without in the meantime. The more relaxed and less hurried you are, the more fun you'll have. Things that may go wrong will have less of an impact since you'll have time to correct them. Delays won't be as stressful.

We've tried to gear the writing of this book towards the average do-it-yourselfer who has no specialized mechanical knowledge. An experienced mechanic in a well equipped shop doesn't need this book. We will prepare you for the job, take you through it step-by-step and make sure that you complete your rebuild successfully.

Can You Do It?

Probably the first real question you're asking yourself is, 'Can I really do this?' The answer is, sure, why not?

You don't have to be an experienced mechanic to rebuild an engine successfully. Really! If you have a basic set of hand tools — ratchets, sockets, wrenches, feeler gauges — and are at all familiar with their use, and, if you have or can get a few special tools, you should have few, if any, real problems.

Physical strength doesn't have much of a bearing on your ability to complete the job either. There is not a lot of heavy lifting involved. A friend is always helpful for lifting items such as manifolds and cylinder heads. Besides, anyone trying to lift heavy parts without either human or mechanical help is just asking for an injury. Using your head is always better than abusing your back!

Location

Hopefully, you have a garage or workshop. You can do the job in your basement, but that's not a good idea for several reasons among which are the job of getting heavy engine parts in and out of the basement, and the presence of flammable chemicals. Therefore, this book will assume that you're working in your garage.

Now, just about any garage will do. It doesn't have to be huge or especially well equipped. If your garage is at all like most peoples' it's more a storage room than anything else. Some garages are so junked up that you can barely walk from one side to the other. So, your first job is to clean the mess up.

You're going to need a clean work area with uncluttered floor space. You're also going to need at least one good, strong workbench, the top of which should be about 3 ft. x 6 ft., at least. Also, you'll need storage shelves to handle the parts, both used and new, as you remove, clean and install them.

Cleanliness is an important factor throughout the job, as is an uncluttered floor. You're going to be working around a large heavy engine, mounted on a workstand, so you don't need anything which would cause you to trip, or knock over the engine stand. You also don't need oil and grease on the floor, which can cause an accident, or worse, which you can track into the house!

Along with space and cleanliness are:

1. At least two 5 lbs. fire extinguishers suitable for chemical and electrical fires
2. A good electrical system which can handle the load of power tools
3. Bright, comfortable lighting
4. Adequate ventilation and
5. If working in the winter, a safe heating system.

Preparing the Work Area

Okay, get rid of the junk! Most of it you don't really need and some of it you probably didn't even know you had. Have a real garage sale! I'll let you handle that. You don't need my advice. If you're like most of us, you never throw anything away, so, just close your eyes and get it over with!

Okay, you're done? Good, let's get busy!

What Type of Engine?

Obviously, since you have this book, you'll want a Chevy V8. That gives you a lot of choices! The primary determining factor will be the vehicle. If you want to do an even-up replacement, that is, you have a 305 and want to replace it with a 305, there's no decision to make. However, if you want to upgrade horsepower and torque there are several limiting factors.

1. The size of the engine compartment
2. The positions of the mounts
3. The bolt pattern of the transmission housing or clutch housing
4. The front suspension load limits, and, if you're really going up in engine size
5. The ability of the driveline and axle to take the torque

In other words, if you have a Chevy II you probably can't put a 454 in it without prohibitively expensive and time consuming work. The engine compartment, mounts, transmission, suspension, driveline and axle will all have to be altered.

However, if you have a 305 pickup, a 454 conversion isn't such a bad thing. There's plenty of engine compartment room, mount adapter kits are available and transmission adapter kits are popular as are transmissions with big block bolt patterns. Heavy duty front springs are inexpensive and the driveline should take the additional torque without modification.

Your situation will fall somewhere in that range. To help you out, there are several companies that supply engine conversion kits, the most experienced of which is Advance Adapters Inc.

Also, check your state's emission laws regarding replacement engines. The engine you install in your vehicle may have to meet the emission regulations pertaining the the year of vehicle manufacture. So, if you have a newer model car or truck and you want to rebuild and install a 327 in it, you may have to extensively modify the engine to meet the emission requirements of your vehicle; something the engine wasn't designed for.

Chevrolet Engines

◆ **See Figures 1, 2 and 3**

One of the most frequently asked questions when dealing with early Chevrolet engines is, 'What is it?' Early Chevy engines were identified by a 3-letter code stamped on the block. So, we've provided identification charts to, hopefully, clear up those questions.

As noted above, there are many different Chevy V8s, not counting those designed exclusively for medium and heavy duty trucks.

These engines range in displacement from 283 cubic inches to 454 cubic inches. Briefly, by displacement and last year manufactured, they are:

- 267, 1984
- 283, 1967
- 305, to present
- 307, 1973
- 327, 1968
- 350, to present
- 396, 1970
- 400, 1976
- 402, 1972
- 454, to present

Design

All Chevrolet engines are water cooled, overhead valve powerplants. Most engines use cast iron blocks and heads, with the exception of some high performance 454s, which use aluminum heads.

Engine Identification
1964–70

No. Cyls.	Cu. In. Displ.	Type	Year and Code						
			1964	1965	1966	1967	1968	1969	1970
8	283	3 Spd.	J	DA	DA	DA			
8	283	4 Spd.	JA	DB	DB	DB			
8	283	PG	JD	DE	DF	DE			
8	283	3 Spd., 4 Bbl.	JH	DG	DG				
8	283	PG, 4 Bbl.	JG	DH	DH				
8	283	w/ex. EM			DI	DI			
8	283	PG, w/ex. EM			DJ	DJ			
8	283	4 Spd., w/ex. EM			DK	DK			
8	283	4 Bbl., w/ex. EM			DL				
8	283	PG, 4 Bbl., w/ex. EM			DM				
8	283	HDC				DN			
8	307	Hyd.						DD	CNF
8	307	M.T.					DA	DA	CNC
8	307	4 Spd.					DE	DE	CND
8	307	PG					DB	DC	CNE
8	307	HDC					DN		
8	327	M.T.	JQ	EA	EA	EA	EA		
8	327	HP	JR	EB					
8	327	w/ex. EM			EB	EB			
8	327	SHP	JS	EC			ES		
8	327	PG, w/ex. EM			EC	EC			
8	327	w/T. Ign.	JT	ED					
8	327	3 or 4 Spd. (325 H.P.)				EP			

87941c01

Fig. 1 Early engine 3-digit identification chart

Engine Identification
1964–70 (cont.)

No. Cyls.	Cu. In. Displ.	Type	1964	1965	1966	1967	1968	1969	1970
						Year and Code			
8	327	HDC, 3 or 4 Spd. w/ex. EM (325 H.P.)				ER			
8	327	HDC (325 H.P.)				ES	ES		
8	327	HDC (275 H.P.)				ED	ED		
8	327	PG	SR	EE	EE	EE	EE		
8	327	PG, HP	SS	EF					
8	350	M.T.						HA	
8	350	Hyd.						HB	
8	350	2-BBL.						HC	
8	350	2-BBL., Hyd.						HD	
8	350	PG						HE	CNM(250)
8	350	PG, 2-BBL.						HF	
8	350	M.T.						HP	CNI(250)
8	350	M.T.						HR	CNJ(300)
8	350	PG						HR	CNK(300)
8	350	Hyd.						HS	CRE(300)
8	396	HDC			ED	ED	ED	ED	
8	396	HP			EF	EF	EF	JC	
8	396	SHP					EG	JD	
8	396	w/ex. EM			EH	EH			
8	396	HP, w/ex. EM			EJ	EJ			
8	396	PG			EK	EK	EK	EK	
8	396	PG, HP			EL	EL	EL	EL	
8	396	PG, w/ex. EM			EM	EM			
8	396	PG, HP, w/ex. EM			EN	EN			
8	396	Hyd. (325 H.P.)				ET	ET	ET	
8	396	Hyd. (350 H.P.)				EU	EU	EU	
8	396	w/ex. EM (325 H.P.)				EV			
8	396	w/ex. EM (350 H.P.)				EW			
8	396	M.T.						JA	CZX(265), CTX(350), CKT(375) CKO(375)
8	396	HP, 3-sp. Hyd. 400						JE	
8	396	Hyd. 400						JK	CTW(350)
8	396	SHP, Hyd. 400. (#–CKP only)						KF	CTY(375), CKP(375), CKU(375)
8	396	M.T.						KG	
8	396	Hyd. 400						KH	CKN(325)
8	396	M.T., HP						KB	
8	396	M.T.						JV	
8	396	SHP, M.T.						KD	
8	396	M.T.						KI	
8	396	M.T., HDC							CTZ(350), CKQ(375)
8	400	M.T. (330 H.P.)							CKR
8	400	M.T., HDC (330 H.P.)							CKS
8	454	M.T. (390 H.P.)							CRN, CRT
8	454	Hyd. 400 (390 H.P.)							CRQ
8	454	Hyd. 400 (450 H.P.)							CRR
8	454	Hyd. 400 #(450 H.P.)							CRS
8	454	M.T. (450 H.P.)							CRV

AC—air conditioned.
HDC—heavy duty clutch.
HP—high performance.
SHP—special high performance.
M.T.—manual transmission.

OD—overdrive.
PG—powerglide transmission.
PCV—positive crankcase ventilation.
w/ex. EM—with exhaust emission

w/T. Ign.—with transistor ignition.
4 Bbl.—four barrel carburetor.
Hyd.—Hydramatic.
#—Aluminum heads.

87941c02

Fig. 2 Early engine 3-digit identification chart, cont.

Engine Identification
1971–75

No. Cyls.	Cu. In. Displ.	Type	Year and Code				
			1971	1972	1973	1974	1975
6	250	PG		CBJ			
6	250	T.H.			CCA	CCX	
6	250	M.T.	CAA	CBG	CCC	CCR	D
6	250	M.T., w/NB2			CCD		
6	250	T.H., w/NB2			CCB	CCW	
8	307	T.H.		CTK	CMA		
8	307	M.T.			CHB		
8	307	PG		CKH			
8	307	M.T.	CCA	CKG			
8	300	T.H., w/NB2			CHC		
8	350	M.T.		CKK, CKA	CKA, CKB		
8	350	2-BBL., M.T.				CMC	H
8	350	2-BBL., T.H.				CMA	
8	350	PG		CKB, CDB			
8	350	T.H.		CT, CKD	CKL, CKJ		
8	350	M.T.	CGA(245)				
8	350	PG	CGB(245)				
8	350	M.T.	CGK(270)				
8	350	T.H. 350	CGL(270) CJD(270)				
8	350	M.T.	CJJ(270)				
8	350	M.T., w/NB2		CKC, CKH			
8	350	T.H., w/NB2		CKD, CKK		CKD	
8	350	3-spd., 4-BBL.				CKH	J, T
8	400	T.H., 4-BBL.				CTC	U
8	400	T.H., 4-BBL., California				CTA	
8	402	M.T., HDC (330 hp)		CLA, CLS			
8	402	T.H. 400 (Mk. IV)	CLB	CLB			
8	402	4-spd. (Mk. IV)	CLL				
8	402	M.T. Police (Mk. IV)	CLR				
8	402	M.T. (Mk. IV)	CLS				
8	402	M.T. (Mk. IV)	CPR				
8	400	M.T. (Mk. IV)	CPA CPG CPD CPP	CPA			
8	454	T.H. 400 (450 hp)		CPD			
8	454	M.T.			CWA	CWA	
8	454	T.H.			CWB	CWX	
8	454	M.T., w/NB2			CWC		
8	454	T.H. w/NB2			CWD	CWD	

AC—air conditioned
HDC—heavy duty clutch
HP—high performance
M.T.—manual transmission
OD—overdrive

PG—powerglide transmission
PCV—positive crankcase ventilation
w/ex. EM—with exhaust emission
w/T. Ign.—with transistor ignition

4-BBL.—four-barrel carburetor
T.H.—Turbo Hydra-Matic
#—Aluminum heads
NB2—Calif. only

87941c03

Fig. 3 Early engine 3-digit identification chart, cont.

The small block family of V8 engines, which has included the 267, 283, 305, 307, 327, 350 and 400 cu. in. blocks, have all evolved from the design of the 1955 265 cu. in. V8. It was this engine that introduced the ball joint type rocker arm design which is now used by many car makers.

This line of engines features a great deal of interchangeability, and later parts may be utilized on earlier engines for increased reliability and/or performance. For example, in 1968 the 283 was dropped and replace by the 307, which is in effect a 327 crankshaft in a 283 block. And the 267, 305, and 350 V8s all share the same stroke, making crankshaft and bore dimensions, the main difference between the engines.

The 396, 402 and 454 engines are known as the big blocks, or less frequently, the Mark IV engines. They are available in the high performance SS versions of the Chevelle, and feature many tuning modifications such as high lift camshafts, solid lifters (in some cases), high compression ratios and large carburetors. These big blocks engines are similar to their small block little brothers in basic design.

Engine Identification

Engine identification can take place using various methods. The VIN, described earlier in this section, contains a code identifying the engine which was originally installed in the vehicle. In most cases, this should be sufficient for determining the engine with which your car is currently equipped. But, some older vehicles may have had the engine replaced or changed by a previous owner. If this is the case, the first step in identification is to locate an engine serial number and code which is stamped on the block or located on adhesive labels that may be present on valve covers or other engine components.

The engine serial number is stamped on an engine block pad in order to identify the place and time of manufacture. In most cases the engine serial number will also contain a 1-3 digit code that identifies the engine type. In the case of single digit codes, this engine code may conform to the code used to identify the engine in the VIN.

On all V8 engines, the serial number is found on a pad at the front right hand side of the cylinder block, just below the cylinder head.

Getting an Engine

If you're going to rebuild a worn or damaged engine you already have, step one is taken care of. Just be certain that the engine is rebuildable. Short of a cracked block, it should be. A good rule of thumb would be to remove a cylinder head and check the ridge at the top of the cylinders. An obvious, pronounced ridge would indicate that the cylinders may be worn beyond reboring and the engine may not be suitable for rebuilding. A cracked block may be obvious..........external leaks, visible cracks, etc., or may be harder to detect. Something which we will discuss later.

If you are beginning a project engine, and you need something to start with, you have several choices:

1. Go to your local junkyards, now called Automotive Parts Recyclers, and hunt for a good, rebuildable engine. Most junkyards are reputable and will tell you the type and year vehicle the engine came from. Many times the engine will still be in the car or truck and you can see it before you buy it. Buying this type of engine will usually also get you all the attached parts such as alternator, carburetor, fuel pump, power steering pump, starter, flywheel and many more. These parts can be used on your rebuilt engine, saved as spares, or used as cores (trade-ins) when you purchase new parts. Junkyard engines can run anywhere between $100.00 and $500.00 dollars.

2. Shop around your local auto parts retailers or rebuilders for a short block or bare block. A short block will be a reconditioned block, bored up to 0.030 in. overbore and comes with new core plugs and a crankshaft installed with ne bearings. All other parts will have to be purchased separately. The short block will cost over $500.00. A bare block is just what it sounds like: a clean, reconditioned, empty block with new core plugs.

3. Purchase a long block from your local rebuilder or parts retailer. A long block will usually come with a crankshaft, pistons and rings, and a camshaft and timing chain and gear set. Long blocks can cost $1500.00 or more. Also, long blocks don't really allow for rebuilding. You will simply be assembling them with the additional parts you'll have to buy.

Parts

For the purposes of this book, let's assume that you're going to purchase and rebuild a recycled (junkyard) engine as a project. You may have the idea that you'll replace everything. That's not a good philosophy unless you have lots of money and can't think of anything else to do with it. With rare exceptions, there are many perfectly good, reusable parts in any engine.

The best (cheapest) place to look for parts would be automotive parts catalogs. Check specialty magazines such as Motor Trend or Four Wheeler for aftermarket vendors. The ads is many of these magazines will contain descriptions and prices as well as ordering information. Delivery is timely and the quality is, usually, high with name brand parts being used.

If you like to see what you're buying first, or don't do catalog shopping, shop around at your local automotive aftermarket retailers for the best selection and quality.

There are many ways to buy parts. Complete rebuild kits are available which contain just about every part that you can think of. However, as stated above, you may not need all these parts. Rebuilding kits with various levels of parts are available. The fewer parts supplied, the less the cost. A good compromise is the kit which supplies all the gaskets and seals along with rings, main bearings, rod bearings, timing chain and gears, and an oil pump. This kit is probably the first thing to order, since these are parts which are replaced, no matter what the circumstances.

Don't decide on such major parts as pistons, rods, crankshaft or camshafts until the engine has been disassembled and the components inspected.

Is the Engine Worth Rebuilding?

The question of whether or not an engine is worth rebuilding is largely a subjective matter and one of personal worth. Is the engine a popular one, or is it an obsolete model? Are parts available? Will it get acceptable gas mileage once it is rebuilt? Is the car it's being put into worth keeping? Would it be less expensive to buy a new engine or a used engine from a junkyard? Or would it be simpler and less expensive to buy another car? If you have considered all these matters and more and have still decided to rebuild the engine, then it is time to decide if you need to rebuild it.

Does the Engine Need Rebuilding?

The usual yardstick for determining whether or not an engine needs rebuilding is mileage. As a very rough guideline, this is a useful method. Most engine rebuilders would consider 100,000 miles as the maximum mileage an average engine can go without a rebuild. The significant word here is average. There is absolutely no reason why a carefully maintained engine cannot easily exceed 100,000 miles and still provide excellent service. Conversely, a poorly maintained or abused engine will never get to 100,000 miles without help. This book, will omit discussion of the mileage factor and concentrate on the symptoms of an engine in trouble.

ISOLATING ENGINE PROBLEMS AND DETERMINING THEIR SEVERITY

Oil Consumption Problems

An engine's oil consumption is probably the single best indicator of the engine's internal condition. An engine's internal parts are tightly fitted, and an inevitable amount of wear occurs as the engine accumulates mileage. Because oil is used as the lubricating agent between the moving parts, excessive wear will invariably result in excessive oil consumption. The consequent question is, what constitutes excessive oil consumption? Any engine, no matter how new or how carefully built, will consume a certain amount of oil. Most rebuilders agree that an engine that uses no more than one quart of oil every 1000 miles is in good condition. This is essentially an optimum figure. An engine can use far more oil than this and still function on a daily basis. Just because the engine continues to run, however, does not mean that it does not need attention.

There are two ways an engine can lose oil. It can be leaking large amounts of oil due to a faulty gasket or external seal, or it can be losing oil 'out of the tailpipe.' The first condition is easy to spot. Simply park the car over a clean, dry area and let it idle for a short time. If any oil accumulates on the floor, the engine is leaking. Once you have fixed the leak, you can look for other causes of oil consumption.

Major internal oil consumption problems are generally caused by either worn or broken piston rings or severely worn valve guides. If oil can get past the oil control ring, it will enter the combustion chamber and be burned along with the fuel/air mixture. It can also be blown right past the rings into the crankcase, creating a condition called blow-by. Before the advent of emission controls, blow-by was vented from the crankcase into the atmosphere by means of a road draft tube or a crankcase vent. Emission-controlled engines have sealed crankcase ventilation systems, and vent excessive blow-by through the PCV valve, into the air cleaner, and eventually back into the combustion chamber. Oil that is at least partially burned in the combustion chamber along with the fuel/air mix-

ture is responsible for the blue smoke that comes from the tailpipe of an engine that needs an overhaul. When you see this kind of 'death smoke' coming from an engine, you know it is time for an overhaul. Ways to isolate and determine piston ring condition will be discussed later in this chapter.

Severely worn valve guides are the other major internal cause of excessive oil consumption. A worn valve guide will allow oil to get past the valve stem and into the combustion chamber or into the exhaust port. In either case, excessive amounts of oil will be lost. Generally speaking, by the time valve guides wear to this extent, the piston rings will be badly worn as well. In fact, rings frequently wear out before valve guides, depending on how often the oil is changed. But do not mistake worn valve stem seals for worn valve guides. Worn seals will create exactly the same conditions as worn guides. So always check the seals before worrying about the guides, especially if the engine has less than 75,000 miles on it. Ways to spot worn guides and seals will be discussed later in this chapter.

Whether it is caused by worn rings, worn valve guides, or anything else, the bottom line on oil consumption is this: if the engine is using a quart or more of oil every 500 miles, it needs some very careful attention. If you discover that the cause of the oil consumption is an internal problem, it is time for a rebuild.

Engine Noises and Their Possible Causes

One of the most common reasons for rebuilding an engine is unusual or excessive engine noise. It is, however, extremely difficult to diagnose engine condition from noises alone. Engine noises are a useful indicator of engine condition, provided other factors, such as oil consumption, test instrument results, and performance loss problems are taken into account. This section will help you to determine which engine noises indicate serious trouble and which do not.

ACCESSORY NOISES

If the engine begins to make an unusual noise, the very first things to check are the engine accessories. Water pumps, alternators, air pumps, and air-conditioning compressors can all make noises that are easily mistaken for more serious engine noises. There is only one sure way to check possible accessory noises, and that is to remove the belt that drives that particular accessory. Of course, most belts drive more than one accessory, but at least you will have narrowed the field. Worn bushings or bearings in any of these accessories will often make a knocking noise that easily can be mistaken for a more serious knock. If you have removed all the belts and the noises remain, the noise is not in the accessories.

CRANKSHAFT OR BOTTOM END NOISES

Crankshaft noises are generally much heavier in volume and tone than other engine noises. They will also occur at engine speed; that is, the noise will rise and fall in perfect synchronization with engine speed. Worn crankshaft bearings will produce an audible knock when the engine is idling, especially if the idle is uneven. If you suspect a bottom end noise, disconnect each spark plug lead one at a time and listen for changes in the noise. If the noise decreases or goes away with a particular plug disconnected, you have located the cylinder and/or bearing with the noise.

ENGINE NOISES

Possible Cause	Correction

NOISY VALVES

Constant loud clacking, light clicking or intermittent noise indicates faulty hydraulic valve lifters (tappets), or mal-adjusted mechanical tappets.

Possible Cause	Correction
1. High or low oil level in crankcase.	Check for correct oil level.
2. Low oil pressure.	Check engine oil level.
3. Dirt in tappets.	Clean tappets.
4. Bend push rods.	Install new push rods.
5. Worn rocker arms.	Inspect oil supply to rockers.
6. Worn tappets.	Install new tappets.
7. Worn valve guides.	Replace guides if removable or ream and install new valves.
8. Excessive run-out of valve seats or valve faces.	Grind valve seats and valves.
9. Incorrect tappet lash.	Adjust to specifications.

CONNECTING ROD NOISE

A metallic knock when idling or retarding engine speed, which disappears under load indicates worn or loose connecting rod bearings. The bearing at fault can be found by shorting out the spark plugs one at a time. The noise will disappear when the cylinder with the faulty bearing is shorted out.

Possible Cause	Correction
1. Insufficient oil supply	Check engine oil level.
2. Low oil pressure.	Check engine oil level.
3. Thin or diluted oil.	Change oil to correct viscosity.
4. Excessive bearing clearance.	Measure bearings for correct clearance or failures.
5. Connecting rod journals out-of-round.	Remove crankshaft and regrind journals.
6. Misaligned connecting rods.	Remove bent connecting rods.

MAIN BEARING NOISE

A main bearing knock is more of a bump than a knock, and it can be located by shorting out the plugs near it. The noise is loudest when the engine is "lugging" (pulling hard at slow speed). The sound is heavier and more dull than a connecting rod knock.

Possible Cause	Correction
1. Insufficient oil supply.	Check engine oil level. Inspect oil pump relief valve damper and spring.
2. Low oil pressure.	Check engine oil level.
3. Thin or diluted oil.	Change the oil to correct viscosity.
4. Excessive bearing clearance.	Check the bearings for correct clearances or failures.
5. Excessive end-play.	Check thrust main bearing for wear on flanges.
6. Crankshaft journals out-of-round or worn.	Remove crankshaft and regrind journals.
7. Loose flywheel.	Tighten correctly.

OTHER ENGINE NOISES

Possible Cause	Correction
1. A sharp rap at idle speed indicates a loose piston pin. The pin at fault can be found by shorting out the spark plugs one at a time. The noise will disappear when the cylinder with the faulty pin is shorted out.	Replace piston pin.
2. A flat slap, when advancing engine speed under load, indicates a loose piston.	Replace piston and rebore cylinder block if necessary.

87931001

PISTON NOISES OR PISTON SLAP

Piston slap is caused by excessive clearance between the piston skirt and the cylinder wall. Generally, piston slap decreases as the engine warms up and the piston expands, so listen for it when the engine is cold. As a general rule, piston slap will create a hollow dull sound, much lower in intensity than a crankshaft noise. A more accurate test of piston slap is to accelerate the engine from low speed under a load; that is, apply a lot of throttle, but do not shift to a lower gear. If the noise increases in intensity, you have located the problem.

You can also check for piston slap by disconnecting each spark plug in turn, or by retarding the spark. If all of the pistons have excessive clearance, retarding the spark should reduce the noise by reducing the load on the pistons. Disconnecting the spark plug leads will do the same thing for each individual piston. Keep in mind, however, that other engine noises are also affected by these operations.

It is sometimes possible to temporarily eliminate piston and ring noises by pouring a small amount of very heavy oil into the cylinder (through the spark plug holes). Crank the engine over (coil wire disconnected) until the oil works past the rings. Start the engine. If the noise has gone away, piston slap is the probable diagnosis.

PISTON PIN NOISES

Excessive piston pin clearance will frequently create a sharp metallic noise or clatter that is usually most audible when the engine is idling. You can check for excessive pin clearance in the same manner as you do for piston slap. Retard the spark and listen for any reduction in the noise. Generally, retarding the spark will reduce the intensity of the knock. Then short out each spark plug in turn. If the piston pin is worn, the sharp metallic knock should become more, not less, pronounced in that particular cylinder. Remember that the same problem exists here that exists with all other internal engine noises: if one component is worn out other components are probably worn out and making noise as well. So keep in mind that the engine is likely making more than one noise, especially if it has well over 100,000 miles on it.

VALVE TRAIN NOISES

Because the camshaft and all related valve train components operate at one-half crankshaft speed, any noise coming from the valve train will occur at one-half the frequency of other noises. If the engine is equipped with hydraulic valve lifters, a sharp rapping or clicking noise probably indicates a worn or collapsed lifter. A somewhat lighter noise may indicate excessive clearance between the rocker arm and the valve stem. Sometimes this clearance is adjustable, and sometimes it is not. (This is only the case with hydraulic lifters; solid lifter valve trains are always adjustable.) Engines equipped with solid lifters will inevitably make a certain amount of noise. It is simply a question of experience and familiarity with a particular engine that will enable you to determine whether or not the noise is excessive.

It is much easier to detect valve train noises with a mechanic's stethoscope or a large, long screwdriver. Place the tip of the screwdriver or stethoscope against the valve cover. Any valve train noises will be greatly amplified. Place the stethoscope against the valve cover at regular intervals along its length, and you may be able to isolate the noise.

If you definitely suspect a valve train noise, and have an engine that is equipped with adjustable rockers, the next step is to remove the valve cover or camshaft cover and check the valve clearance. The valve clearance should be checked as a normal part of a good tune-up anyway.

If you find that the valve clearances are correct and you still hear excessive valve train noises, the engine may have severely worn lifters or a worn camshaft. If you cannot adjust the excessive clearance out of the valve train, the engine's rocker arms are probably worn out. And remember that worn rockers usually mean worn valve stems or lifters as well.

CONNECTING ROD BEARING NOISES

Connecting rod bearing noises are similar to main bearing noises in that they occur in exact synchronization with engine speed. However, they are much lighter in intensity than main bearing noises. In terms of noise intensity, they fall somewhere between valve train noises and main bearing noises. Check for rod bearing noises by shorting out each cylinder in turn and listening for a reduction in the noise. Remember, you may not be able to eliminate the noise entirely, but you will be able to reduce it considerably. A stethoscope or long screwdriver held against the block is a big help, provided you can reach it.

DETONATION AND PREIGNITION

Detonation and preignition are not the same thing, but both can create the same symptoms, and both can severely damage an engine's performance. In addition, both can create a rapid metallic rattle, generally called 'ping' or 'spark knock.' Preignition occurs when the combustion process is initiated by any source other than the spark plug. In other words, preignition is caused by the presence of any hot spot in the combustion chamber. A piece of glowing carbon, the sharp edge of a valve, a hot spot on the piston crown--any of these can cause premature ignition of the fuel/air mixture. As a result, the fuel/air mixture ignites while the piston is on the way up in the cylinder on the compression stroke. The resultant pressure attempts to force the piston back down while it is still trying to come up. This places a tremendous load on the piston, connecting rod, and the bearings, as well as resulting in a sharp knocking sound.

To understand detonation, you must remember that the ignition of the fuel/air mixture is not an explosion, but a very rapid, controlled burning process. The spark plug ignites the fuel/air mixture, which spreads very rapidly out in a specific pattern. This is what occurs during normal ignition of the fuel/air charge. Detonation occurs when part of the charge auto-ignites from excessive combustion chamber heat and pressure. This explosion spreads out and meets the oncoming flame front created by normal ignition. The resultant collision creates extremely high combustion chamber pressures, places great strain on the piston, connecting rod and bearings, eats away metal where it occurs, and causes a sharp knocking sound.

A number of things can cause preignition or detonation, including excessive carbon deposits or poor quality fuel. For the purposes of this book, it should be noted that excessively high combustion chamber temperatures or pressures can be detected by a careful spark plug analysis. If the engine is pinging or rattling, and you suspect it might be preignition or detonation, the first thing to do is to analyze the spark plugs and give the car a good tune-up. Pay particular attention to correct

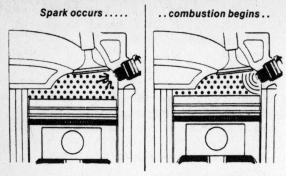

Normal combustion (Courtesy Champion Spark Plug Co.)

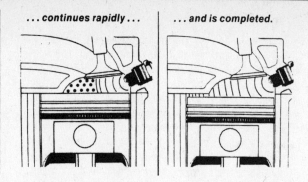

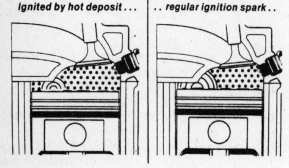

Preignition (Courtesy Champion Spark Plug Co.)

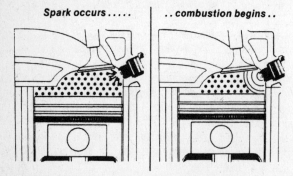

Detonation (Courtesy Champion Spark Plug Co.)

87931002

ignition timing and spark plug heat range. In the end, you may find that the car is pinging and rattling simply because of poor quality gas, a common problem today.

If you find that the car is in a good state of tune, and you have switched to high octane gas but still have rattling noises coming from the engine, the problem may be excessive carbon deposits on the valves or on the tops of the pistons. There are gasoline additives on the market that will loosen carbon deposits. It is not uncommon, however, for these additives to work all too well, loosening the carbon from the piston crown and the valves and allowing it to bounce around in the combustion chamber. The point to remember is that carbon is a symptom of a problem rather than the problem itself. This does not mean that carbon buildup cannot cause problems, only that simply getting rid of the carbon does not necessarily solve the problem. Frequently, carbon deposits are caused by vehicle usage: if you do a lot of low-speed driving and stop-and-go driving, you stand a good chance of developing carbon deposits in the engine.

Carbon deposits can also be caused by worn piston rings or valve stems, allowing oil to get into the combustion chamber

where a certain amount of it will be glazed onto the valves or the piston crown by combustion chamber heat. Carbon deposits can cause knocks that easily may be mistaken for more serious noises. The only positive way to determine whether or not the engine has developed excessive carbon deposits is to remove the cylinder heads, but that is going far beyond simple diagnosis.

Types of Piston Damage

Damaged pistons, after thorough examination, can many times be attributed to some form of abnormal combustion.

PERFORMANCE LOSS PROBLEMS AND POSSIBLE CAUSES

▶ See Figure 4

The possible causes of poor performance are almost limitless, but this book will discuss only serious internal engine problems that will directly and obviously affect engine performance. If, for instance, the engine is using a lot more gas and showing serious power losses, it could have a blown head gasket or a warped cylinder head. If the engine is using coolant but there is no leak, that may also indicate a blown head gasket or warped head. Check for the presence of water in the oil or oil in the water. If coolant is getting into the oil supply, oil on the dipstick will be whitish and foamy. The presence of oil in the cooling system will be immediately obvious because there will be an oily scum apparent when the radiator cap is removed. Use a pressure tester to locate any coolant leaks.

Burned valves will definitely affect an engine's performance. Keep in mind, however, that larger, more powerful engines show less effect from a burned valve than a small engine. In other words, a burned valve on a four-cylinder car is immediately apparent, but you may not notice the power loss on a large V8. A compression test will reveal a burned valve. Vacuum gauge readings will also detect burned valves, assuming that the engine is in a good state of tune to begin with.

A worn timing chain or a worn camshaft can also drastically affect performance, yet not be noticeable when the engine is idling. Unfortunately, it is almost impossible to detect this problem with external diagnosis. A badly worn timing chain may give a late valve timing reading on the vacuum gauge, but it is entirely possible that it may not.

USING TEST INSTRUMENTS TO DETERMINE ENGINE CONDITION

Test instruments are the most reliable and accurate way to determine an engine's condition. There are three very important tests that you must perform on any engine before you decide to rebuild it. They are the vacuum gauge readings, compression test results, and spark plug analysis.

Vacuum Gauge Readings
◆ See Figure 5

A vacuum gauge simply measures how well the engine is pumping air. To use it, locate a vacuum gauge fitting on the intake manifold and connect the vacuum gauge to the fitting. Variations in atmospheric pressure will affect vacuum gauge

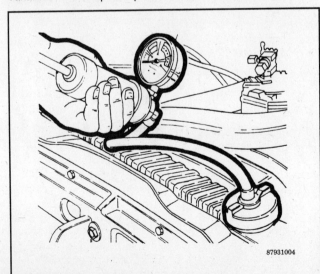

87931004

Fig. 4 Pressure testing the cooling system

readings, so remember that the action of the needle is more important than the actual reading.

Checking Engine Compression
◆ See Figure 6

A noticeable lack of engine power, excessive oil consumption and/or poor fuel mileage measured over an extended period are all indicators of internal engine wear. Worn piston rings, scored or worn cylinder bores, blown head gaskets, sticking or burnt valves and worn valve seats are all possible culprits here. A check of each cylinder's compression will help you locate the problems.

As mentioned earlier, a screw-in type compression gauge is more accurate that the type you simply hold against the spark plug hole, although it takes slightly longer to use. It's worth it to obtain a more accurate reading. Follow the procedures below.

1. Warm up the engine to normal operating temperature.
2. Remove all the spark plugs.
3. Disconnect the high tension lead from the ignition coil and ground it.
4. Screw the compression gauge into the no.1 spark plug hole until the fitting is snug.

✱✱WARNING

Be careful not to crossthread the plug hole. On aluminum cylinder heads use extra care, as the threads in these heads are easily ruined.

5. Fully open the throttle either by operating the carburetor throttle linkage by hand or by having an assistant floor the accelerator pedal.
6. While you read the compression gauge, ask the assistant to crank the engine two or three times in short bursts using the ignition switch or a remote starter switch.
7. Read the compression gauge at the end of each series of cranks, and record the highest of these readings. Repeat this procedure for each of the engine's cylinders. Compare the highest reading of each cylinder.

The difference between any two cylinders should be no more than 12-14 pounds.

8. If a cylinder is unusually low, pour a tablespoon of clean engine oil into the cylinder through the spark plug hole and repeat the compression test. If the compression comes up after adding the oil, it appears that the cylinder's piston rings or bore are damaged or worn. If the pressure remains low, the valves may not be seating properly (a valve job is needed), or the head gasket may be blown near that cylinder. If compression in any two adjacent cylinders is low, and if the addition of oil doesn't help the compression, there is leakage past the head gasket. Oil and coolant water in the combustion chamber can result from this problem. There may be evidence of water droplets on the engine dipstick when a head gasket has blown.

CHECKING THE RESULTS

Now that you have all your compression readings, it is time to decide what they mean. Depending on the engine, you may observe readings anywhere from 80 to 200 or even 250 psi. Specific readings, however, are not as important as the spread

Normal engine

Late ignition timing

Stuck throttle valve, leaking intake manifold or carburetor gaskets

Leaking head gasket

Worn valve guides

Burnt or leaking valves

Sticking valves

Weak valve springs

Carburetor needs adjustment

Late valve timing

Choked muffler

Normal engine—(opened and closed throttle, rings and valves OK)

87931003

Fig. 5 Analyzing the engine with a vacuum gauge

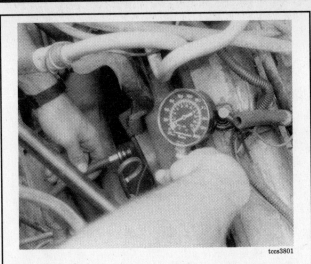

Fig. 6 The screw-in type compression gauge is more accurate.

between cylinders. In other words, no one cylinder should be appreciably lower than any other. All cylinder readings should be within a range of 25 percent. If, for example, the highest reading is 100 psi and the lowest is 75 psi, the compression readings are within tolerance.

If the compression readings do not fall within this range, the first thing to do is to perform a 'wet test.' Squirt a teaspoonful or two of heavy oil into the cylinder and give it a couple of minutes to seep down around the rings. Then recheck the compression. If the readings improve appreciably, the piston rings (at least) are worn out. You may also have worn pistons and cylinder bores.

If you discover two adjacent cylinders with low compression, chances are that there is a blown head gasket or a warped cylinder head--probably a blown gasket-between the two cylinders. Keep in mind that there should be other indications of a blown head gasket, such as water in the oil or oil in the water. It is also possible for a blown head gasket to affect only one cylinder. Run the engine to operating temperature and then carefully remove the radiator cap. If you see a lot of bubbles, that is another indication of a blown gasket.

If compression buildup is erratic on any of the cylinders, the problem could be sticky valves. Check for this condition by removing the valve or camshaft cover and connecting a timing light to the spark plug lead of the suspect cylinder. Aim the timing light at the valves of the cylinder in question. Loosen the distributor and vary the timing gradually in order to observe the motion of the valve or valves. If the valve appears to be operating erratically, it could possibly be sticking. Keep in mind that it is a tricky test (not to mention a messy one), and it takes a lot of experience to detect a sticky valve.

Spark Plugs

▶ See Figure 7

A typical spark plug consists of a metal shell surrounding a ceramic insulator. A metal electrode extends downward through the center of the insulator and protrudes a small distance. Located at the end of the plug and attached to the side of the outer metal shell is the side electrode. The side electrode bends in at a 90° angle so that its tip is just past and parallel

to the tip of the center electrode. The distance between these two electrodes (measured in thousandths of an inch or hundredths of a millimeter) is called the spark plug gap. The spark plug does not produce a spark but instead provides a gap across which the current can arc. The coil produces anywhere from 20,000-25,000 volts (the HEI transistorized ignition produces considerably more voltage than the standard type, approximately 50,000 volts) which travels through the wires to the spark plugs. The current passes along the center electrode and jumps the gap to the side electrode, and in doing so, ignites the fuel/air mixture in the combustion chamber. All plugs used since 1969 have a resistor built into the center electrode to reduce interference to any nearby radio and television receivers. The resistor also cuts down on erosion of plug electrodes caused by excessively long sparking. Resistor spark plug wiring is original equipment on all models.

SPARK PLUG HEAT RANGE

▶ See Figure 8

Spark plug life and efficiency depend upon condition of the engine and the temperatures to which the plug is exposed. Combustion chamber temperatures are affected by many factors such as compression ratio of the engine, fuel/air mixtures, exhaust emission equipment, and the type of driving you do. Spark plugs are designed and classified by number according to the heat range at which they will operate most efficiently. The amount of heat that the plug absorbs is determined by the length of the lower insulator. The longer the insulator (it extends farther into the engine), the hotter the plug will operate; the shorter it is, the cooler it will operate. A plug that has a short path for heat transfer and remains too cool will quickly accumulate deposits of oil and carbon since it is not hot enough to burn them off. This leads to plug fouling and consequently to misfiring. A plug that has a long path of heat transfer will have no deposits but, due to the excessive heat, the electrodes will burn away quickly and, in some instances, pre-ignition may result. Pre-ignition takes place when plug tips get so hot that they glow sufficiently to ignite the fuel/air mixture before the spark does. This early ignition will usually cause a

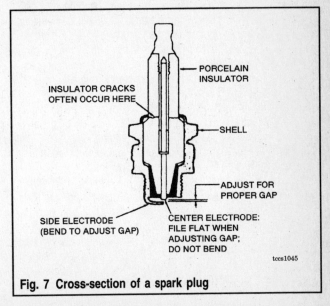

Fig. 7 Cross-section of a spark plug

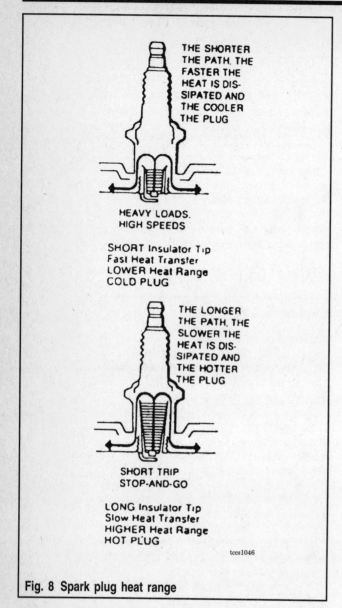

THE SHORTER
THE PATH, THE
FASTER THE
HEAT IS DIS-
SIPATED AND
THE COOLER
THE PLUG

HEAVY LOADS.
HIGH SPEEDS

SHORT Insulator Tip
Fast Heat Transfer
LOWER Heat Range
COLD PLUG

THE LONGER
THE PATH, THE
SLOWER THE
HEAT IS DIS-
SIPATED AND
THE HOTTER
THE PLUG

SHORT TRIP
STOP-AND-GO

LONG Insulator Tip
Slow Heat Transfer
HIGHER Heat Range
HOT PLUG

tccs1046

Fig. 8 Spark plug heat range

pinging (sounding much like castanets) during low speeds and heavy loads. In severe cases, the heat may become enough to start the fuel/air mixture burning throughout the combustion chamber rather than just to the front of the plug as in normal operation. At this time, the piston is rising in the cylinder making its compression stroke. The burning mass is compressed and an explosion results producing tremendous pressure. Something has to give, and it does; pistons are often damaged. Obviously, this detonation (explosion) is a destructive condition that can be avoided by installing a spark plug designed and specified for your particular engine.

A set of spark plugs usually requires replacement after 10,000-12,000 miles depending on the type of driving (this interval has been increased to 22,500 miles for all 1975-79 models and 30,000 miles for all 1980 and later models). The electrode on a new spark plug has a sharp edge but, with use, this edge becomes rounded by erosion causing the plug gap to increase. In normal operation, plug gap increases about 0.001 in. (0.0254mm) for every 1,000-2,000 miles. As the gap increases, the plug's voltage requirement also increases. It requires a greater voltage to jump the wider gap and about 2-4

times as much voltage to fire a plug at high speed and acceleration than at idle.

The higher voltage produced by the HEI ignition coil is one of the primary reasons for the prolonged replacement interval for spark plugs in 1975 and later cars. A consistently hotter spark prevents the fouling of plugs for much longer than could normally be expected; this spark is also able to jump across a larger gap more efficiently than a spark from a conventional system. However, even plugs used with the HEI system wear after time in the engine.

Worn plugs become obvious during acceleration. Voltage requirement is greatest during acceleration and a plug with an enlarged gap may require more voltage than the coil is able to produce. As a result, the engine misses and sputters until acceleration is reduced. Reducing acceleration reduces the plug's voltage requirement and the engine runs smoother. Slow, city driving is hard on plugs. The long periods of idle experienced in traffic creates an overly rich gas mixture. The engine does not run fast enough to completely burn the gas and, consequently, the plugs become fouled with gas deposits and engine idle becomes rough. In many cases, driving under the right conditions can effectively clean these fouled plugs.

To help clean fouled plugs in a running engine, first accelerate you car to the speed where the engine begins to miss and then slow down to the point where the engine smooths out. Run at this speed for a few minutes and then accelerate again to the point of engine miss. With each repetition this engine miss should occur at increasingly higher speeds and then disappear altogether. Do not attempt to shortcut this procedure by hard acceleration. This approach will compound problems by fusing deposits into a hard permanent glaze. Dirty, fouled plugs may be cleaned by sandblasting. Many shops have a spark plug sandblaster and there are a few inexpensive models that are designed for home use and available from aftermarket sources. After sandblasting, the electrode should be filed to a sharp, square shape and then gapped to specifications. Gapping a plug too close will produce a rough idle while gapping it too wide will increase its voltage requirement and cause missing at high speed and during acceleration.

➡**There are several reasons why a spark plug will foul and you can usually learn what is at fault by just looking at the plug.**

The type of driving you do may require a change in spark plug heat range. If the majority of your driving is done in the city and rarely at high speeds, plug fouling may necessitate changing to a plug with a heat range one number higher than that specified by the car manufacturer. For example, a 1970 Chevelle with a 350 cu. in. (300 hp) engine requires an R44 plug. Frequent city driving may foul these plugs making engine operation rough. An R45 is the next hottest plug in the AC heat range (the higher the AC number, the hotter the plug) and its insulator is longer than the R44 so that it can absorb and retain more heat than the shorter R44. This hotter R45 burns off deposits even at low city speeds but would be too hot for prolonged turnpike driving. Using this plug at high speed would create dangerous pre-ignition. On the other hand, if the aforementioned Chevelle were used almost exclusively for long distance high speed driving, the specified R44 might be too hot resulting in rapid electrode wear and dangerous pre-ignition. In this case, it might be wise to change to a colder R43. If the car is used for abnormal driving (as in the examples above), or the engine has been modified for higher performance, then a change to a plug with a different heat range may be necessary. For a modified car it is always wise to go to a colder plug as a protection against pre-ignition. It will require more frequent plug cleaning, but destructive detonation during acceleration will be avoided.

REMOVAL

▶ See Figures 9 and 10

When you're removing spark plugs, you should work on one at a time. Don't start by removing the plug wires all at once because unless you number them, or they're going to get mixed up. On some models though, it will be more convenient for you to remove all the wires before you start to work on the plugs. If this is necessary, take a minute before you begin and number the wires with tape before you take them off. The time you spend doing this will pay off later when it comes time to reconnect the wires to the plugs.

1. Disconnect the negative battery cable from the negative battery terminal.

2. Twist the spark plug boot slightly in either direction to break loose the seal, then remove the boot from the plug. You may also use a plug wire removal tool designed especially for this purpose. Do not pull on the wire itself or you may separate the plug connector from the end of the wire. When the wire has been removed, take a wire brush and clean the area around the plug. An evaporative spray cleaner such as those designed for brake applications will also work well. Make sure that all the foreign material is removed so that none will enter the cylinder after the plug has been removed.

➡If you have access to a compressor, use the air hose to blow all material away from the spark plug bores before loosening the plug. Always protect your eyes with safety glasses when using compressed air.

3. Remove the plug using the proper size socket, extensions, and universals as necessary. Be careful to hold the socket or the extension close to the plug with your free hand as this will help lessen the possibility of applying a shear force

which might snap the spark plug in half. If the cylinder heads on the engine are original, then for all 1964-69 engines, and all V8s 1964-71, use a $\frac{13}{16}$ in. spark plug socket. V8s from 1972 and later are equipped with tapered seat plugs which require a $\frac{5}{8}$ in. socket.

4. If removing the plug is difficult, drip some penetrating oil on the plug threads, allow it to work, then remove the plug. Also, be sure that the socket is straight on the plug, especially on those hard to reach plugs. Again, if the socket is cocked to one side, a shear force may be applied to the plug and could snap the plug in half.

INSPECTION

▶ See Figures 11, 12 and 13

Check the plugs for deposits and wear. If they are not going to be replaced, clean the plugs thoroughly. Remember that any kind of deposit will decrease the efficiency of the plug. Plugs can be cleaned on a spark plug cleaning machine, which can sometimes be found in service stations, or you can do an acceptable job of cleaning with a stiff brush. If the plugs are cleaned, the electrodes must be filed flat. Use an ignition points file, not an emery board or the like, which will leave deposits. The electrodes must be filed perfectly flat with sharp edges; rounded edges reduce the spark plug voltage by as much as 50%.

Check and adjust the spark plug gap immediately before installation. The ground electrode (the L-shaped one connected to the body of the plug) must be parallel to the center electrode and the specified size gauge (see Tune-Up Specifications in Chapter 6) should pass through the gap with a slight drag. Always check the gap on new plugs, too; since they are not always set correctly at the factory.

➡NEVER adjust the gap on a used platinum type spark plug.

Do not use a flat feeler gauge when measuring the gap on used plugs, because the reading may be inaccurate. The ground electrode on a used plug is often rounded on the face closest to the center electrode. A flat gauge will not be able to

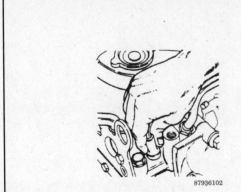

Fig. 9 Twist and pull on the rubber boot to disconnect the spark plug wires; never pull on the wire itself

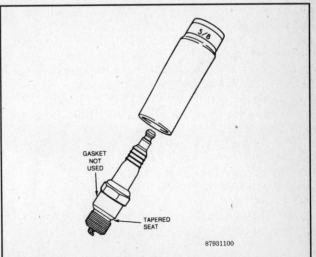

Fig. 10 Remove the spark plug using a suitable socket and driver

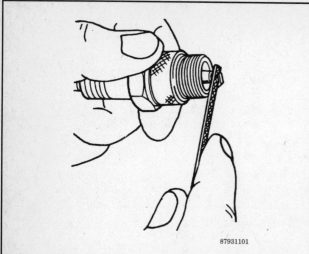

87931101

Fig. 11 Spark plugs that are in good condition can be filed and re-used

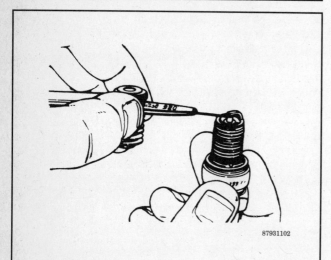

87931102

Fig. 12 Always use a wire gauge to check the electrode gap on used plugs

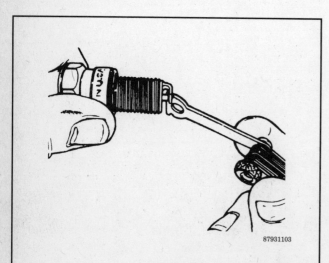

87931103

Fig. 13 Adjust the gap by bending the side electrode very slightly towards or away from the center electrode

accurately measure this distance as well as a wire gauge. Most gapping tools usually have a bending tool attached. This tool may be used to adjust the side electrode until the proper distance is obtained. Never attempt to move or bend the center electrode or spark plug damage will likely occur. Also, be careful not to bend the side electrode too far or too often; if it is overstressed it may weaken and break off within the engine, requiring removal of the cylinder head to retrieve it.

CHECKING SPARK PLUGS

▶ **See Figure 14**

The single most accurate indicator of the engine's condition is the firing end of the spark plugs. Although the spark plug has no moving parts. It is exposed to more stress than any other engine part. It is required to deliver a high-voltage spark thousands of times a minute, at precisely timed intervals, under widely varying conditions. Because it is inside the combustion chamber, it is exposed to the corrosive effects from chemical additives in fuel and oil and to extremes of temperature and pressure. The terminal end may be as cold as ice, but the firing tip will be exposed to flame temperatures in excess of 3000°F (1650°C).

READING SPARK PLUGS

A close examination of spark plugs will provide many clues to the condition of an engine. Keeping the plugs in order according to cylinder location will make the diagnosis even more effective and accurate. The following diagrams illustrate some of the conditions that spark plugs will reveal.

APPEARANCE

▶ **See Figure 15**

This plug is typical of one operating normally. The insulator nose varies from a light tan to grayish color with slight electrode wear. The presence of slight deposits is normal on used plugs and will have no adverse effect or engine performance. The spark plug heat range is correct for the engine and the engine is running correctly.

CAUSE

Properly running engine.

RECOMMENDATION

Before reinstalling this plug, the electrodes should be cleaned and filed square. Set the gap to specifications If the plug has been in service for more than 10,000 to 12,000 miles, the entire set should probably be replaced with a fresh set of the same heat range.

APPEARANCE

▶ **See Figure 16**

The firing end of the plug is covered with a wet, oily coating.

CAUSE

The problem is poor oil control. On high-mileage engines, oil is leaking past the rings or valve guides into the combustion chamber. A common cause also is a plugged PCV valve, and a ruptured fuel pump diaphragm also can cause this condition.

Tracking Arc
High voltage arcs between a fouling deposit on the insulator tip and spark plug shell. This ignites the fuel/air mixture at some point along the insulator tip, retarding the ignition timing which causes a power and fuel loss.

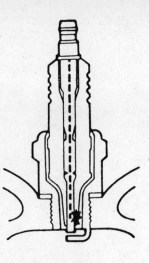

Wide Gap
Spark plug electrodes are worn so that the high voltage charge cannot arc across the electrodes. Improper gapping of electrodes on new or "cleaned" spark plugs could cause a similar condition. Fuel remains unburned and a power loss results.

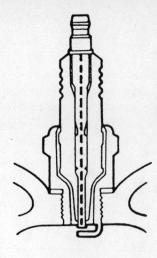

Flashover
A damaged spark plug boot, along with dirt and moisture, could permit the high voltage charge to short over the insulator to the spark plug shell or the engine. AC's buttress insulator design helps prevent high voltage flashover.

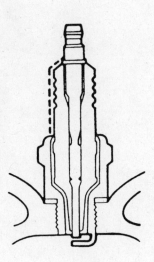

Fouled Spark Plug
Deposits that have formed on the insulator tip may become conductive and provide a "shunt" path to the shell. This prevents the high voltage from arcing between the electrodes. A power and fuel loss is the result.

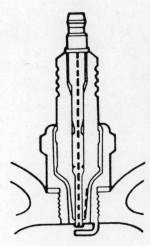

Bridged Electrodes
Fouling deposits between the electrodes "ground out" the high voltage needed to fire the spark plug. The arc between the electrodes does not occur and the fuel air mixture is not ignited. This causes a power loss and exhausting of raw fuel.

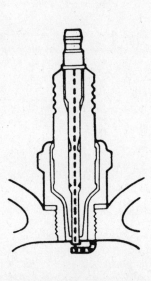

Cracked Insulator
A crack in the spark plug insulator could cause the high voltage charge to "ground out." Here, the spark does not jump the electrode gap and the fuel air mixture is not ignited. This causes a power loss and raw fuel is exhausted.

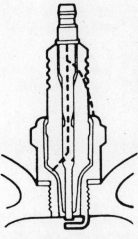

tccs2001

Fig. 14 Used spark plugs which show damage may indicate engine problems

tccs2135

Fig. 15 A normally worn spark plug should have light tan or grey deposits on the firing tip

tccs2138

Fig. 16 An oil fouled spark plug indicates an engine with worn piston rings and/or bad valve seals allowing excessive oil to enter the combustion chamber

Oil-fouled plugs such as these are often found in new or recently overhauled engines, before normal oil control is achieved, and can be cleaned and reinstalled.

RECOMMENDATION

A hotter spark plug may temporarily relieve the problem, but the engine is probably in need of repair.

APPEARANCE

▶ See Figure 17

Carbon fouling is easily identified by the presence of dry, soft, black, sooty deposits.

CAUSE

Changing the heat range can often lead to carbon fouling, as can prolonged slow, stop-and-start driving. If the heat range is correct, carbon fouling can be attributed to a rich fuel mixture, sticking choke, clogged air cleaner, worn breaker points, retarded timing, or low compression. If only one or two plugs

are carbon-fouled, check for corroded or cracked wires on the affected plugs. Also look for cracks in the distributor cap between the towers of affected cylinders.

RECOMMENDATION

After the problem is corrected, these plugs can be cleaned and reinstalled if not worn severely.

APPEARANCE

▶ See Figure 18

Splash deposits occur in varying degrees as spotty deposits on the insulator.

CAUSE

By-products of combustion have accumulated on pistons and valves because of a delayed tune-up. Following tune-up or during hard acceleration, the deposits loosen and are thrown against the hot surface of the plug. If sufficient deposits accumulate, misfiring can occur.

Fig. 17 A carbon fouled plug, identified by soft, sooty, black deposits, may indicate an improperly tuned engine. Check the air cleaner, ignition components and engine control systems

Fig. 18 A bridged gap or almost bridged spark plug, identified by a build-up of deposits between the electrodes, caused by excessive carbon or oil build-up on the plug

RECOMMENDATION

These plugs can be cleaned, gapped, and reinstalled.

APPEARANCE

▶ See Figure 19

Excessive gap.

CAUSE

During hard, fast acceleration, plug temperatures rise suddenly. Deposits from normal combustion have no chance to burn off; instead, they melt on the insulator forming an electrically conductive coating that causes misfiring.

RECOMMENDATION

Glazed plugs are not easily cleaned. They should be replaced with a fresh set of plugs of the correct heat range. If the condition recurs, using plugs with a heat range one step colder may cure the problem.

APPEARANCE

▶ See Figure 20

Detonation is usually characterized by a broken plug insulator.

CAUSE

A portion of the fuel charge will begin to burn spontaneously from the increased heat following ignition. The explosion that results applies extreme pressure to engine components, frequently damaging spark plugs and pistons.

Detonation can result from over-advanced ignition timing, inferior gasoline (low octane), lean fuel/air mixture, poor carburetion, engine lugging, or an increase in compression ratio due to combustion chamber deposits or engine modification.

RECOMMENDATION

Replace the plugs after correcting the problem.

Fig. 19 This plug has been left in the engine too long causing an excessive gap between the electrodes. Plugs with an excessive gap can cause misfiring, stumble, poor fuel economy and a lack of power

Fig. 20 A physically damaged spark plug may be evidence of severe detonation in that cylinder. Watch that cylinder carefully since continued detonation will not only damage the plug, but could also damage the engine

Spark Plug Wires

TESTING

♦ See Figures 21 and 22

Visually check the spark plug cables for burns cuts, or breaks in the insulation. Check the boots and the nipples on the distributor cap and coil. Replace any damaged wiring.

Every 50,000 miles (80,000 Km) or 60 months, the resistance of the wires should be checked with an ohmmeter. Wires with excessive resistance will cause misfiring, and may make the engine difficult to start in damp weather.

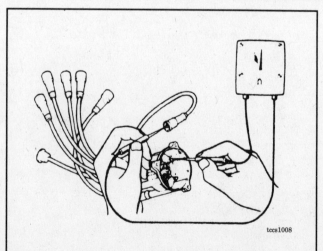

Fig. 21 Checking plug wire resistance through the distributor cap with an ohmmeter

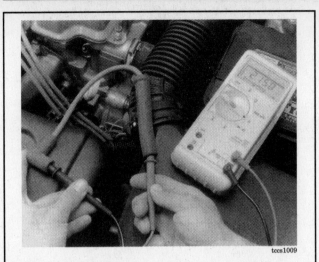

Fig. 22 Checking individual plug wire resistance with an digital ohmmeter

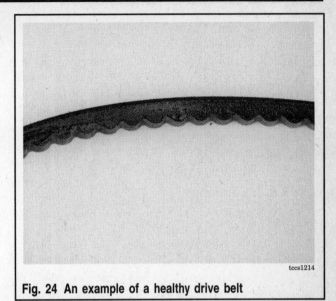

Fig. 24 An example of a healthy drive belt

Accessory Drive Belts

INSPECTION

▶ See Figures 23, 24, 25, 26 and 27

Inspect the belts for signs of glazing or cracking. A glazed belt will be perfectly smooth from slippage, while a good belt will have a slight texture of fabric visible. Cracks will usually start at the inner edge of the belt and run outward. All worn or damaged drive belts should be replaced immediately. It is best to replace all drive belts at one time, as a preventive maintenance measure, during this service operation.

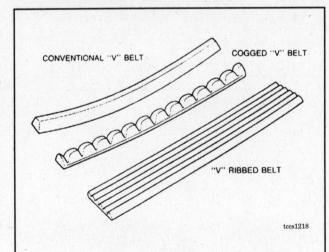

Fig. 23 There are typically 3 types of accessory drive belts found on vehicles today

Timing Belts

INSPECTION

▶ See Figures 28, 29, 30, 31, 32 and 33

Timing belts are found with increasing frequency on most domestic and imported vehicles. It is important to periodically check the condition of the timing belt, but when overhauling and engine equipped with a timing belt, always change it. A broken timing belt can cause major internal damage.

Hoses

INSPECTION

▶ See Figures 34, 35, 36 and 37

Upper and lower radiator hoses along with the heater hoses should be checked for deterioration, leaks and loose hose clamps at least every 15,000 miles (24,000 km). It is also wise to check the hoses periodically in early spring and at the beginning of the fall or winter when you are performing other maintenance. A quick visual inspection could discover a weakened hose which might have left you stranded if it had remained unrepaired.

Whenever you are checking the hoses, make sure the engine and cooling system are cold. Visually inspect for cracking, rotting or collapsed hoses, and replace as necessary. Run your hand along the length of the hose. If a weak or swollen spot is noted when squeezing the hose wall, the hose should be replaced.

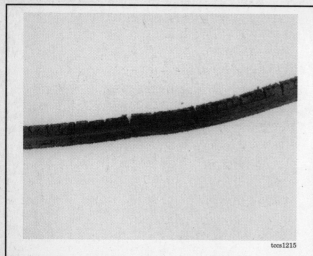

Fig. 25 Deep cracks in this belt will cause flex, building up heat that will eventually lead to belt failure

Fig. 26 The cover of this belt is worn, exposing the critical reinforcing cords to excessive wear

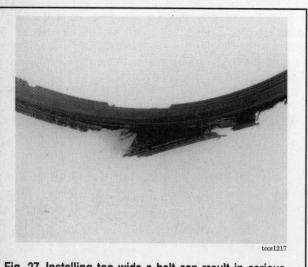

Fig. 27 Installing too wide a belt can result in serious belt wear and/or breakage

Fig. 28 Do not bend, twist or turn the timing belt inside out. Never allow oil, water or steam to contact the belt

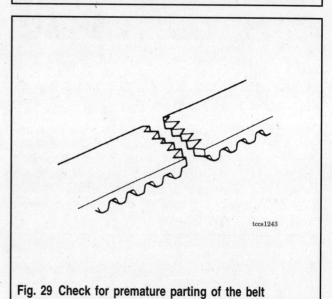

Fig. 29 Check for premature parting of the belt

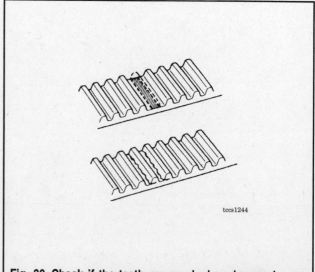

Fig. 30 Check if the teeth are cracked or damaged

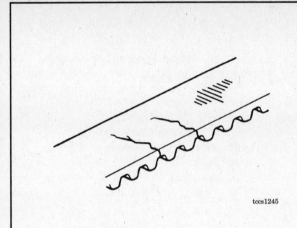

Fig. 31 Look for noticeable cracks or wear on the belt face

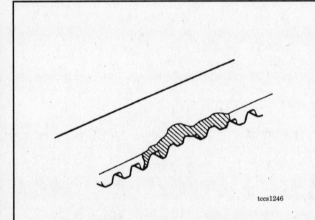

Fig. 32 You may only have damage on one side of the belt; if so, the guide could be the culprit

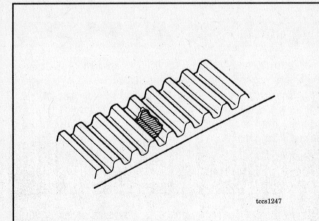

Fig. 33 Foreign materials can get in between the teeth and cause damage

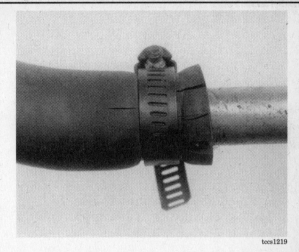

Fig. 34 The cracks developing along this hose are a result of age-related hardening

Fig. 35 A hose clamp that is too tight can cause older hoses to separate and tear on either side of the clamp

Fig. 36 A soft spongy hose (identifiable by the swollen section) will eventually burst and should be replaced

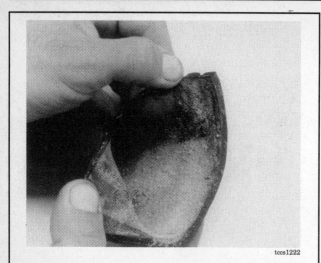
tccs1222

Fig. 37 Hoses are likely to deteriorate from the inside if the cooling system is not periodically flushed

REMOVAL & INSTALLATION

1. Remove the radiator pressure cap.

❉❉CAUTION

Never remove the pressure cap while the engine is running, or personal injury from scalding hot coolant or steam may result. If possible, wait until the engine has cooled to remove the pressure cap. If this is not possible, wrap a thick cloth around the pressure cap and turn it slowly to the stop. Step back while the pressure is released from the cooling system. When you are sure all the pressure has been released, use the cloth to turn and remove the cap.

2. Position a clean container under the radiator and/or engine draincock or plug, then open the drain and allow the cooling system to drain to an appropriate level. For some upper hoses, only a little coolant must be drained. To remove hoses positioned lower on the engine, such as a lower radiator hose, the entire cooling system must be emptied.

❉❉CAUTION

When draining coolant, keep in mind that cats and dogs are attracted by ethylene glycol antifreeze, and are quite likely to drink any that is left in an uncovered container or in puddles on the ground. This will prove fatal in sufficient quantity. Always drain coolant into a sealable container. Coolant may be reused unless it is contaminated or several years old.

3. Loosen the hose clamps at each end of the hose requiring replacement. Clamps are usually either of the spring tension type (which require pliers to squeeze the tabs and loosen) or of the screw tension type (which require screw or hex drivers to loosen). Pull the clamps back on the hose away from the connection.

4. Twist, pull and slide the hose off the fitting, taking care not to damage the neck of the component from which the hose is being removed.

➡If the hose is stuck at the connection, do not try to insert a screwdriver or other sharp tool under the hose end in an effort to free it, as the connection and/or hose may become damaged. Heater connections especially may be easily damaged by such a procedure. If the hose is to be replaced, use a single-edged razor blade to make a slice along the portion of the hose which is stuck on the connection, perpendicular to the end of the hose. Do not cut deep so as to prevent damaging the connection. The hose can then be peeled from the connection and discarded.

5. Clean both hose mounting connections. Inspect the condition of the hose clamps and replace them, if necessary.
To install:
6. Dip the ends of the new hose into clean engine coolant to ease installation.
7. Slide the clamps over the replacement hose, then slide the hose ends over the connections into position.
8. Position and secure the clamps at least ¼ in. (6.35mm) from the ends of the hose. Make sure they are located beyond the raised bead of the connector.
9. Close the radiator or engine drains and properly refill the cooling system with the clean drained engine coolant or a suitable mixture of ethylene glycol coolant and water.
10. If available, install a pressure tester and check for leaks. If a pressure tester is not available, run the engine until normal operating temperature is reached (allowing the system to naturally pressurize), then check for leaks.

❉❉CAUTION

If you are checking for leaks with the system at normal operating temperature, BE EXTREMELY CAREFUL not to touch any moving or hot engine parts. Once temperature has been reached, shut the engine OFF, and check for leaks around the hose fittings and connections which were removed earlier.

Air Conditioning

➡Be sure to consult the laws in your area before servicing the air conditioning system. In most areas, it is illegal to perform repairs involving refrigerant unless the work is done by a certified technician. Also, it is quite likely that you will not be able to purchase refrigerant without proof of certification.

SAFETY PRECAUTIONS

There are two major hazards associated with air conditioning systems and they both relate to the refrigerant gas. First, the refrigerant gas (R-12 or R-134a) is an extremely cold substance. When exposed to air, it will instantly freeze any surface it comes in contact with, including your eyes. The other hazard relates to fire (if your vehicle is equipped with R-12. Although normally non-toxic, the R-12 gas becomes highly poisonous in the presence of an open flame. One good whiff of the vapor formed by burning R-12 can be fatal. Keep all forms of fire (including cigarettes) well clear of the air conditioning system.

Because of the inherent dangers involved with working on air conditioning systems, these safety precautions must be strictly followed.

- Avoid contact with a charged refrigeration system, even when working on another part of the air conditioning system or vehicle. If a heavy tool comes into contact with a section of tubing or a heat exchanger, it can easily cause the relatively soft material to rupture.
- When it is necessary to apply force to a fitting which contains refrigerant, as when checking that all system couplings are securely tightened, use a wrench on both parts of the fitting involved, if possible. This will avoid putting torque on refrigerant tubing. (It is also advisable to use tube or line wrenches when tightening these flare nut fittings.)

➡R-12 refrigerant is a chlorofluorocarbon which, when released into the atmosphere, can contribute to the depletion of the ozone layer in the upper atmosphere. Ozone filters out harmful radiation from the sun.

- Do not attempt to discharge the system without the proper tools. Precise control is possible only when using the service gauges and a proper A/C refrigerant recovery station. Wear protective gloves when connecting or disconnecting service gauge hoses.
- Discharge the system only in a well ventilated area, as high concentrations of the gas which might accidentally escape can exclude oxygen and act as an anesthetic. When leak testing or soldering, this is particularly important, as toxic gas is formed when R-12 contacts any flame.
- Never start a system without first verifying that both service valves are properly installed, and that all fittings throughout the system are snugly connected.
- Avoid applying heat to any refrigerant line or storage vessel. Charging may be aided by using water heated to less than 125°F (50°C) to warm the refrigerant container. Never allow a refrigerant storage container to sit out in the sun, or near any other source of heat, such as a radiator or heater.
- Always wear goggles to protect your eyes when working on a system. If refrigerant contacts the eyes, it is advisable in all cases to consult a physician immediately.
- Frostbite from liquid refrigerant should be treated by first gradually warming the area with cool water, and then gently applying petroleum jelly. A physician should be consulted.
- Always keep refrigerant drum fittings capped when not in use. If the container is equipped with a safety cap to protect the valve, make sure the cap is in place when the can is not being used. Avoid sudden shock to the drum, which might occur from dropping it, or from banging a heavy tool against it. Never carry a drum in the passenger compartment of a vehicle.
- Always completely discharge the system into a suitable recovery unit before painting the vehicle (if the paint is to be baked on), or before welding anywhere near refrigerant lines.
- When servicing the system, minimize the time that any refrigerant line or fitting is open to the air in order to prevent moisture or dirt from entering the system. Contaminants such as moisture or dirt can damage internal system components. Always replace O-rings on lines or fittings which are disconnected. Prior to installation coat, but do not soak, replacement O-rings with suitable compressor oil.

GENERAL SERVICING PROCEDURES

➡It is recommended, and possibly required by law, that a qualified technician perform the following services.

✲✲WARNING

Some of the vehicles covered by this manual may be equipped with R-134a refrigerant systems, rather than R-12. Be ABSOLUTELY SURE what type of system you are working on before attempting to add refrigerant. Use of the wrong refrigerant or oil will cause damage to the system.

The most important aspect of air conditioning service is the maintenance of a pure and adequate charge of refrigerant in the system. A refrigeration system cannot function properly if a significant percentage of the charge is lost. Leaks are common because the severe vibration encountered underhood in an automobile can easily cause a sufficient cracking or loosening of the air conditioning fittings; allowing, the extreme operating pressures of the system to force refrigerant out.

The problem can be understood by considering what happens to the system as it is operated with a continuous leak. Because the expansion valve regulates the flow of refrigerant to the evaporator, the level of refrigerant there is fairly constant. The receiver/drier stores any excess refrigerant, and so a loss will first appear there as a reduction in the level of liquid. As this level nears the bottom of the vessel, some refrigerant vapor bubbles will begin to appear in the stream of liquid supplied to the expansion valve. This vapor decreases the capacity of the expansion valve very little as the valve opens to compensate for its presence. As the quantity of liquid in the condenser decreases, the operating pressure will drop there and throughout the high side of the system. As the refrigerant continues to be expelled, the pressure available to force the liquid through the expansion valve will continue to decrease, and, eventually, the valve's orifice will prove to be too much of a restriction for adequate flow even with the needle fully withdrawn.

At this point, low side pressure will start to drop, and a severe reduction in cooling capacity, marked by freeze-up of the evaporator coil, will result. Eventually, the operating pressure of the evaporator will be lower than the pressure of the atmosphere surrounding it, and air will be drawn into the system wherever there are leaks in the low side.

Because all atmospheric air contains at least some moisture, water will enter the system mixing with the refrigerant and oil. Trace amounts of moisture will cause sludging of the oil, and corrosion of the system. Saturation and clogging of the filter/drier, and freezing of the expansion valve orifice will eventually result. As air fills the system to a greater and greater extent, it will interfere more and more with the normal flows of refrigerant and heat.

From this description, it should be obvious that much of the repairman's focus in on detecting leaks, repairing them, and then restoring the purity and quantity of the refrigerant charge. A list of general rules should be followed in addition to all safety precautions:

• Keep all tools as clean and dry as possible.

• Thoroughly purge the service gauges/hoses of air and moisture before connecting them to the system. Keep them capped when not in use.

• Thoroughly clean any refrigerant fitting before disconnecting it, in order to minimize the entrance of dirt into the system.

• Plan any operation that requires opening the system beforehand, in order to minimize the length of time it will be exposed to open air. Cap or seal the open ends to minimize the entrance of foreign material.

• When adding oil, pour it through an extremely clean and dry tube or funnel. Keep the oil capped whenever possible. Do not use oil that has not been kept tightly sealed.

• Purchase refrigerant intended for use only in automatic air conditioning systems.

• Completely evacuate any system that has been opened for service, or that has leaked sufficiently to draw in moisture and air. This requires evacuating air and moisture with a good vacuum pump for at least one hour. If a system has been open for a considerable length of time it may be advisable to evacuate the system for up to 12 hours (overnight).

• Use a wrench on both halves of a fitting that is to be disconnected, so as to avoid placing torque on any of the refrigerant lines.

• When overhauling a compressor, pour some of the oil into a clean glass and inspect it. If there is evidence of dirt, metal particles, or both, flush all refrigerant components with clean refrigerant before evacuating and recharging the system. In addition, if metal particles are present, the compressor should be replaced.

• Schrader valves may leak only when under full operating pressure. Therefore, if leakage is suspected but cannot be located, operate the system with a full charge of refrigerant and look for leaks from all Schrader valves. Replace any faulty valves.

Additional Preventive Maintenance

USING THE SYSTEM

The easiest and most important preventive maintenance for your A/C system is to be sure that it is used on a regular basis. Running the system for five minutes each month (no matter what the season) will help assure that the seals and all internal components remain lubricated.

ANTIFREEZE

▶ See Figure 38

In order to prevent heater core freeze-up during A/C operation, it is necessary to maintain a proper antifreeze protection. Use a hand-held antifreeze tester (hydrometer) to periodically check the condition of the antifreeze in your engine's cooling system.

➡**Antifreeze should not be used longer than the manufacturer specifies.**

Fig. 38 An antifreeze tester can be use to determine the freezing and boiling level of the coolant in your vehicle

RADIATOR CAP

For efficient operation of an air conditioned vehicle's cooling system, the radiator cap should have a holding pressure which meets manufacturer's specifications. A cap which fails to hold these pressures should be replaced.

CONDENSER

Any obstruction of or damage to the condenser configuration will restrict the air flow which is essential to its efficient operation. It is therefore a good rule to keep this unit clean and in proper physical shape.

➡**Bug screens which are mounted in front of the condenser (unless they are original equipment) are regarded as obstructions.**

CONDENSATION DRAIN TUBE

This single molded drain tube expels the condensation, which accumulates on the bottom of the evaporator housing, into the engine compartment. If this tube is obstructed, the air conditioning performance can be restricted and condensation buildup can spill over onto the vehicle's floor.

SYSTEM INSPECTION

➡**R-12 refrigerant is a chlorofluorocarbon which, when released into the atmosphere, can contribute to the depletion of the ozone layer in the upper atmosphere. Ozone filters out harmful radiation from the sun.**

The easiest and often most important check for the air conditioning system consists of a visual inspection of the system components. Visually inspect the air conditioning system for refrigerant leaks, damaged compressor clutch, compressor drive belt tension and condition, plugged evaporator drain tube, blocked condenser fins, disconnected or broken wires, blown fuses, corroded connections and poor insulation.

A refrigerant leak will usually appear as an oily residue at the leakage point in the system. The oily residue soon picks up dust or dirt particles from the surrounding air and appears greasy. Through time, this will build up and appear to be a heavy dirt impregnated grease. Most leaks are caused by damaged or missing O-ring seals at the component connections, damaged charging valve cores or missing service gauge port caps.

For a thorough visual and operational inspection, check the following:

1. Check the surface of the radiator and condenser for dirt, leaves or other material which might block air flow.

2. Check for kinks in hoses and lines. Check the system for leaks.

3. Make sure the drive belt is under the proper tension. When the air conditioning is operating, make sure the drive belt is free of noise or slippage.

4. Make sure the blower motor operates at all appropriate positions, then check for distribution of the air from all outlets with the blower on **HIGH**.

➡**Keep in mind that under conditions of high humidity, air discharged from the A/C vents may not feel as cold as expected, even if the system is working properly. This is because the vaporized moisture in humid air retains heat more effectively than does dry air, making the humid air more difficult to cool.**

5. Make sure the air passage selection lever is operating correctly. Start the engine and warm it to normal operating temperature, then make sure the hot/cold selection lever is operating correctly.

DISCHARGING, EVACUATING AND CHARGING

Discharging, evacuating and charging the air conditioning system must be performed by a properly trained and certified mechanic in a facility equipped with refrigerant recovery/recycling equipment that meets SAE standards for the type of system to be serviced.

If you don't have access to the necessary equipment, we recommend that you take your vehicle to a reputable service station to have the work done. If you still wish to perform repairs on the vehicle, have them discharge the system, then take your vehicle home and perform the necessary work. When you are finished, return the vehicle to the station for evacuation and charging. Just be sure to cap ALL A/C system fittings immediately after opening them and keep them protected until the system is recharged.

ENGLISH TO METRIC CONVERSION: MASS (WEIGHT)

Current **mass** measurement is expressed in pounds and ounces (lbs. & ozs.). The metric unit of mass (or weight) is the kilogram (kg). Even although this table does not show conversion of masses (weights) larger than 15 lbs, it is easy to calculate larger units by following the data immediately below.

To convert ounces (oz.) to grams (g): multiply th number of ozs. by 28
To convert grams (g) to ounces (oz.): multiply the number of grams by .035

To convert pounds (lbs.) to kilograms (kg): multiply the number of lbs. by .45
To convert kilograms (kg) to pounds (lbs.): multiply the number of kilograms by 2.2

lbs	kg	lbs	kg	oz	kg	oz	kg
0.1	0.04	0.9	0.41	0.1	0.003	0.9	0.024
0.2	0.09	1	0.4	0.2	0.005	1	0.03
0.3	0.14	2	0.9	0.3	0.008	2	0.06
0.4	0.18	3	1.4	0.4	0.011	3	0.08
0.5	0.23	4	1.8	0.5	0.014	4	0.11
0.6	0.27	5	2.3	0.6	0.017	5	0.14
0.7	0.32	10	4.5	0.7	0.020	10	0.28
0.8	0.36	15	6.8	0.8	0.023	15	0.42

ENGLISH TO METRIC CONVERSION: TEMPERATURE

To convert Fahrenheit (°F) to Celsius (°C): take number of °F and subtract 32; multiply result by 5; divide result by 9

To convert Celsius (°C) to Fahrenheit (°F): take number of °C and multiply by 9; divide result by 5; add 32 to total

Fahrenheit (F)	Celsius (C)			Fahrenheit (F)	Celsius (C)			Fahrenheit (F)	Celsius (C)		
°F	°C	°C	°F	°F	°C	°C	°F	°F	°C	°C	°F
−40	−40	−38	−36.4	80	26.7	18	64.4	215	101.7	80	176
−35	−37.2	−36	−32.8	85	29.4	20	68	220	104.4	85	185
−30	−34.4	−34	−29.2	90	32.2	22	71.6	225	107.2	90	194
−25	−31.7	−32	−25.6	95	35.0	24	75.2	230	110.0	95	202
−20	−28.9	−30	−22	100	37.8	26	78.8	235	112.8	100	212
−15	−26.1	−28	−18.4	105	40.6	28	82.4	240	115.6	105	221
−10	−23.3	−26	−14.8	110	43.3	30	86	245	118.3	110	230
−5	−20.6	−24	−11.2	115	46.1	32	89.6	250	121.1	115	239
0	−17.8	−22	−7.6	120	48.9	34	93.2	255	123.9	120	248
1	−17.2	−20	−4	125	51.7	36	96.8	260	126.6	125	257
2	−16.7	−18	−0.4	130	54.4	38	100.4	265	129.4	130	266
3	−16.1	−16	3.2	135	57.2	40	104	270	132.2	135	275
4	−15.6	−14	6.8	140	60.0	42	107.6	275	135.0	140	284
5	−15.0	−12	10.4	145	62.8	44	112.2	280	137.8	145	293
10	−12.2	−10	14	150	65.6	46	114.8	285	140.6	150	302
15	−9.4	−8	17.6	155	68.3	48	118.4	290	143.3	155	311
20	−6.7	−6	21.2	160	71.1	50	122	295	146.1	160	320
25	−3.9	−4	24.8	165	73.9	52	125.6	300	148.9	165	329
30	−1.1	−2	28.4	170	76.7	54	129.2	305	151.7	170	338
35	1.7	0	32	175	79.4	56	132.8	310	154.4	175	347
40	4.4	2	35.6	180	82.2	58	136.4	315	157.2	180	356
45	7.2	4	39.2	185	85.0	60	140	320	160.0	185	365
50	10.0	6	42.8	190	87.8	62	143.6	325	162.8	190	374
55	12.8	8	46.4	195	90.6	64	147.2	330	165.6	195	383
60	15.6	10	50	200	93.3	66	150.8	335	168.3	200	392
65	18.3	12	53.6	205	96.1	68	154.4	340	171.1	205	401
70	21.1	14	57.2	210	98.9	70	158	345	173.9	210	410
75	23.9	16	60.8	212	100.0	75	167	350	176.7	215	414

ENGLISH TO METRIC CONVERSION: LENGTH

To convert inches (ins.) to millimeters (mm): multiply number of inches by 25.4

To convert millimeters (mm) to inches (ins.): multiply number of millimeters by .04

Inches	Decimals	Milli-meters	Inches to millimeters inches	mm	Inches	Decimals	Milli-meters	Inches to millimeters inches	mm
1/64	0.051625	0.3969	0.0001	0.00254	33/64	0.515625	13.0969	0.6	15.24
1/32	0.03125	0.7937	0.0002	0.00508	17/32	0.53125	13.4937	0.7	17.78
3/64	0.046875	1.1906	0.0003	0.00762	35/64	0.546875	13.8906	0.8	20.32
1/16	0.0625	1.5875	0.0004	0.01016	9/16	0.5625	14.2875	0.9	22.86
5/64	0.078125	1.9844	0.0005	0.01270	37/64	0.578125	14.6844	1	25.4
3/32	0.09375	2.3812	0.0006	0.01524	19/32	0.59375	15.0812	2	50.8
7/64	0.109375	2.7781	0.0007	0.01778	39/64	0.609375	15.4781	3	76.2
1/8	0.125	3.1750	0.0008	0.02032	5/8	0.625	15.8750	4	101.6
9/64	0.140625	3.5719	0.0009	0.02286	41/64	0.640625	16.2719	5	127.0
5/32	0.15625	3.9687	0.001	0.0254	21/32	0.65625	16.6687	6	152.4
11/64	0.171875	4.3656	0.002	0.0508	43/64	0.671875	17.0656	7	177.8
3/16	0.1875	4.7625	0.003	0.0762	11/16	0.6875	17.4625	8	203.2
13/64	0.203125	5.1594	0.004	0.1016	45/64	0.703125	17.8594	9	228.6
7/32	0.21875	5.5562	0.005	0.1270	23/32	0.71875	18.2562	10	254.0
15/64	0.234375	5.9531	0.006	0.1524	47/64	0.734375	18.6531	11	279.4
1/4	0.25	6.3500	0.007	0.1778	3/4	0.75	19.0500	12	304.8
17/64	0.265625	6.7469	0.008	0.2032	49/64	0.765625	19.4469	13	330.2
9/32	0.28125	7.1437	0.009	0.2286	25/32	0.78125	19.8437	14	355.6
19/64	0.296875	7.5406	0.01	0.254	51/64	0.796875	20.2406	15	381.0
5/16	0.3125	7.9375	0.02	0.508	13/16	0.8125	20.6375	16	406.4
21/64	0.328125	8.3344	0.03	0.762	53/64	0.828125	21.0344	17	431.8
11/32	0.34375	8.7312	0.04	1.016	27/32	0.84375	21.4312	18	457.2
23/64	0.359375	9.1281	0.05	1.270	55/64	0.859375	21.8281	19	482.6
3/8	0.375	9.5250	0.06	1.524	7/8	0.875	22.2250	20	508.0
25/64	0.390625	9.9219	0.07	1.778	57/64	0.890625	22.6219	21	533.4
13/32	0.40625	10.3187	0.08	2.032	29/32	0.90625	23.0187	22	558.8
27/64	0.421875	10.7156	0.09	2.286	59/64	0.921875	23.4156	23	584.2
7/16	0.4375	11.1125	0.1	2.54	15/16	0.9375	23.8125	24	609.6
29/64	0.453125	11.5094	0.2	5.08	61/64	0.953125	24.2094	25	635.0
15/32	0.46875	11.9062	0.3	7.62	31/32	0.96875	24.6062	26	660.4
31/64	0.484375	12.3031	0.4	10.16	63/64	0.984375	25.0031	27	690.6
1/2	0.5	12.7000	0.5	12.70					

ENGLISH TO METRIC CONVERSION: TORQUE

To convert foot-pounds (ft. lbs.) to Newton-meters: multiply the number of ft. lbs. by 1.3

To convert inch-pounds (in. lbs.) to Newton-meters: multiply the number of in. lbs. by .11

in lbs	N-m	in lbs	N-m	in lbs	N-m	in lbs	N-m	in lbs	N-m
0.1	0.01	1	0.11	10	1.13	19	2.15	28	3.16
0.2	0.02	2	0.23	11	1.24	20	2.26	29	3.28
0.3	0.03	3	0.34	12	1.36	21	2.37	30	3.39
0.4	0.04	4	0.45	13	1.47	22	2.49	31	3.50
0.5	0.06	5	0.56	14	1.58	23	2.60	32	3.62
0.6	0.07	6	0.68	15	1.70	24	2.71	33	3.73
0.7	0.08	7	0.78	16	1.81	25	2.82	34	3.84
0.8	0.09	8	0.90	17	1.92	26	2.94	35	3.95
0.9	0.10	9	1.02	18	2.03	27	3.05	36	4.0/

tccs1c02

ENGLISH TO METRIC CONVERSION: TORQUE

Torque is now expressed as either foot-pounds (ft./lbs.) or inch-pounds (in./lbs.). The metric measurement unit for torque is the Newton-meter (Nm). This unit—the Nm—will be used for all SI metric torque references, both the present ft./lbs. and in./lbs.

ft lbs	N-m	ft lbs	N-m	ft lbs	N-m	ft lbs	N-m
0.1	0.1	33	44.7	74	100.3	115	155.9
0.2	0.3	34	46.1	75	101.7	116	157.3
0.3	0.4	35	47.4	76	103.0	117	158.6
0.4	0.5	36	48.8	77	104.4	118	160.0
0.5	0.7	37	50.7	78	105.8	119	161.3
0.6	0.8	38	51.5	79	107.1	120	162.7
0.7	1.0	39	52.9	80	108.5	121	164.0
0.8	1.1	40	54.2	81	109.8	122	165.4
0.9	1.2	41	55.6	82	111.2	123	166.8
1	1.3	42	56.9	83	112.5	124	168.1
2	2.7	43	58.3	84	113.9	125	169.5
3	4.1	44	59.7	85	115.2	126	170.8
4	5.4	45	61.0	86	116.6	127	172.2
5	6.8	46	62.4	87	118.0	128	173.5
6	8.1	47	63.7	88	119.3	129	174.9
7	9.5	48	65.1	89	120.7	130	176.2
8	10.8	49	66.4	90	122.0	131	177.6
9	12.2	50	67.8	91	123.4	132	179.0
10	13.6	51	69.2	92	124.7	133	180.3
11	14.9	52	70.5	93	126.1	134	181.7
12	16.3	53	71.9	94	127.4	135	183.0
13	17.6	54	73.2	95	128.8	136	184.4
14	18.9	55	74.6	96	130.2	137	185.7
15	20.3	56	75.9	97	131.5	138	187.1
16	21.7	57	77.3	98	132.9	139	188.5
17	23.0	58	78.6	99	134.2	140	189.8
18	24.4	59	80.0	100	135.6	141	191.2
19	25.8	60	81.4	101	136.9	142	192.5
20	27.1	61	82.7	102	138.3	143	193.9
21	28.5	62	84.1	103	139.6	144	195.2
22	29.8	63	85.4	104	141.0	145	196.6
23	31.2	64	86.8	105	142.4	146	198.0
24	32.5	65	88.1	106	143.7	147	199.3
25	33.9	66	89.5	107	145.1	148	200.7
26	35.2	67	90.8	108	146.4	149	202.0
27	36.6	68	92.2	109	147.8	150	203.4
28	38.0	69	93.6	110	149.1	151	204.7
29	39.3	70	94.9	111	150.5	152	206.1
30	40.7	71	96.3	112	151.8	153	207.4
31	42.0	72	97.6	113	153.2	154	208.8
32	43.4	73	99.0	114	154.6	155	210.2

tccs1c03

ENGLISH TO METRIC CONVERSION: FORCE

Force is presently measured in pounds (lbs.). This type of measurement is used to measure spring pressure, specifically how many pounds it takes to compress a spring. Our present force unit (the pound) will be replaced in SI metric measurements by the Newton (N). This term will eventually see use in specifications for electric motor brush spring pressures, valve spring pressures, etc.

To convert pounds (lbs.) to Newton (N): multiply the number of lbs. by 4.45

lbs	N	lbs	N	lbs	N	oz	N
0.01	0.04	21	93.4	59	262.4	1	0.3
0.02	0.09	22	97.9	60	266.9	2	0.6
0.03	0.13	23	102.3	61	271.3	3	0.8
0.04	0.18	24	106.8	62	275.8	4	1.1
0.05	0.22	25	111.2	63	280.2	5	1.4
0.06	0.27	26	115.6	64	284.6	6	1.7
0.07	0.31	27	120.1	65	289.1	7	2.0
0.08	0.36	28	124.6	66	293.6	8	2.2
0.09	0.40	29	129.0	67	298.0	9	2.5
0.1	0.4	30	133.4	68	302.5	10	2.8
0.2	0.9	31	137.9	69	306.9	11	3.1
0.3	1.3	32	142.3	70	311.4	12	3.3
0.4	1.8	33	146.8	71	315.8	13	3.6
0.5	2.2	34	151.2	72	320.3	14	3.9
0.6	2.7	35	155.7	73	324.7	15	4.2
0.7	3.1	36	160.1	74	329.2	16	4.4
0.8	3.6	37	164.6	75	333.6	17	4.7
0.9	4.0	38	169.0	76	338.1	18	5.0
1	4.4	39	173.5	77	342.5	19	5.3
2	8.9	40	177.9	78	347.0	20	5.6
3	13.4	41	182.4	79	351.4	21	5.8
4	17.8	42	186.8	80	355.9	22	6.1
5	22.2	43	191.3	81	360.3	23	6.4
6	26.7	44	195.7	82	364.8	24	6.7
7	31.1	45	200.2	83	369.2	25	7.0
8	35.6	46	204.6	84	373.6	26	7.2
9	40.0	47	209.1	85	378.1	27	7.5
10	44.5	48	213.5	86	382.6	28	7.8
11	48.9	49	218.0	87	387.0	29	8.1
12	53.4	50	224.4	88	391.4	30	8.3
13	57.8	51	226.9	89	395.9	31	8.6
14	62.3	52	231.3	90	400.3	32	8.9
15	66.7	53	235.8	91	404.8	33	9.2
16	71.2	54	240.2	92	409.2	34	9.4
17	75.6	55	244.6	93	413.7	35	9.7
18	80.1	56	249.1	94	418.1	36	10.0
19	84.5	57	253.6	95	422.6	37	10.3
20	89.0	58	258.0	96	427.0	38	10.6

tccs1c04

ENGLISH TO METRIC CONVERSION: LIQUID CAPACITY

Liquid or fluid capacity is presently expressed as pints, quarts or gallons, or a combination of all of these. In the metric system the liter (l) will become the basic unit. Fractions of a liter would be expressed as deciliters, centiliters, or most frequently (and commonly) as milliliters.

To convert pints (pts.) to liters (l): multiply the number of pints by .47
To convert liters (l) to pints (pts.): multiply the number of liters by 2.1
To convert quarts (qts.) to liters (l): multiply the number of quarts by .95

To convert liters (l) to quarts (qts.): multiply the number of liters by 1.06
To convert gallons (gals.) to liters (l): multiply the number of gallons by 3.8
To convert liters (l) to gallons (gals.): multiply the number of liters by .26

gals	liters	qts	liters	pts	liters
0.1	0.38	0.1	0.10	0.1	0.05
0.2	0.76	0.2	0.19	0.2	0.10
0.3	1.1	0.3	0.28	0.3	0.14
0.4	1.5	0.4	0.38	0.4	0.19
0.5	1.9	0.5	0.47	0.5	0.24
0.6	2.3	0.6	0.57	0.6	0.28
0.7	2.6	0.7	0.66	0.7	0.33
0.8	3.0	0.8	0.76	0.8	0.38
0.9	3.4	0.9	0.85	0.9	0.43
1	3.8	1	1.0	1	0.5
2	7.6	2	1.9	2	1.0
3	11.4	3	2.8	3	1.4
4	15.1	4	3.8	4	1.9
5	18.9	5	4.7	5	2.4
6	22.7	6	5.7	6	2.8
7	26.5	7	6.6	7	3.3
8	30.3	8	7.6	8	3.8
9	34.1	9	8.5	9	4.3
10	37.8	10	9.5	10	4.7
11	41.6	11	10.4	11	5.2
12	45.4	12	11.4	12	5.7
13	49.2	13	12.3	13	6.2
14	53.0	14	13.2	14	6.6
15	56.8	15	14.2	15	7.1
16	60.6	16	15.1	16	7.6
17	64.3	17	16.1	17	8.0
18	68.1	18	17.0	18	8.5
19	71.9	19	18.0	19	9.0
20	75.7	20	18.9	20	9.5
21	79.5	21	19.9	21	9.9
22	83.2	22	20.8	22	10.4
23	87.0	23	21.8	23	10.9
24	90.8	24	22.7	24	11.4
25	94.6	25	23.6	25	11.8
26	98.4	26	24.6	26	12.3
27	102.2	27	25.5	27	12.8
28	106.0	28	26.5	28	13.2
29	110.0	29	27.4	29	13.7
30	113.5	30	28.4	30	14.2

ENGLISH TO METRIC CONVERSION: PRESSURE

The basic unit of pressure measurement used today is expressed as pounds per square inch (psi). The metric unit for psi will be the kilopascal (kPa). This will apply to either fluid pressure or air pressure, and will be frequently seen in tire pressure readings, oil pressure specifications, fuel pump pressure, etc.

To convert pounds per square inch (psi) to kilopascals (kPa): multiply the number of psi by 6.89

Psi	kPa	Psi	kPa	Psi	kPa	Psi	kPa
0.1	0.7	37	255.1	82	565.4	127	875.6
0.2	1.4	38	262.0	83	572.3	128	882.5
0.3	2.1	39	268.9	84	579.2	129	889.4
0.4	2.8	40	275.8	85	586.0	130	896.3
0.5	3.4	41	282.7	86	592.9	131	903.2
0.6	4.1	42	289.6	87	599.8	132	910.1
0.7	4.8	43	296.5	88	606.7	133	917.0
0.8	5.5	44	303.4	89	613.6	134	923.9
0.9	6.2	45	310.3	90	620.5	135	930.8
1	6.9	46	317.2	91	627.4	136	937.7
2	13.8	47	324.0	92	634.3	137	944.6
3	20.7	48	331.0	93	641.2	138	951.5
4	27.6	49	337.8	94	648.1	139	958.4
5	34.5	50	344.7	95	655.0	140	965.2
6	41.4	51	351.6	96	661.9	141	972.2
7	48.3	52	358.5	97	668.8	142	979.0
8	55.2	53	365.4	98	675.7	143	985.9
9	62.1	54	372.3	99	682.6	144	992.8
10	69.0	55	379.2	100	689.5	145	999.7
11	75.8	56	386.1	101	696.4	146	1006.6
12	82.7	57	393.0	102	703.3	147	1013.5
13	89.6	58	399.9	103	710.2	148	1020.4
14	96.5	59	406.8	104	717.0	149	1027.3
15	103.4	60	413.7	105	723.9	150	1034.2
16	110.3	61	420.6	106	730.8	151	1041.1
17	117.2	62	427.5	107	737.7	152	1048.0
18	124.1	63	434.4	108	744.6	153	1054.9
19	131.0	64	441.3	109	751.5	154	1061.8
20	137.9	65	448.2	110	758.4	155	1068.7
21	144.8	66	455.0	111	765.3	156	1075.6
22	151.7	67	461.9	112	772.2	157	1082.5
23	158.6	68	468.8	113	779.1	158	1089.4
24	165.5	69	475.7	114	786.0	159	1096.3
25	172.4	70	482.6	115	792.9	160	1103.2
26	179.3	71	489.5	116	799.8	161	1110.0
27	186.2	72	496.4	117	806.7	162	1116.9
28	193.0	73	503.3	118	813.6	163	1123.8
29	200.0	74	510.2	119	820.5	164	1130.7
30	206.8	75	517.1	120	827.4	165	1137.6
31	213.7	76	524.0	121	834.3	166	1144.5
32	220.6	77	530.9	122	841.2	167	1151.4
33	227.5	78	537.8	123	848.0	168	1158.3
34	234.4	79	544.7	124	854.9	169	1165.2
35	241.3	80	551.6	125	861.8	170	1172.1
36	248.2	81	558.5	126	868.7	171	1179.0

tccs1c06

ENGLISH TO METRIC CONVERSION: PRESSURE

The basic unit of pressure measurement used today is expressed as pounds per square inch (psi). The metric unit for psi will be the kilopascal (kPa). This will apply to either fluid pressure or air pressure, and will be frequently seen in tire pressure readings, oil pressure specifications, fuel pump pressure, etc.

To convert pounds per square inch (psi) to kilopascals (kPa): multiply the number of psi by 6.89

Psi	kPa	Psi	kPa	Psi	kPa	Psi	kPa
172	1185.9	216	1489.3	260	1792.6	304	2096.0
173	1192.8	217	1496.2	261	1799.5	305	2102.9
174	1199.7	218	1503.1	262	1806.4	306	2109.8
175	1206.6	219	1510.0	263	1813.3	307	2116.7
176	1213.5	220	1516.8	264	1820.2	308	2123.6
177	1220.4	221	1523.7	265	1827.1	309	2130.5
178	1227.3	222	1530.6	266	1834.0	310	2137.4
179	1234.2	223	1537.5	267	1840.9	311	2144.3
180	1241.0	224	1544.4	268	1847.8	312	2151.2
181	1247.9	225	1551.3	269	1854.7	313	2158.1
182	1254.8	226	1558.2	270	1861.6	314	2164.9
183	1261.7	227	1565.1	271	1868.5	315	2171.8
184	1268.6	228	1572.0	272	1875.4	316	2178.7
185	1275.5	229	1578.9	273	1882.3	317	2185.6
186	1282.4	230	1585.8	274	1889.2	318	2192.5
187	1289.3	231	1592.7	275	1896.1	319	2199.4
188	1296.2	232	1599.6	276	1903.0	320	2206.3
189	1303.1	233	1606.5	277	1909.8	321	2213.2
190	1310.0	234	1613.4	278	1916.7	322	2220.1
191	1316.9	235	1620.3	279	1923.6	323	2227.0
192	1323.8	236	1627.2	280	1930.5	324	2233.9
193	1330.7	237	1634.1	281	1937.4	325	2240.8
194	1337.6	238	1641.0	282	1944.3	326	2247.7
195	1344.5	239	1647.8	283	1951.2	327	2254.6
196	1351.4	240	1654.7	284	1958.1	328	2261.5
197	1358.3	241	1661.6	285	1965.0	329	2268.4
198	1365.2	242	1668.5	286	1971.9	330	2275.3
199	1372.0	243	1675.4	287	1978.8	331	2282.2
200	1378.9	244	1682.3	288	1985.7	332	2289.1
201	1385.8	245	1689.2	289	1992.6	333	2295.9
202	1392.7	246	1696.1	290	1999.5	334	2302.8
203	1399.6	247	1703.0	291	2006.4	335	2309.7
204	1406.5	248	1709.9	292	2013.3	336	2316.6
205	1413.4	249	1716.8	293	2020.2	337	2323.5
206	1420.3	250	1723.7	294	2027.1	338	2330.4
207	1427.2	251	1730.6	295	2034.0	339	2337.3
208	1434.1	252	1737.5	296	2040.8	240	2344.2
209	1441.0	253	1744.4	297	2047.7	341	2351.1
210	1447.9	254	1751.3	298	2054.6	342	2358.0
211	1454.8	255	1758.2	299	2061.5	343	2364.9
212	1461.7	256	1765.1	300	2068.4	344	2371.8
213	1468.7	257	1772.0	301	2075.3	345	2378.7
214	1475.5	258	1778.8	302	2082.2	346	2385.6
215	1482.4	259	1785.7	303	2089.1	347	2392.5

tccs1c07

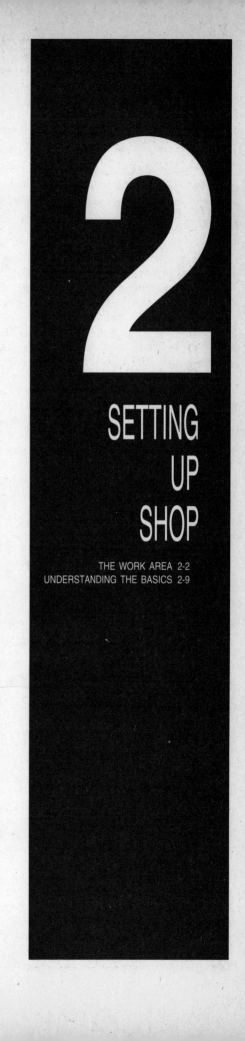

2

SETTING UP SHOP

THE WORK AREA

Floor Space and Working Height

The average one car garage will give you more than enough work space. A floor plan of 16 ft. X 12 ft. is more than sufficient for shelving, work benches, tool shelves or boxes and parts storage areas. 12 X 16 works out to 192 square feet. You may think that this sounds like a lot of room, but when you start building shelves, and constructing work benches almost most half of that can be eaten up!

Also, you may wonder why a lot of floor space is needed. There are several reasons, not the least of which is the safety factor. You'll be working around a large, heavy, metal object mounted on a work stand. The work stand has wheels so that it can be moved to allow easy work angles. The work stand allows the engine to be rotated for the same reason and the work stand has legs and supports that take up floor space. Accidents can happen! Even the best engine stand can tip over; you can easily trip over a work stand leg or drop a heavy part or tool. You'll need room to take evasive action!

Most garages have concrete floors. The engine and stand can weigh 800 lbs. or more when fully assembled. Engine stands have small steel wheels which roll best on smooth concrete. If your garage floor has cracks with raised sections or blocks with deep grooves, you may have a problem. The wheels can hang up on these cracks or grooves causing the whole thing to tip over.

As for working height, overhead clearance is necessary for the engine crane. To lift an engine from or install an engine in a vehicle, the crane cane need as much as 10 ft. overhead. If you don't have this much room, you might want to lift the engine out of or into the vehicle outside an roll it to or from the garage mounted on an engine dolly. DON'T roll the crane any great distance with the engine suspended! A tipover or crane damage can easily occur. Plus, once an engine starts swinging on the crane boom, it's tough to control.

Storage Areas

▶ See Figures 2 and 3

SHELVES

You can't have enough shelf space. Adequate shelf space means that you don't have to stack anything on the floor, where it would be in the way.

Shelves aren't tough. You can make your own or buy modular or prefab units. The best modular units are those made of interlocking shelves and uprights of ABS plastic. They're lightweight and easy to assemble, and their load-bearing capacity is more than sufficient. Also, they are not subject the rust or rot as are wood and metal shelves.

Probably the cheapest and best shelves are ones that you make yourself from one inch shelving with 2X4 uprights. You can make them as long, wide and high as you want. For at least the uprights, use pressure treated wood. Its resistance to rot is more than worth the additional cost.

Fig. 1 Typical home-made wood shelves, crammed with stuff. These shelves are made from spare $5/4$ x 6 in. pressure treated decking

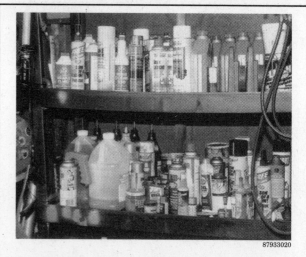

Fig. 2 Modular plastic shelves, such as these are inexpensive, weather-proof and easy to assemble

TOOL CHESTS

▶ See Figures 4 and 5

There are many types and sizes of tool chests. Their greatest advantage is that they can hold a lot of tools, securely, in a relatively small area. If you decide that you need one, make sure that you buy one that's big enough and mobile enough for the work area. Also, you get what you pay for, so purchase a good brand name. It will last a lifetime.

WORK BENCHES

▶ See Figure 6

As with the shelving, work benches can be either store-bought or home-made. The store-bought work benches can be

Fig. 3 These shelves were made from the frame of old kitchen cabinets

Fig. 4 Different types of mobile, steel tool chests

Fig. 5 A good tool chest has several drawers, each designed to hold a different type tool

87933512

Fig. 6 Homemade workbenches

steel or precut wood kits. Either are fine and are available at most building supply stores or through tool catalogs.

Home-made benches, as with the shelves have the advantage of being made-to-fit your workshop. A free-standing workbench is best, as opposed to one attached to an outside wall. The free-standing bench can take more abuse since it doesn't transfer the shock or vibration to wall supports.

A good free-standing workbench should be constructed using 4X4 pressure treated wood as legs, 2X6 planking as header boards and ¾ inch plywood sheathing as a deck. Diagonal supports can be 2X4 studs and it's always helpful to construct a full size ¾ inch plywood shelf under the bench. Not only can you use the shelf for storage but it gives great rigidity to the whole bench structure. Assembling the bench with screws rather than nails takes longer but adds strength and gives you the ability to take the whole thing apart if you ever want to move it.

LIGHTING

▶ **See Figures 7 and 8**

The importance of adequate lighting can't be over emphasized. Good lighting is not only a convenience but a safety feature. If you can see what your working on you're less likely to make mistakes, have a wrench slip or trip over an obstacle. On most engines, everything is about the same color and usually dirty. During disassembly, a lot of frustration can be avoided if you can see all the bolts, some of which may be hidden or obscured.

For overhead lighting, at least 2 twin tube 36 inch fluourescent shop lights should be in place. Most garages are wired with standard light bulbs attached to the wall studs at intervals. Four or five of these lights, at about a 6 foot height combined with the overhead lighting should suffice. However, no matter where the lights are, your body is going to block some of it so a droplight or clip-on type work light is a great idea. These lights can be mounted on the engine stand, or even the engine itself.

Fig. 7 At least two of this type of twin tube fluorescent light is essential

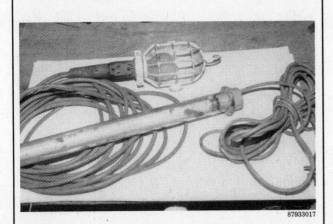

Fig. 8 Two types of droplights. Incandescent and fluorescent

VENTILATION

At one time or another, be working with chemicals which may require adequate ventilation. Now, just about all garages have a big car-sized door and all sheds or workshops have a door. In bad weather the door will have to be closed so at least one window that opens is a necessity. An exhaust fan or regular ventilation fan is a great help, especially in hot weather.

HEATERS

If you live in an area where the winters are cold, as do most of us, it's nice to have some sort of heat where we work. If your workshop or garage is attached to the house, you'll probably be okay. If your garage or shop is detached, then a space heater of some sort — electric, propane or kerosene

— will be necessary. NEVER run a space heater in the presence of flammable vapors! When running a space heater, always allow for some means of venting the carbon monoxide!

ELECTRICAL REQUIREMENTS

Obviously, your workshop should be wired according to all local codes. As to what type of service you need, that depends on your electrical load. If you have a lot of power equipment and maybe a refrigerator, TV, stereo or whatever, not only do you have a great shop, but your amperage requirements may exceed your wiring's capacity. If you are at all in doubt, consult your local electrical contractor.

Shop Safety

▶ **See Figures 9, 10, 11 and 12**

It is virtually impossible to anticipate all of the hazards involved with automotive maintenance and service but care and common sense will prevent most accidents.

The rules of safety for mechanics range from 'don't smoke around gasoline' to 'use the proper tool for the job.' The trick to avoiding injuries is to develop safe work habits and take every possible precaution.

Do's

• Do keep a fire extinguisher and first aid kit within easy reach.
• Do wear safety glasses or goggles when cutting, drilling, grinding, or prying, even if you have 20/20 vision. If you wear glasses for the sake of vision, then they should be made of hardened glass that can serve also as safety glasses, or wear safety glasses over your regular glasses.
• Do shield your eyes whenever you work around the battery. Batteries contain sulfuric acid; in case of contact with the eyes or skin, flush the area with water or a mixture of water and baking soda and get medical attention immediately.

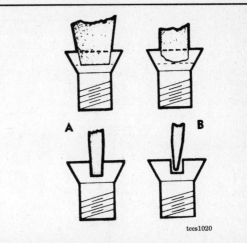

Fig. 9 Screwdrivers should be kept in good condition to prevent injury or damage which could result if the blade slips from the screw

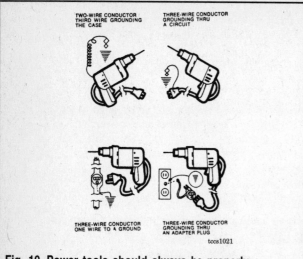

TWO-WIRE CONDUCTOR
THIRD WIRE GROUNDING
THE CASE

THREE-WIRE CONDUCTOR
GROUNDING THRU
A CIRCUIT

THREE-WIRE CONDUCTOR
ONE WIRE TO A GROUND

THREE-WIRE CONDUCTOR
GROUNDING THRU
AN ADAPTER PLUG

tccs1021

Fig. 10 Power tools should always be properly grounded

tccs1022

Fig. 11 Using the correct size wrench will help prevent the possibility of rounding-off a nut

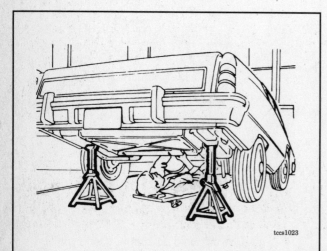

tccs1023

Fig. 12 NEVER work under a vehicle unless it is supported using safety stands (jackstands)

• Do use safety stands for any under-truck service. Jacks are for raising vehicles; safety stands are for making sure the vehicle stays raised until you want it to come down. Whenever the vehicle is raised, block the wheels remaining on the ground and set the parking brake.

• Do use adequate ventilation when working with any chemicals. Like carbon monoxide, the asbestos dust resulting from brake lining wear can be poisonous in sufficient quantities.

• Do disconnect the negative battery cable when working on the electrical system. The primary ignition system can contain up to 40,000 volts.

• Do follow manufacturer's directions whenever working with potentially hazardous materials. Both brake fluid and antifreeze are poisonous if taken internally.

• Do properly maintain your tools. Loose hammerheads, mushroomed punches and chisels, frayed or poorly grounded electrical cords, excessively worn screwdrivers, spread wrenches (open end), cracked sockets, slipping ratchets, or faulty droplight sockets can cause accidents.

• Do use the proper size and type of tool for the job being done.

• Do when possible, pull on a wrench handle rather than push on it, and adjust your stance to prevent a fall.

• Do be sure that adjustable wrenches are tightly adjusted on the nut or bolt and pulled so that the face is on the side of the fixed jaw.

• Do select a wrench or socket that fits the nut or bolt. The wrench or socket should sit straight, not cocked.

• Do strike squarely with a hammer. Avoid glancing blows.

• Do set the parking brake and block the drive wheels if the work requires that the engine be running.

Don't's

• Don't run an engine in a garage or anywhere else without proper ventilation — EVER! Carbon monoxide is poisonous; it takes a long time to leave the human body and you can build up a deadly supply of it in your system by simply breathing in a little every day. You may not realize you are slowly poisoning yourself. Always use proper vents, window, fans or open the garage door.

• Don't work around moving parts while wearing a necktie or other loose clothing. Short sleeves are much safer than long, loose sleeves and hard-toed shoes with neoprene soles protect your toes and give a better grip on slippery surfaces. Jewelry such as watches, fancy belt buckles, beads or body adornment of any kind is not safe working around a truck. Long hair should be hidden under a hat or cap.

• Don't use pockets for toolboxes. A fall or bump can drive a screwdriver deep into your body. Even a wiping cloth hanging from the back pocket can wrap around a spinning shaft or fan.

• Don't smoke when working around gasoline, cleaning solvent or other flammable material.

• Don't smoke when working around the battery. When the battery is being charged, it gives off explosive hydrogen gas.

• Don't use gasoline to wash your hands; there are excellent soaps available. Gasoline removes all the natural oils from the skin so that bone dry hands will such up oil and grease.

• Don't service the air conditioning system unless you are equipped with the necessary tools and training. The refrigerant,

R-12, is extremely cold and when exposed to the air, will instantly freeze any surface it comes in contact with, including your eyes. Although the refrigerant is normally non-toxic, R-12 becomes a deadly poisonous gas in the presence of an open flame. One good whiff of the vapors from burning refrigerant can be fatal.

• Don't ever use a bumper jack (the jack that comes with the vehicle) for anything other than changing tires! If you are serious about maintaining your truck yourself, invest in a hydraulic floor jack of at least 1½ ton capacity. It will pay for itself many times over through the years.

SAFETY EQUIPMENT

▶ **See Figures 13 and 14**

Fire Extinguishers

There are many types of safety equipment. The most important of these is the fire extinguisher. You'll be well off with two 5 lbs. extinguishers rated for oil, chemical and wood.

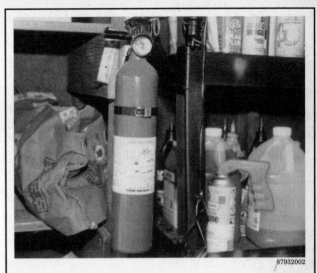

Fig. 14 A good, all-purpose fire extinguisher

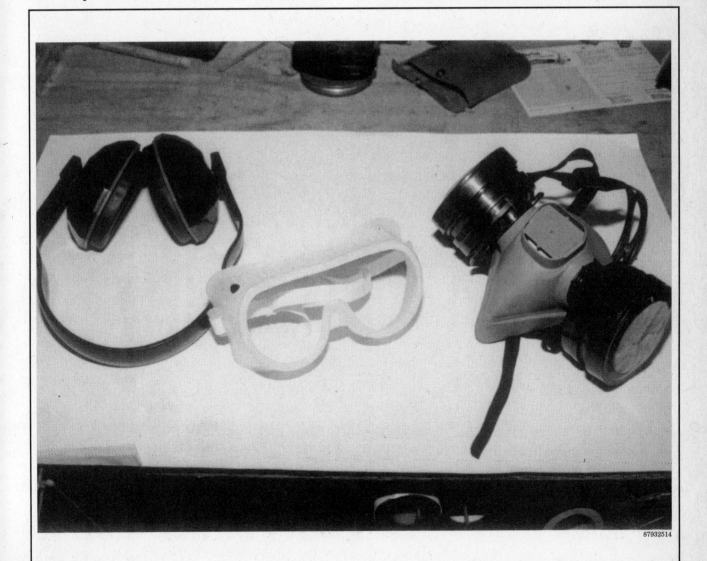

Fig. 13 Three essential pieces of safety equipment. Left to right: ear protectors, safety goggles and respirator

First Aid

Next you'll need a good first aid kit. Any good kit which can purchase from the local drug store will be fine. It's a good idea, in addition, to have something easily accessible in the event of a minor injury, such a hydrogen peroxide or other antiseptic that can be poured onto or applied to a wound immediately.

Work Gloves

▶ **See Figure 15**

Unless you think scars on your hands are cool, enjoy pain and like wearing bandages, get a good pair of work gloves. Canvass or leather are the best. And yes, I realize that there are some jobs involving small parts that can't be done while wearing work gloves. These jobs are not the ones usually associated with hand injuries.

A good pair of rubber gloves such as those usually associated with dish washing is also a great idea. There are some liquids such as solvent and penetrants that don't belong on your skin. Avoid burns and rashes. Wear these gloves.

And lastly, an option. If you're tired of being greasy and dirty all the time, go to the drug store and buy a box of disposable latex gloves like medical professionals wear. You can handle greasy parts, perform small tasks, wash parts, etc. all without getting dirty! These gloves take a surprising amount of abuse without tearing and aren't expensive. Note however, that it has been reported that some people are allergic to the latex.

Eye Protection

Don't begin this, or for that matter any, job without a good pair of work goggles or impact resistant glasses! When doing any kind of work, it's all too easy to avoid eye injury through this simple precaution. And don't just buy eye protection and leave it on the shelf. Wear it all the time! Things have a habit of breaking, chipping, splashing, spraying, splintering and flying around. And, for some reason, your eye is always in the way!

Ear Protection

Often overlooked is hearing protection. Power equipment is noisy! Loud noises damage your ears. It's as simple as that!

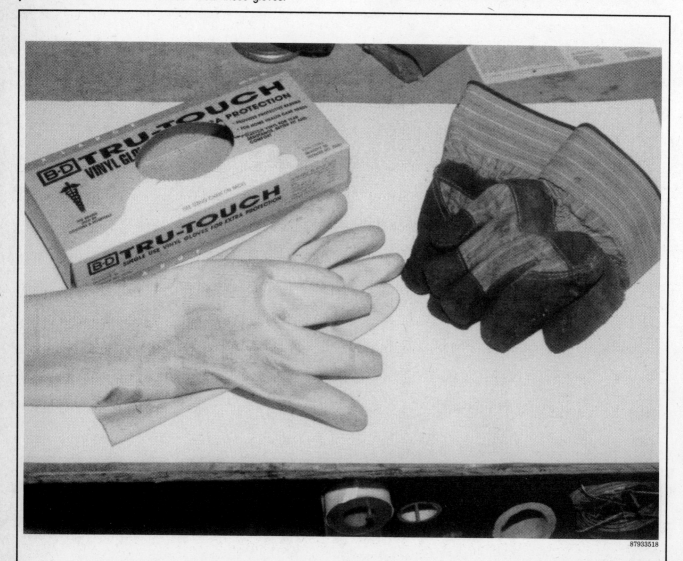

87933518

Fig. 15 Three different types of work gloves. The box contains latex gloves

The simplest and cheapest form of ear protection is a pair of noise-reducing ear plugs. Cheap insurance for your ears. And, they even come with their own, cute little carrying case.

More substantial, more protection and more money is a good pair of noise reducing ear muffs. They protect from all but the loudest sounds. Hopefully those are sounds that you'll never encounter since they're usually associated with disasters or rock concerts.

Work Boots

It's up to you, but I think that a good, comfortable pair of steel-toed work boots is a sensible idea. Primarily because heavy parts always get dropped sooner or later. A manifold can do significant damage to a sneaker-clad foot.

Good work boots also provide better support — you're going to be on your feet a lot — are oil-resistant, and they keep your feet warm and dry.

Work Clothes

Everyone has 'work clothes'. Usually this consists of old jeans and a shirt that has seen better days. That's fine. In addition, a denim work apron is a nice accessory. It's rugged, can hold some tools, and you don't feel bad wiping your hands or tools on it. That's what it's for.

UNDERSTANDING THE BASICS

To do a good job when performing any automotive work, you have to be capable of more than just turning a wrench. When you get around to installing and trying to start your new engine, a lot of things can go wrong. Among the most mysterious is the electrical system. Read the following paragraphs to gain some basic start on understanding automotive electrical systems.

Understanding Electricity

For any electrical system to operate, there must be a complete circuit. This simply means that the power flow from the battery must make a full circle. When an electrical component is operating, power flows from the battery to the components, passes through the component (load) causing it to function, and returns to the battery through the ground path of the circuit. This ground may be either another wire or a metal part of the vehicle (depending upon how the component is designed).

BASIC CIRCUITS

▶ **See Figure 16**

Perhaps the easiest way to visualize a circuit is to think of connecting a light bulb (with two wires attached to it) to the battery. If one of the two wires was attached to the negative post (-) of the battery and the other wire to the positive post (+), the circuit would be complete and the light bulb would illuminate. Electricity could follow a path from the battery to the bulb and back to the battery. It's not hard to see that with longer wires on our light bulb, it could be mounted anywhere on the vehicle. Further, one wire could be fitted with a switch so that the light could be turned on and off. Various other items could be added to our primitive circuit to make the light flash, become brighter or dimmer under certain conditions, or advise the user that it's burned out.

Ground

Some automotive components are grounded through their mounting points. The electrical current runs through the chassis of the vehicle and returns to the battery through the ground (-) cable; if you look, you'll see that the battery ground cable connects between the battery and the body of the vehicle.

Load

▶ **See Figure 17**

Every complete circuit must include a 'load' (something to use the electricity coming from the source). If you were to connect a wire between the two terminals of the battery (DON'T do this, but take out word for it) without the light bulb, the battery would attempt to deliver its entire power supply from one pole to another almost instantly. This is a short circuit. The electricity is taking a short cut to get to ground and is not being used by any load in the circuit. This sudden and uncontrolled electrical flow can cause great damage to other components in the circuit and can develop a tremendous amount of heat. A short in an automotive wiring harness can develop sufficient heat to melt the insulation on all the surrounding wires and reduce a multiple wire cable to one sad lump of plastic and copper. Two common causes of shorts are broken insulation (thereby exposing the wire to contact with surrounding metal surfaces or other wires) or a failed switch (the pins inside the switch come out of place and touch each other).

Switches and Relays

Some electrical components which require a large amount of current to operate also have a relay in their circuit. Since these circuits carry a large amount of current (amperage or amps), the thickness of the wire in the circuit (wire gauge) is also greater. If this large wire were connected from the load to the control switch on the dash, the switch would have to carry the high amperage load and the dash would be twice as large to accommodate wiring harnesses as thick as your wrist. To prevent these problems, a relay is used. The large wires in the circuit are connected from the battery to one side of the relay and from the opposite side of the relay to the load. The relay is normally open, preventing current from passing through the circuit. An additional, smaller wire is connected from the relay to the control switch for the circuit. When the control switch is turned on, it grounds the smaller wire to the relay and completes its circuit. The main switch inside the relay closes, sending power to the component without routing the main power through the inside of the vehicle. Some common circuits which may use relays are the horn, headlights, starter and rear window defogger systems.

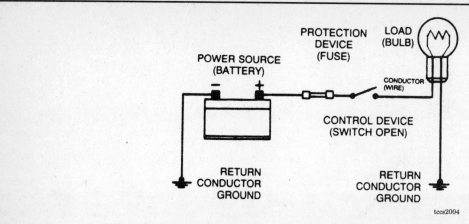

Fig. 16 Here is an example of a simple automotive circuit. When the switch is closed, power from the positive battery terminal flows through the fuse, then the switch and to the load (light bulb), the light illuminates and then, the circuit is completed through the return conductor and the vehicle ground. If the light did not work, the tests could be made with a voltmeter or test light at the battery, fuse, switch or bulb socket

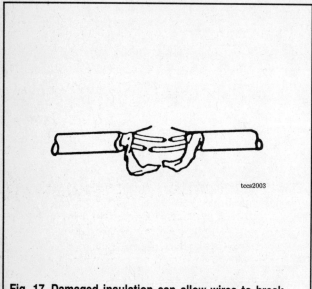

Fig. 17 Damaged insulation can allow wires to break (causing an open circuit) or touch (causing a short)

Protective Devices

It is possible for larger surges of current to pass through the electrical system of your vehicle. If this surge of current were to reach the load in the circuit, it could burn it out or severely damage it. To prevent this, fuses, circuit breakers and/or fusible links are connected into the supply wires of the electrical system. These items are nothing more than a built-in weak spot in the system. It's much easier to go to a known location (the fusebox) to see why a circuit is inoperative than to dissect 15 feet of wiring under the dashboard, looking for what happened.

When an electrical current of excessive power passes through the fuse, the fuse blows (the conductor melts) and breaks the circuit, preventing the passage of current and protecting the components.

A circuit breaker is basically a self repairing fuse. It will open the circuit in the same fashion as a fuse, but when either the

short is removed or the surge subsides, the circuit breaker resets itself and does not need replacement.

A fuse link (fusible link or main link) is a wire that acts as a fuse. One of these is normally connected between the starter relay and the main wiring harness under the hood. Since the starter is usually the highest electrical draw on the vehicle, an internal short during starting could direct about 130 amps into the wrong places. Consider the damage potential of introducing this current into a system whose wiring is rated at 15 amps and you'll understand the need for protection. Since this link is very early in the electrical path, it's the first place to look if nothing on the vehicle works, but the battery seems to be charged and is properly connected.

TROUBLESHOOTING

▶ See Figures 18, 19 and 20

Electrical problems generally fall into one of three areas:
• The component that is not functioning is not receiving current.
• The component is receiving power but is not using it or is using it incorrectly (component failure).
• The component is improperly grounded.

The circuit can be can be checked with a test light and a jumper wire. The test light is a device that looks like a pointed screwdriver with a wire on one end and a bulb in its handle. A jumper wire is simply a piece of wire with alligator clips or special terminals on each end. If a component is not working, you must follow a systematic plan to determine which of the three causes is the villain.

1. Turn ON the switch that controls the item not working.

➡Some items only work when the ignition switch is turned ON.

2. Disconnect the power supply wire from the component.
3. Attach the ground wire of a test light or a voltmeter to a good metal ground.
4. Touch the end probe of the test light (or the positive lead of the voltmeter) to the power wire; if there is current in the wire, the light in the test light will come on (or the voltme-

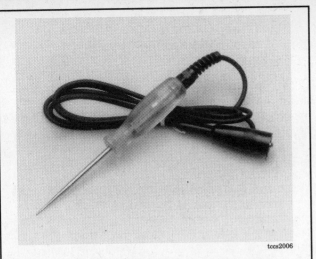

Fig. 18 A 12 volt test light is useful when checking parts of a circuit for power

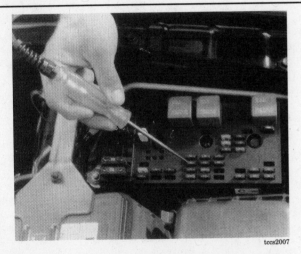

Fig. 19 Here, someone is checking a circuit by making sure there is power to the component's fuse

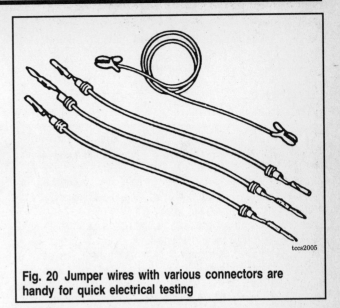

Fig. 20 Jumper wires with various connectors are handy for quick electrical testing

ate with less voltage and connecting them to 12 volts could destroy them. Jumper wires are best used to bypass a portion of the circuit (such as a stretch of wire or a switch) that DOES NOT contain a resistor and is suspected to be bad.

If all the fuses are good and the component is not receiving power, find the switch for the circuit. Bypass the switch with the jumper wire. This is done by connecting one end of the jumper to the power wire coming into the switch and the other end to the wire leaving the switch. If the component comes to life, the switch has failed.

✳✳WARNING

Never substitute the jumper for the component. The circuit needs the electrical load of the component. If you bypass it, you will cause a short circuit.

Checking the ground for any circuit can mean tracing wires to the body, cleaning connections or tightening mounting bolts for the component itself. If the jumper wire can be connected to the case of the component or the ground connector, you can ground the other end to a piece of clean, solid metal on the vehicle. Again, if the component starts working, you've found the problem.

A systematic search through the fuse, connectors, switches and the component itself will almost always yield an answer. Loose and/or corroded connectors, particularly in ground circuits, are becoming a larger problem in modern vehicles. The computers and on-board electronic (solid state) systems are highly sensitive to improper grounds and will change their function drastically if one occurs.

Remember that for any electrical circuit to work, ALL the connections must be clean and tight.

ter will indicate the amount of voltage). You have now established that current is getting to the component.

5. Turn the ignition or dash switch **OFF** and reconnect the wire to the component.

If there was no power, then the problem is between the battery and the component. This includes all the switches, fuses, relays and the battery itself. The next place to look is the fusebox; check carefully either by eye or by using the test light across the fuse clips. The easiest way to check is to simply replace the fuse. If the fuse is blown, and upon replacement, immediately blows again, there is a short between the fuse and the component. This is generally (not always) a sign of an internal short in the component. Disconnect the power wire at the component again and replace the fuse; if the fuse holds, the component is the problem.

✳✳WARNING

DO NOT test a component by running a jumper wire from the battery UNLESS you are certain that it operates on 12 volts. Many electronic components are designed to oper-

Battery, Starting and Charging Systems

BASIC OPERATING PRINCIPLES

Battery

The battery is the first link in the chain of mechanisms which work together to provide cranking of the automobile engine. In most modern vehicles, the battery is a lead/acid electrochemical device consisting of six 2v subsections (cells) connected in series so the unit is capable of producing approximately 12v of electrical pressure. Each subsection consists of a series of positive and negative plates held a short distance apart in a solution of sulfuric acid and water.

The two types of plates are of dissimilar metals. This sets-up a chemical reaction, and it is this reaction which produces current flow from the battery when its positive and negative terminals are connected to an electrical accessory such as a lamp or motor. The continued transfer of electrons would eventually convert the sulfuric acid to water, and make the two plates identical in chemical composition. As electrical energy is removed from the battery, its voltage output tends to drop. Thus, measuring battery voltage and battery electrolyte composition are two ways of checking the ability of the unit to supply power. During engine cranking, electrical energy is removed from the battery. However, if the charging circuit is in good condition and the operating conditions are normal, the power removed from the battery will be replaced by the alternator which will force electrons back through the battery, reversing the normal flow, and restoring the battery to its original chemical state.

Starting System

The battery and starting motor are linked by very heavy electrical cables designed to minimize resistance to the flow of current. Generally, the major power supply cable that leaves the battery goes directly to the starter, while other electrical system needs are supplied by a smaller cable. During starter operation, power flows from the battery to the starter and is grounded through the vehicle's frame/body or engine and the battery's negative ground strap.

The starter is a specially designed, direct current electric motor capable of producing a great amount of power for its size. One thing that allows the motor to produce a great deal of power is its tremendous rotating speed. It drives the engine through a tiny pinion gear (attached to the starter's armature), which drives the very large flywheel ring gear at a greatly reduced speed. Another factor allowing it to produce so much power is that only intermittent operation is required of it. Thus, little allowance for air circulation is necessary, and the windings can be built into a very small space.

The starter solenoid is a magnetic device which employs the small current supplied by the start circuit of the ignition switch. This magnetic action moves a plunger which mechanically engages the starter and closes the heavy switch connecting it to the battery. The starting switch circuit usually consists of the starting switch contained within the ignition switch, a neutral safety switch or clutch pedal switch, and the wiring necessary to connect these in series with the starter solenoid or relay.

The pinion, a small gear, is mounted to a one way drive clutch. This clutch is splined to the starter armature shaft. When the ignition switch is moved to the **START** position, the solenoid plunger slides the pinion toward the flywheel ring gear via a collar and spring. If the teeth on the pinion and flywheel match properly, the pinion will engage the flywheel immediately. If the gear teeth butt one another, the spring will be compressed and will force the gears to mesh as soon as the starter turns far enough to allow them to do so. As the solenoid plunger reaches the end of its travel, it closes the contacts that connect the battery and starter, then the engine is cranked.

As soon as the engine starts, the flywheel ring gear begins turning fast enough to drive the pinion at an extremely high rate of speed. At this point, the one-way clutch begins allowing the pinion to spin faster than the starter shaft so that the starter will not operate at excessive speed. When the ignition switch is released from the starter position, the solenoid is de-energized, and a spring pulls the gear out of mesh interrupting the current flow to the starter.

Some starters employ a separate relay, mounted away from the starter, to switch the motor and solenoid current on and off. The relay replaces the solenoid electrical switch, but does not eliminate the need for a solenoid mounted on the starter used to mechanically engage the starter drive gears. The relay is used to reduce the amount of current the starting switch must carry.

Charging System

The automobile charging system provides electrical power for operation of the vehicle's ignition system, starting system and all electrical accessories. The battery serves as an electrical surge or storage tank, storing (in chemical form) the energy originally produced by the engine driven generator. The system also provides a means of regulating output to protect the battery from being overcharged and to avoid excessive voltage to the accessories.

The storage battery is a chemical device incorporating parallel lead plates in a tank containing a sulfuric acid/water solution. Adjacent plates are slightly dissimilar, and the chemical reaction of the two dissimilar plates produces electrical energy when the battery is connected to a load such as the starter motor. The chemical reaction is reversible, so that when the generator is producing a voltage (electrical pressure) greater than that produced by the battery, electricity is forced into the battery, and the battery is returned to its fully charged state.

Newer automobiles use alternating current generators or alternators, because they are more efficient, can be rotated at higher speeds, and have fewer brush problems. In an alternator, the field usually rotates while all the current produced passes only through the stator winding. The brushes bear against continuous slip rings. This causes the current produced to periodically reverse the direction of its flow. Diodes (electrical one way valves) block the flow of current from traveling in the wrong direction. A series of diodes is wired together to permit the alternating flow of the stator to be rectified back to 12 volts DC for use by the vehicle's electrical system.

The voltage regulating function is performed by a regulator. The regulator is often built in to the alternator; this system is termed an integrated or internal regulator.

Fusible Links

The fuse link is a short length of special, Hypalon (high temperature) insulated wire, integral with the engine compartment wiring harness and should not be confused with standard wire. It is several wire gauges smaller than the circuit which it protects. Under no circumstances should a fuse link replacement repair be made using a length of standard wire cut from bulk stock or from another wiring harness.

To repair any blown fuse link use the following procedure:

1. Determine which circuit is damaged, its location and the cause of the open fuse link. If the damaged fuse link is one of three fed by a common No. 10 or 12 gauge feed wire, determine the specific affected circuit.

2. Disconnect the negative battery cable.

3. Cut the damaged fuse link from the wiring harness and discard it. If the fuse link is one of three circuits fed by a single feed wire, cut it out of the harness at each splice end and discard it.

4. Identify and procure the proper fuse link with butt connectors for attaching the fuse link to the harness.

➡**Heat shrink tubing must be slipped over the wire before crimping and soldering the connection.**

5. To repair any fuse link in a 3-link group with one feed:

a. After cutting the open link out of the harness, cut each of the remaining undamaged fuse links close to the feed wire weld.

b. Strip approximately ½ in. (13mm) of insulation from the detached ends of the two good fuse links. Insert two wire ends into one end of a butt connector, then carefully push one stripped end of the replacement fuse link into the same end of the butt connector and crimp all three firmly together.

➡**Care must be taken when fitting the three fuse links into the butt connector as the internal diameter is a snug fit for three wires. Make sure to use a proper crimping tool. Pliers, side cutters, etc. will not apply the proper crimp to retain the wires and withstand a pull test.**

c. After crimping the butt connector to the three fuse links, cut the weld portion from the feed wire and strip approximately ½ in. (13mm) of insulation from the cut end. Insert the stripped end into the open end of the butt connector and crimp very firmly.

d. To attach the remaining end of the replacement fuse link, strip approximately ½ in. (13mm) of insulation from the wire end of the circuit from which the blown fuse link was removed, and firmly crimp a butt connector or equivalent to the stripped wire. Then, insert the end of the replacement link into the other end of the butt connector and crimp firmly.

e. Using rosin core solder with a consistency of 60 percent tin and 40 percent lead, solder the connectors and the wires at the repairs then insulate with electrical tape or heat shrink tubing.

6. To replace any fuse link on a single circuit in a harness, cut out the damaged portion, strip approximately ½ in. (13mm) of insulation from the two wire ends and attach the appropriate replacement fuse link to the stripped wire ends with two proper size butt connectors. Solder the connectors and wires, then insulate.

7. To repair any fuse link which has an eyelet terminal on one end such as the charging circuit, cut off the open fuse link behind the weld, strip approximately ½ in. (13mm) of insulation from the cut end and attach the appropriate new eyelet fuse link to the cut stripped wire with an appropriate size butt connector. Solder the connectors and wires at the repair, then insulate.

8. Connect the negative battery cable to the battery and test the system for proper operation.

➡**Do not mistake a resistor wire for a fuse link. The resistor wire is generally longer and has print stating, 'Resistor-don't cut or splice."**

When attaching a single No. 16, 17, 18 or 20 gauge fuse link to a heavy gauge wire, always double the stripped wire end of the fuse link before inserting and crimping it into the butt connector for positive wire retention.

Add-On Electrical Equipment

The electrical system in your vehicle is designed to perform under reasonable operating conditions without interference between components. Before any additional electrical equipment is installed, it is recommended that you consult your dealer or a reputable repair facility that is familiar with the vehicle and its systems.

If the vehicle is equipped with mobile radio equipment and/or mobile telephone, it may have an effect upon the operation of any on-board computer control modules. Radio Frequency Interference (RFI) from the communications system can be picked up by the vehicle's wiring harnesses and conducted into the control module, giving it the wrong messages at the wrong time. Although well shielded against RFI, the computer should be further protected by taking the following measures:

• Install the antenna as far as possible from the control module. For instance, if the module is located behind the center console area, then the antenna should be mounted at the rear of the vehicle.

• Keep the antenna wiring a minimum of eight inches away from any wiring running to control modules and from the module itself. NEVER wind the antenna wire around any other wiring.

• Mount the equipment as far from the control module as possible. Be very careful during installation not to drill through any wires or short a wire harness with a mounting screw.

• Insure that the electrical feed wire(s) to the equipment are properly and tightly connected. Loose connectors can cause interference.

• Make certain that the equipment is properly grounded to the vehicle. Poor grounding can damage expensive equipment.

Troubleshooting Basic Starting System Problems

Problem	Cause	Solution
Starter motor rotates engine slowly	• Battery charge low or battery defective	• Charge or replace battery
	• Defective circuit between battery and starter motor	• Clean and tighten, or replace cables
	• Low load current	• Bench-test starter motor. Inspect for worn brushes and weak brush springs.
	• High load current	• Bench-test starter motor. Check engine for friction, drag or coolant in cylinders. Check ring gear-to-pinion gear clearance.
Starter motor will not rotate engine	• Battery charge low or battery defective	• Charge or replace battery
	• Faulty solenoid	• Check solenoid ground. Repair or replace as necessary.
	• Damaged drive pinion gear or ring gear	• Replace damaged gear(s)
	• Starter motor engagement weak	• Bench-test starter motor
	• Starter motor rotates slowly with high load current	• Inspect drive yoke pull-down and point gap, check for worn end bushings, check ring gear clearance
	• Engine seized	• Repair engine
Starter motor drive will not engage (solenoid known to be good)	• Defective contact point assembly	• Repair or replace contact point assembly
	• Inadequate contact point assembly ground	• Repair connection at ground screw
	• Defective hold-in coil	• Replace field winding assembly
Starter motor drive will not disengage	• Starter motor loose on flywheel housing	• Tighten mounting bolts
	• Worn drive end busing	• Replace bushing
	• Damaged ring gear teeth	• Replace ring gear or driveplate
	• Drive yoke return spring broken or missing	• Replace spring
Starter motor drive disengages prematurely	• Weak drive assembly thrust spring	• Replace drive mechanism
	• Hold-in coil defective	• Replace field winding assembly
Low load current	• Worn brushes	• Replace brushes
	• Weak brush springs	• Replace springs

tccs2c01

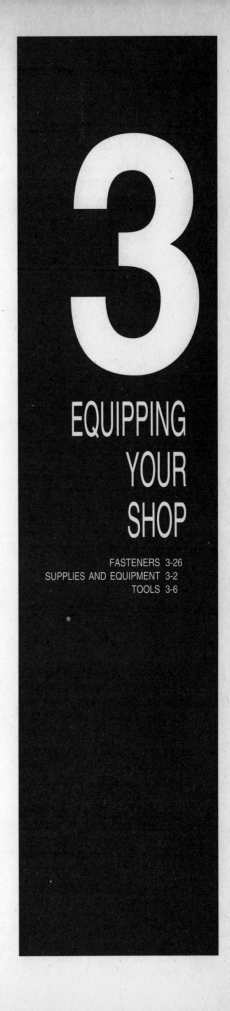

3

EQUIPPING
YOUR
SHOP

SUPPLIES AND EQUIPMENT

Fluid Disposal

Used fluids such as engine oil, transmission fluid, antifreeze and brake fluid are hazardous wastes and must be disposed of properly. Before draining any fluids, consult with your local authorities; in many areas waste oil, etc. is being accepted as a part of recycling programs. A number of service stations and auto parts stores are also accepting waste fluids for recycling.

Be sure of the recycling center's policies before draining any fluids, as many will not accept different fluids that have been mixed together.

Chemicals

There is a whole range of chemicals that you'll be needing. The most common types are, lubricants, penetrants and sealers. Keep these handy, on some convenient shelf. You'll be using each type throughout the rebuild.

When a particular chemical is not being used, keep it capped, upright and in a safe place. These substances may be flammable or irritants or caustic and should always be stored properly, used properly and handled with care. Always read and follow all label directions and wear hand and eye protection!

Lubricants and Penetrants

▶ See Figure 1

In this category you'll need:
• Clean engine oil. Whatever you use regularly in your engine will be fine.
• Lithium grease.
• Chassis lube
• Assembly lube
• Silicone grease
• Silicone spray
• Penetrating oil

Clean engine oil is used to coat most bolts, screws and nuts prior to installation. This is always a good practice since the less friction there is on a fastener, the less chance there will be of breakage and crossthreading. Also, an oiled bolt will give a truer torque value and be less likely to rust or seize. An obvious exception would be exhaust manifold bolts or studs. These are not oiled.

Lithium grease, chassis lube and silicone grease can all be used pretty much interchangeably. All can be used for coating rust-prone fasteners and for facilitating the assembly of parts which are a tight fit. Silicone grease is the most versatile and should always be used on the inside of spark plug wire boots as a release agent.

Silicone spray is a good lubricant for hard-to-reach places and parts that shouldn't be gooped up with grease.

Penetrating oil may turn out to be one of your best friends during disassembly. The most familiar penetrating oils are Liquid Wrench® and WD-40®. These products have hundreds of uses. For your purposes, they are vital!

Before disassembling any part, check the fasteners. If any appear rusted, soak them thoroughly with the penetrant and let them stand while you do something else. This simple act can save you hours of tedious work trying to extract a broken bolt or stud.

Assembly lube. There are several types of this product available. Essentially it is a heavy bodied lubricant used for coating moving parts prior to assembly. The idea is that is stays in place until the engine starts for the first time and dissolves in the engine oil as oil pressure is achieved. This way, expensive parts receive needed protection until everything is working.

Sealants

▶ See Figure 2

Sealants are an indispensible part of almost all automotive work. The purpose of sealants is to establish a leak-proof bond between or around assembled parts. Most sealers are used in conjunction with gaskets, but some are used instead of conventional gasket material in newer engines.

The most common sealers are the non-hardening types such as Permatex®No.2 or its equivalents. These sealers are applied to the mating surfaces of each part to be joined, then a gasket is put in place and the parts are assembled.

One very helpful type of non-hardening sealer is the 'high tack' type. This type is a very sticky material which holds the gasket in place while the parts are being assembled. This stuff is really a good idea when you don't have enough hands or fingers to keep everything where it should be.

The stand-alone sealers are the RTV (Room Temperature Vulcanizing) silicone gasket makers. On may newer engines, this material is used instead of a gasket. In those instances, a gasket amy not be available or, because of the shape of the mating surfaces, a gasket shouldn't be used. This stuff, when used in conjunction with a conventional gasket, produces the surest bonds.

It does have its limitations though. When using this material, you will have a time limit. It starts to set-up within 15 minutes or so, so you have to assemble the parts without delay. In addition, when squeezing the material out of the tube, don't drop any glops into the engine. The stuff will form and set and travel around the oil gallery, possibly plugging up a passage. Also, most types are not fuel-proof. Check the tube for all cautions.

Cleaners

▶ See Figures 3, 4 and 5

You'll have two types of cleaners to deal with: parts cleaners and hand cleaners.

The parts cleaners are for the engine; the hand cleaners are for you.

There are many good, non-flammable, biodegradable parts cleaners on the market. These cleaning agents are safe for you, the parts and the environment. Therefore, there is no

87933516

Fig. 1 Penetrants and lubricants

reason to use flammable, caustic or toxic substances to clean your parts or tools.

As far as hand cleaners go, the waterless types are the best. They have always been efficient at cleaning, but left behind a pretty smelly odor. Recently though, just about all of them have eliminated the odor and added stuff that actually smells good. Make sure that you pick one that contains lanolin or some other moisture-replenishing additive. Cleaners not only remove grease and oil but also skin oil.

One other note: most women know this already but most men don't. Use a hand lotion when you're all cleaned up. It's okay. Real men DO use hand lotion!

Shop Towels

One of the most important elements in doing shop work is a good supply of shop towels. Paper towels just don't cut it! Most auto parts stores sell packs of shop towels, usually 50-100 in a pack. They are relatively cheap and can be washed over and over. Always keep them handy.

Fig. 2 Sealants are essential. These four types are all that you'll need

Fig. 3 Three types of cleaners. Some are caustic; some are not

Fig. 4 This is one type of hand cleaner that not only works well but smells pretty good too

Fig. 5 Along with cleaners, you'll need clean-up material. The best thing for all types of spills is 'kitty litter'

TOOLS

▶ **See Figures 7, 8, 9 and 10**

Every do-it-yourselfer loves to accumulate tools. So gathering the tools necessary for engine work can be real fun!

When buying tools, the saying 'You get what you pay for' is absolutely true! Don't go cheap! Any hand tool that you buy should be drop forged and/or chrome vanadium. These two qualities tell you that the tool is strong enough for the job. With any tool, power or not, go with a name that you've heard of before, or, that is recommended buy your local professional retailer. Let's go over a list of tools that you'll need.

87933065

Fig. 6 A pack of shop towels

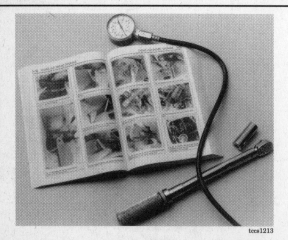

tccs1213

Fig. 7 The most important tool you need to do the job is the proper information, so always have a Chilton Total Car Care manual handy

Hands Tools

Socket sets

▶ **See Figures 11, 12, 13 and 14**

Socket sets are the most basic, necessary hand tools for engine work. For our purposes, socket sets come in three drive sizes: 1/4 inch, 3/8 inch and 1/2 inch. Drive size refers to the size of the drive lug on the ratchet, breaker bar or speed handle.

You'll need a good 1/2 inch set since this size drive lug assure that you won't break a ratchet or socket. Also, torque wrenches with a torque scale high enough are all 1/2 inch drive. The socket set that you'll need should range is sizes from 7/16 inch through 1 inch.

A 3/8 set is very handy to have since it allows you to get into tight places that the larger drive ratches can't. Also, it gives you a range of smaller socket sizes that are still strong enough to do heavy work.

1/4 inch drive sets aren't really necessary or applicable for engine work, but they're good to have for other, light work around the car or house. Besides, they're tools...you NEED them!

As for the sockets themselves, they come in standard and deep lengths, standard and thin walled and 6 and 12 point.

Standard length sockets are good for just about all jobs, however, some stud-head bolts, hard-to-reach bolts, nuts on long studs, etc., require the deep sockets.

Thin-walled sockets are not too common and aren't usually needed in engine work. They are exactly what you think, sockets made with thinner wall to fit into tighter places. They don't have the wall strength of a standard socket, of course, but their usefulness in a tight spot can make them worth it.

6 and 12 points. This refers to how many sides are in the socket itself. Each has advantages. The 6 point socket is stronger and less prone to slipping which would strip a bolt head or nut. 12 point sockets are more common, usually less expensive and can operate better in tight places where the ratchet handle can't swing far.

Torque Wrenches
▶ **See Figure 15**

In most applications, a torque wrench can be used to assure proper installation of a fastener. Torque wrenches come in various designs and most automotive supply stores will carry a variety to suit your needs. A torque wrench should be used any time we supply a specific torque value for a fastener. A torque wrench can also be used if you are following the general guidelines in the accompanying charts. Keep in mind that because there is no worldwide standardization of fasteners, the charts are a general guideline and should be used with caution. Again, the general rule of "if you are using the right tool for the job, you should not have to strain to tighten a fastener" applies here.

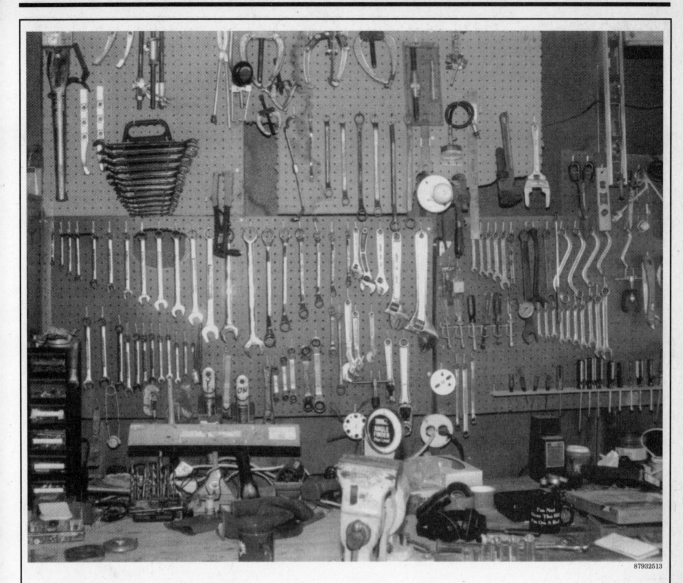

Fig. 8 The well-stocked garage pegboard

BEAM TYPE

▶ See Figure 16

The beam type torque wrench is one of the most popular types. It consists of a pointer attached to the head that runs the length of the flexible beam (shaft) to a scale located near the handle. As the wrench is pulled, the beam bends and the pointer indicates the torque using the scale.

CLICK (BREAKAWAY) TYPE

▶ See Figure 17

Another popular design of torque wrench is the click type. To use the click type wrench you pre-adjust it to a torque setting. Once the torque is reached, the wrench has a reflex signalling feature that causes a momentary breakaway of the torque wrench body, sending an impulse to the operator's hand.

PIVOT HEAD TYPE

▶ See Figure 18

Some torque wrenches (usually of the click type) may be equipped with a pivot head which can allow it to be used in areas of limited access. BUT, it must be used properly. To hold a pivot head wrench, grasp the handle lightly, and as you pull on the handle, it should be floated on the pivot point. If the handle comes in contact with the yoke extension during the process of pulling, there is a very good chance the torque readings will be inaccurate because this could alter the wrench

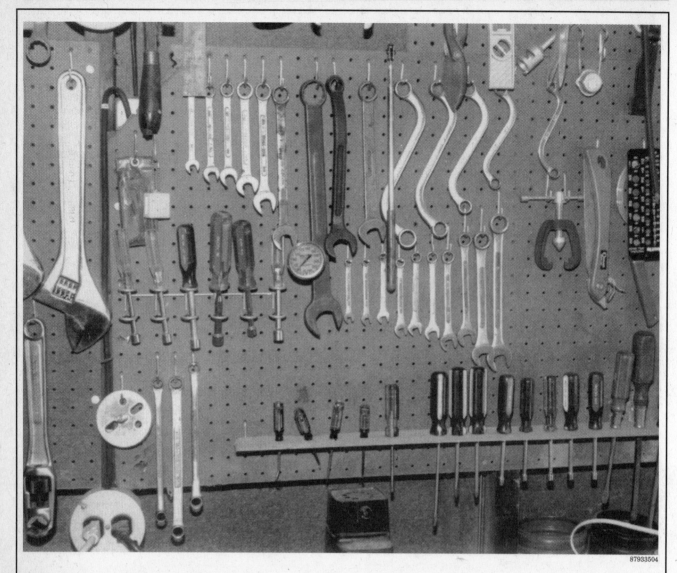

Fig. 9 You can arrange the pegboard any way you like, but it's best to hang the most used tools closest to you

Fig. 10 A good set of handy storage cabinets for fasteners and small parts makes any job easier

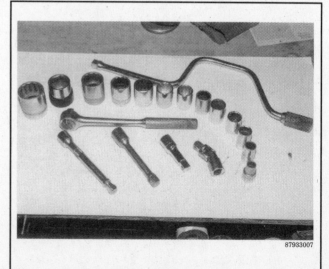

Fig. 11 A good half inch drive socket set

Fig. 12 Left, a hex drive socket; right, a Torx drive socket

Fig. 13 Two types of drive adapters and a swivel (U-joint) adapter

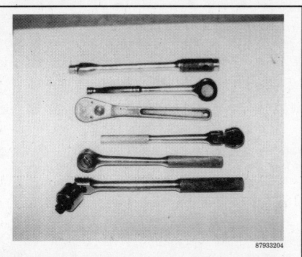

Fig. 14 Ratchets come in all sizes from rigid to swivel-headed

loading point. The design of the handle is usually such as to make it inconvenient to deliberately misuse the wrench.

➡It should be mentioned that the use of any U-joint, wobble or extension will have an effect on the torque readings, no matter what type of wrench you are using. For the most accurate readings, install the socket directly on the wrench driver. If necessary, straight extensions (which hold a socket directly under the wrench driver) will have the least effect on the torque reading. Avoid any extension that alters the length of the wrench from the handle to the head/driving point (such as a crow's foot). U-joint or Wobble extensions can greatly affect the readings; avoid their use at all times.

RIGID CASE (DIRECT READING)
▸ See Figure 19

A rigid case or direct reading torque wrench is equipped with a dial indicator to show torque values. One advantage of these wrenches is that they can be held at any position on the wrench without affecting accuracy. These wrenches are often preferred because they tend to be compact, easy to read and have a great degree of accuracy.

TORQUE ANGLE METERS
▸ See Figure 20

Because the frictional characteristics of each fastener or threaded hole will vary, clamp loads which are based strictly on torque will vary as well. In most applications, this variance is not significant enough to cause worry. But, in certain applications, a manufacturer's engineers may determine that more precise clamp loads are necessary (such is the case with many aluminum cylinder heads). In these cases, a torque angle method of installation would be specified. When installing fasteners which are torque angle tightened, a predetermined seating torque and standard torque wrench are usually used first to remove any compliance from the joint. The fastener is then tightened the specified additional portion of a turn measured in degrees. A torque angle gauge (mechanical protractor) is used for these applications.

Breaker Bars

Breaker bars are long handles with a drive lug. Their main purpose is to provide extra turning force when breaking loose tight bolts or nuts. They come in all drive sizes and lengths. Always wear gloves when using a breaker bar

Speed Handles
▸ See Figure 21

Speed handles are tools with a drive lug and angled turning handle which allow you to quickly remove or install a bolt or nut. They don't, however have much torque ability. You might consider one when installing a number of similar bolts such as head bolts or main bearing cap nuts.

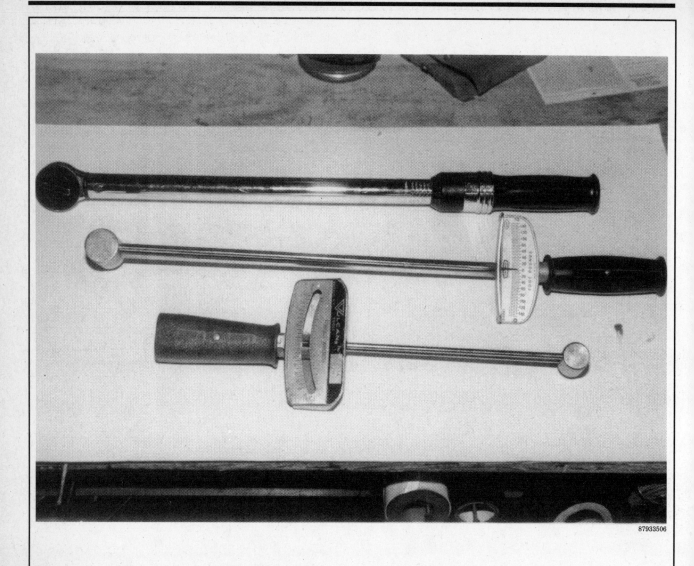

87933506

Fig. 15 Three types of torque wrenches. Top to bottom: a half inch drive clicker type, a half inch drive beam type and a three-eights in drive beam type that read in inch lbs.

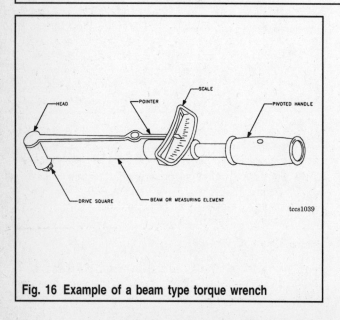

Fig. 16 Example of a beam type torque wrench

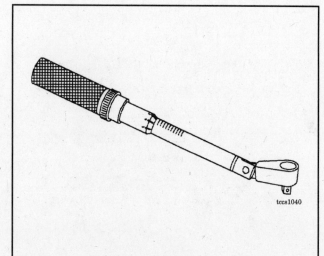

Fig. 17 A click type or breakaway torque wrench — note this one has a pivoting head

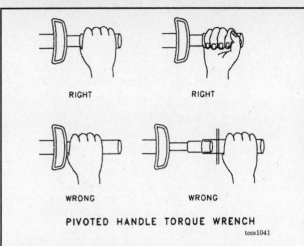

Fig. 18 Torque wrenches with pivoting heads must be grasped and used properly to prevent an incorrect reading

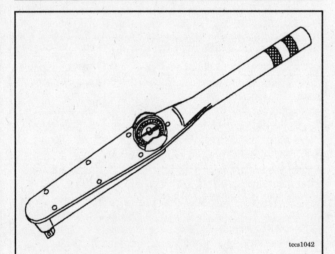

Fig. 19 The rigid case (direct reading) torque wrench uses a dial indicator to show torque

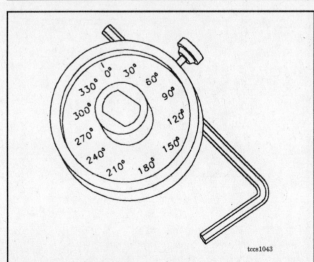

Fig. 20 Some specifications require the use of a torque angle meter (mechanical protractor)

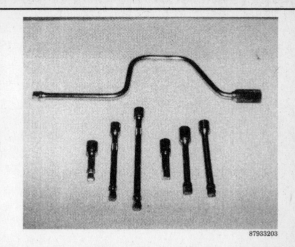

Fig. 21 A speed driver and drive extensions. The three extensions on the left are called 'wobble' extensions since they allow some lateral movement

Wrenches

▶ See Figures 22, 23, 24 and 25

Basically, there are 3 kinds of fixed wrenches: open end, box end, and combination.

Open end wrenches have 2-jawed end ends at each end of the wrench. These wrenches are able to fit onto just about any nut or bolt. They are extremely versatile but have one major drawback. They can slip on a worn or rounded bolt head or nut and cause bleeding knuckles and a useless fastener.

Box-end wrenches have a 360° circular jaw at each end of the wrench. They come in both 6 and 12 point versions just like sockets and each type has the same advantages and disadvantages as sockets.

Combination wrenches have the best of both. They have a 2-jawed open end and a box end. These wrenches are probably the most versatile.

As for sizes, you'll need a range of ¼ inch through 1 inch. As for numbers, you'll need 2 of each size, since, in many instances, one wrench holds the nut while the other turns the bolt. On most fasteners, the nut and bolt are the same size.

One extremely valuable type of wrench is the adjustable wrench. An adjustable wrench has a fixed upper jaw and a moveable lower jaw. The lower jaw is moved by turning a threaded drum. The advantage of an adjustable wrench is its ability to be adjusted to just about any size fastener. The main drawback of an adjustable wrench is the lower jaw's tendency to move slightly under heavy pressure. This can cause the wrench to slip. Adjustable wrenches come in a large range of sizes, measured by the wrench length.

Pliers

▶ See Figure 26

At least 2 pair of standard pliers is an absolute necessity. Pliers are simply mechanical fingers. They are, more than anything, an extension of your hand.

INCHES	DECIMAL		DECIMAL	MILLIMETERS
1/8"	.125		.118	3mm
3/16"	.187		.157	4mm
1/4"	.250		.236	6mm
5/16"	.312		.354	9mm
3/8"	.375		.394	10mm
7/16"	.437		.472	12mm
1/2"	.500		.512	13mm
9/16"	.562		.590	15mm
5/8"	.625		.630	16mm
11/16"	.687		.709	18mm
3/4"	.750		.748	19mm
13/16"	.812		.787	20mm
7/8"	.875		.866	22mm
15/16"	.937		.945	24mm
1"	1.00		.984	25mm

87933106

Fig. 22 Comparison of U.S. measure and metric wrench sizes

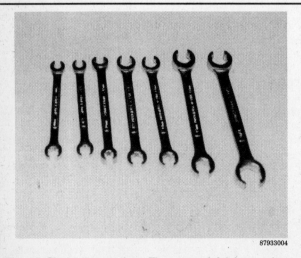

87933004

Fig. 23 Flarenut wrenches. They are useful for turning nuts mounted on tubing

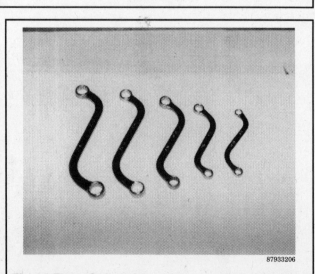

87933206

Fig. 24 These S-shaped wrenches are called obstruction wrenches

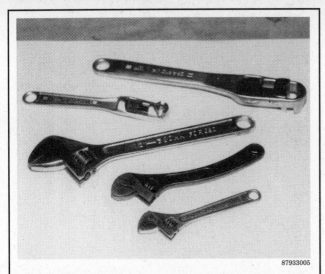

Fig. 25 **Several types and sizes of adjustable wrenches**

In addition to standard pliers there are the slip-joint, multi-position pliers such as ChannelLock® pliers and locking pliers, such as Vise Grips®.

Slip joint pliers are extremely valuable in grasping oddly sized parts and fasteners. Just make sure that you don't use them instead of a wrench too often since they can easily round off a bolt head or nut.

Locking pliers are usually used for gripping bolt or stud that can't be removed conventionally. You can get locking pliers in square jawed, needle-nosed and pipe-jawed. Pipe jawed have slightly curved jaws for gripping more than just pipes. Locking pliers can rank right up behind duct tape as the handy-man's best friend.

Screwdrivers

You can't have too many screwdrivers. Screwdrivers are either standard or Phillips. Standard blades come in various sizes and thicknesses for all types of slotted fasteners. Phillips

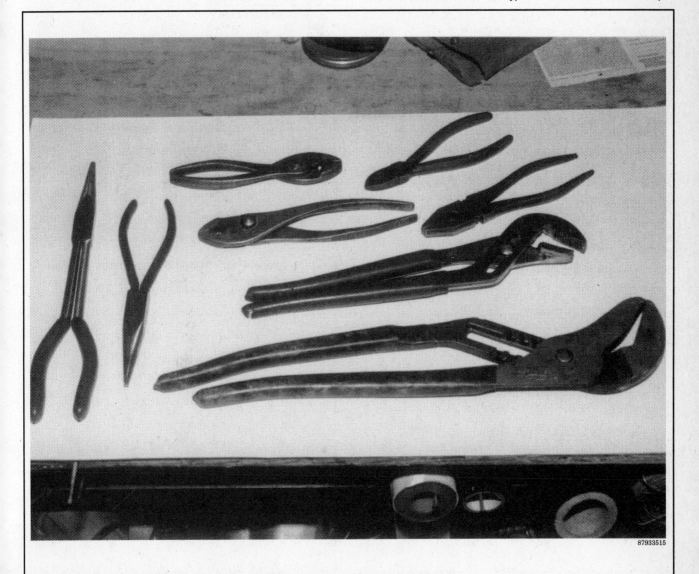

Fig. 26 **Pliers come in many shapes and sizes. Here are the most common types**

screwdrivers come in three sizes: No. 1, 2 and 3; 3 being the largest. Screwdrivers can be purchased separately or in sets.

Hammers

▶ See Figure 27

You always need a hammer — for just about any kind of work. For engine work, you need a ball-peen hammer for using drivers and other like tools, a plastic hammer for hitting things safely, and a soft-faced dead-blow hammer for hitting things safely and hard.

Other Common Tools

▶ See Figures 28, 29, 30 and 31

There are a lot of other tools that every workshop should have for automotive work. The include:
- Chisels
- Punches
- Files
- Hacksaw
- Bench Vise
- Tap and Die Set
- Gasket scraper
- Putty Knife
- Screw/Bolt Extractors
- Pry Bar

Chisel, punches and files are repair tools. There uses will come up during the rebuilding operation.

Hacksaws have just one use, cutting things off. You may wonder why you'd need one for something as precise as engine work, but the chances are you will. Among other things, guide studs for parts installation can be made from old bolts with their heads cut off.

A large bench vise — 4 inch capacity is good — is essential. A vise is needed to hold anything being worked on.

A tap and die set might be something you've never needed, but you can't get along without it when rebuilding. It's a good

Fig. 28 A good quality, heavy-duty bench vise, like this 5½ in. type, with reversible jaws, is ideal for shop work

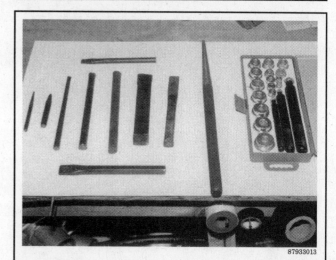

Fig. 29 Punches, chisels and drivers can be purchased separately or in sets

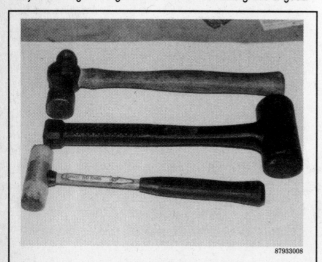

Fig. 27 Three types of hammers. Top to bottom: ball peen, rubber dead-blow, and plastic

Fig. 30 Two good tap and die sets; US measure (left) and metric

rule, when everything is apart, to run clean-up all threads, on bolts, screws and threaded holes. Also, you'll likely run across a situation in which stripped threads will be encountered. The tap and die set will handle that for you.

Gasket scrapers are just what you'd think, tools made for scraping old gasket material off of parts. You don't absolutely need one. Old gasket material can be remove with a putty knife or single edge razor blade. However, putty knives may not be sharp enough for some really stuck gaskets and razor blades have a knack of breaking just when you don't want them to, inevitably slicing the nearest body part!

Putty knives really do have a use in automotive work. Just because you remove all the bolts from a rocker cover or oil pan doesn't mean it's going to come off. Most of the time, the gasket and sealer will hold it tightly. Lightly driving a putty knife at various points between the two parts will break the seal without damage to the parts.

A small — 8-10 inches long — pry bar is extremely useful for removing stuck parts such as cylinder heads, timing cases, intake manifolds, etc. NEVER, NEVER, use a screwdriver as a pry bar! Screwdrivers are not meant for prying. Screwdrivers, used for prying, can break, sending the broken shaft flying!

Screw/bolt extractors are used for removing broken bolts or studs that have broke off flush with the surface of the part. Their function will be explained in Chapter 4.

Automotive Tools

In addition to the common hand tools, there are a number of tools designed specifically for automotive work. They are:
- ring groove cleaner
- piston ring compressor
- piston ring spreader
- valve spring compressor
- valve lifter magnet
- oil filter wrench
- cylinder hone
- ridge reamer
- valve lapper
- 2 in. 2-jaw puller
- 2-jaw pullers
- 3-jaw pullers
- damper puller set
- O-Ring Picks

Piston Ring Expander
▶ See Figure 32

The piston ring spreader is used for removing and installing the rings. Unlike piston ring compressors, a piston ring installer is not absolutely necessary. But if you are a little doubtful of your ability, you should get one. They are not that expensive (certainly not as much as a new set of rings), and they will add immeasurably to your peace of mind.

Ring Groove Cleaner

The ring groove cleaner is used for cleaning the ring grooves in the pistons after the rings are removed. Some engine rebuilders will say that a ring groove cleaner is not necessary; that an old piece of broken piston ring will work just as well. While a broken piston ring will accomplish the same

thing, it will take three times as long, and you will wear your hands out. Buy the ring groove cleaner.

Piston Ring Compressor

There are two basic types of ring compressor. The most common utilizes an allen wrench to activate the compression process. The other uses a pliers. The ring compressor is used for pushing the rings within the ring grooves so that the piston can be installed in the cylinder. This tool is indispensable. There is simply no way to get a ringed piston into the cylinder without a compressor. It's use will be discussed further in Chapter 5.

Cylinder Hone or Glaze Breaker

There are two types of cylinder hones: those that follow the existing bore (spring-loaded or ball-type hones) and those that remain rigid and cut their own path. Rigid hones are used to hone cylinders that have a pronounced amount of wear and out-of-roundness. Spring loaded or ball-type hones are used for cylinders that are not as badly worn or to get a good cross-hatch pattern on a recently rebored cylinder. Ball-type hones are generally acknowledged to give a better result, but they are not as versatile as the spring-loaded type because each particular ball-type hone will only fit a certain range of bore sizes.

Ridge Reamer
▶ See Figure 33

A ridge reamer is the sort of tool you will not know you are going to need until you get the cylinder heads off the engine. Engines with well over 100,000 miles on them sometimes won't have a ridge, and some with 50,000 miles on them will. A cylinder ridge is a combination of unworn cylinder bore and some carbon buildup. Because the top piston ring cannot get all the way to the top of the cylinder, there will always be a slight (or not so slight) amount of unworn bore here. It has to be removed before you can remove the pistons from the engine. A ridge reamer is essentially a cutting tool designed to do this particular job. The cutter can be expanded to fit a variety of bore sizes.

Most ridge reamers have 3 or 4 cutting blades. The tool is placed in the top of a cylinder and turned with a wrench to remove the ridge caused by cylinder wear.

Valve Lappers
▶ See Figure 34

The valve lapper is basically a handle with a suction cup. When installing reground or new valves, the valve lapper is used, in conjunction with lapping compound, to effectively mate the valves with their seats in the head. The precise use will be explained in Chapter 5.

Pullers
▶ See Figures 35 and 36

The 2- and 3-jawed pullers are used mainly for removing bearings, gears and sprockets, although you'll find they come in handy for a number of other things. Pullers come in various sizes. We'd recommend that you have 2 in., 4 in., 6 in., and 8 in. pullers.

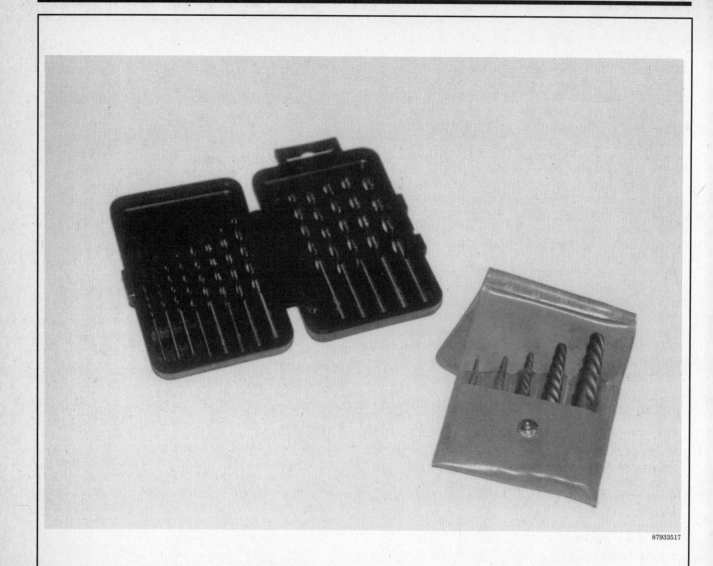

87933517

Fig. 31 A set of drill bits and a set of screw extractors

The damper puller is essential for removing the crankshaft damper. You can't do the job without it. Complete instructions are supplied with the damper kit.

Gauges and Testers

▶ **See Figures 37, 38 and 39**

- spark plug gauge
- 30 in. machinist's straightedge
- 40-piece flat feeler gauge set
- starter/alternator tester
- auto-ranging, digital multi-tester
- Tach/Dwell/Voltmeter
- vacuum gauge
- vacuum pump
- timing light
- compression tester

Everybody knows what a spark plug gauge set is. But, if you don't, it's used for checking the gap between the spark plug's center and ground electrodes.

The machinist's straightedge is used to check the flatness of cylinder heads, block surfaces and intake manifold surfaces. You'll need one that is at least 30 inches long.

A set of flat feeler gauges is needed to measure the gap between parts where gapping is critical or part of the part's function. A 40-piece set will give you all the feelers that you'll ever need.

The uses of the testers will be explained in Chapter 6.

Micrometers and Calipers

Outside Micrometers

Outside micrometers are used to check the diameters of such components as the pistons and crankshaft. The most common type of micrometer reads in 1/1000 of an inch. Micrometers that use a vernier scale can estimate to 1/10 of an inch. The illustrations show the various part names.

Micrometers and calipers are devices used to make extremely precise measurements. The success of any rebuild is

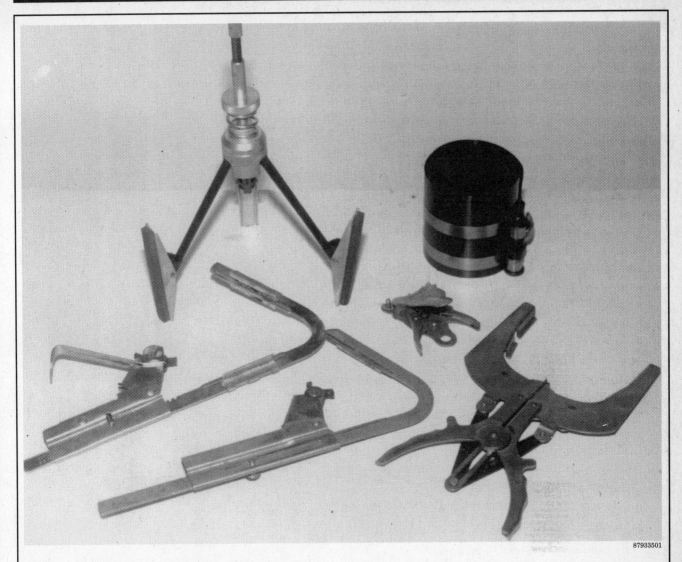

Fig. 32 An assortment of piston-related tools. From the top, clockwise: cylinder hone, piston ring compressor, ring expanders, and 2 types of ring groove cleaners

87933501

dependent, to a great extent on the ability to check the size and fit of components as specified by the engine manufacturer. These measurements are made in thousandths and ten-thousandths of an inch.

A micrometer is an instrument made up of a precisely machined spindle which is rotated in a fixed nut, opening and closing the distance between the end of the spindle and a fixed anvil.

To make a measurement, you back off the spindle until you can place the piece to be measured between the spindle and anvil. You then rotate the spindle until the part is contacted by both the spindle and anvil. The measurement is then found by reading the gradations in the handle of the micrometer.

Here's the hard part. I'll try to explain how to read a micrometer. The spindle is threaded. Most micrometers use a thread pitch of 40 threads per inch. One complete revolution of the spindle move the spindle toward or away from the anvil 0.025 in. ($^1/_{40}$ in.).

The fixed part of the handle (called, the sleeve) is marked with 40 gradations per inch of handle length, so each line is 0.025 in. apart. Okay so far?

Every 4th line is marked with a number. The first long line marked 1 represents 0.100 in., the second is 0.200 in., and so on.

The part of the handle that turns is called the thimble. The beveled end of the thimble is marked with gradations, each of which corresponds to 0.001 in. and, usually, every 5th line is numbered.

Turn the thimble until the 0 lines up with the 0 on the sleeve. Now, rotate the thimble one complete revolution and look at the sleeve. You'll see that one complete thimble revolution moved the thimble 0.025 in. down the sleeve.

To read the micrometer, multiply the number of gradations exposed on the sleeve by 0.025 and add that to the number of thousandths indicated by the thimble line that is lined up with the horizontal line on the sleeve. So, if you've measured a part and there are 6 vertical gradations exposed on the sleeve and the 7th gradation on the thimble is lined up with the horizontal line on the sleeve, the thickness of the part is 0.157 in. (6 x 0.025 = 0.150 . Add to that 0.007 representing the 7 lines on the thimble and you get 0.157). See?

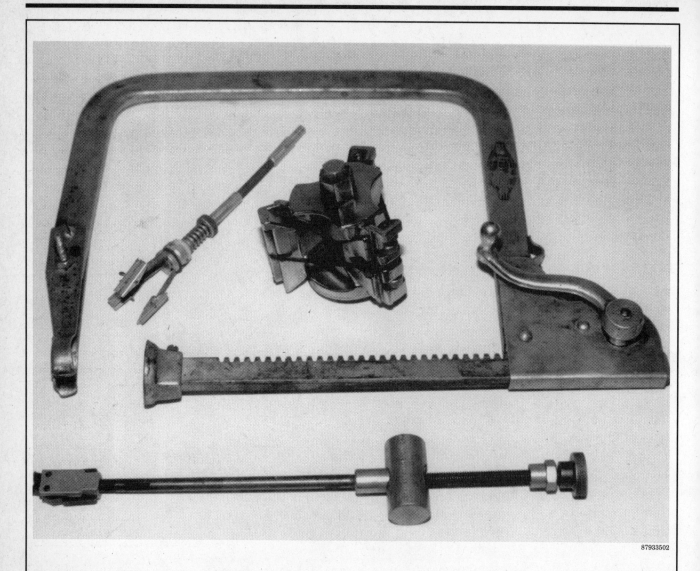

Fig. 33 More special tools. The big thing is a valve spring compressor. Positioned within it are a small hone (left) and a ridge reamer. Underneath is a lifter puller.

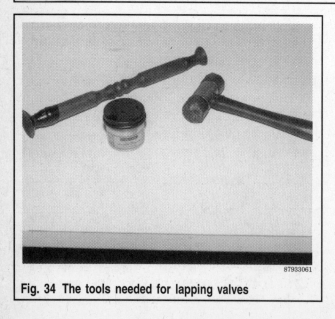

Fig. 34 The tools needed for lapping valves

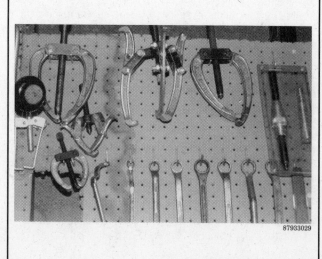

Fig. 35 Several sizes of 2- and 3-jawed pullers

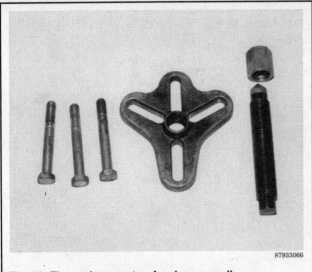

Fig. 36 The various parts of a damper puller

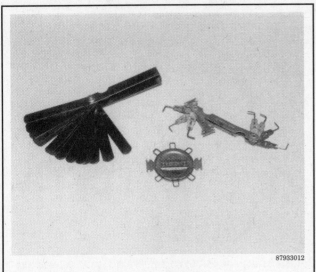

Fig. 37 Flat and round feeler gauges

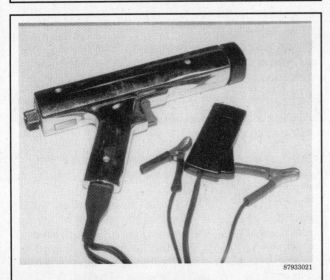

Fig. 38 A typical inductive timing light

If you didn't understand that, try the instructions that come with the micrometer or ask someone that knows, to show you how to work it.

Inside Micrometers

Inside micrometers are used to measure the distance between two parallel surfaces. In engine rebuilding work, the inside mike measures cylinder bore wear, connecting rod big end wear, and block main bearing bore sizes. Inside mikes are graduated the same way as outside mikes and are read the same way as well.

Remember that an inside mike must be absolutely perpendicular to the work being measured. When you measure with an inside mike, rock the mike gently from side to side and tip it back and forth slightly so that you span the widest part of the bore. Just to be on the safe side, take several readings. It takes a certain amount of experience to work any mike with confidence.

Metric Micrometers

Metric micrometers are read in the same way as inch micrometers, except that the measurements are in millimeters. Each line on the main scale equals 1 mm. Each fifth line is stamped 5, 10, 15, and so on. Each line on the thimble scale equals 0.01 mm. It will take a little practice, but if you can read an inch mike, you can read a metric mike.

Inside and Outside Calipers

Inside and outside calipers are useful devices to have if you need to measure something quickly and precise measurement is not necessary. Simply take the reading and then hold the calipers on an accurate steel rule.

DIAL INDICATORS

A dial indicator is a gauge that utilizes a dial face and a needle to register measurements. There is a movable contact arm on the dial indicator. When the arms moves, the needle rotates on the dial. Dial indicators are calibrated to show readings in thousandths of an inch and typically, are used to measure end play and runout on camshafts, crankshafts, gears, and so on.

Dial indicators are quite easy to use, although they are relatively expensive. A variety of mounting devices are available so that the indicator can be used in a number of situations. Make certain that the contact arm is always parallel to the movement of the work being measured.

TELESCOPING GAUGES

A telescope gauge is used to measure the inside of bores, connecting rod big ends, and so on. They can take the place of an inside mike for some of these jobs. Simply insert the gauge in the hole to be measured and lock the plungers after they have contacted the walls. Remove the tool and measure across the plungers with an outside micrometer.

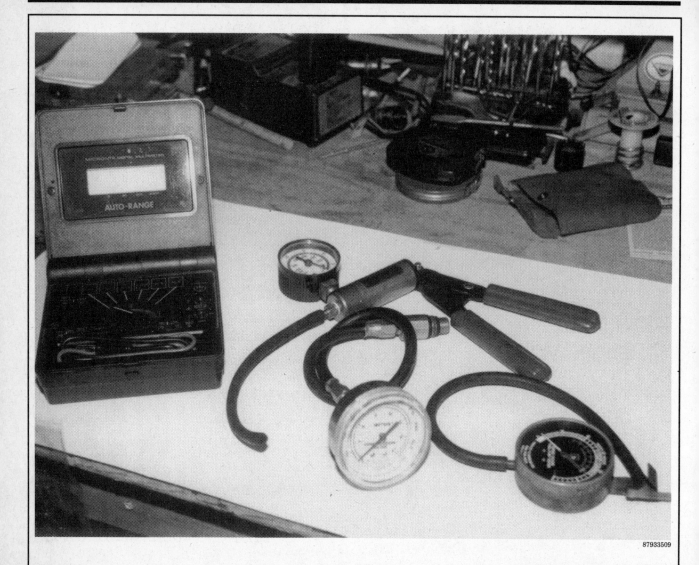

Fig. 39 Several types of test equipment. Left to right: digital multi-tester, vacuum pump, compression tester and vacuum gauge

87933509

PLASTIGAGE

Plastigage is a sort of soft plastic that will flatten out to predetermined widths when subjected to torquing. These widths will equal a specific clearance. Plastigage is normally used to check main and rod-bearing clearance. It is sold in a paper sleeve that also doubles as the scale upon which it is measured. The scale reads out in thousandths of an inch. The most common type is green Plastigage which is used to measure clearances from 0.001 to 0.003 in. Its use will be discussed later, in Chapter 5.

Special Tools

Normally, the use of special factory tools is avoided for repair procedures, since these are not readily available for the do-it-yourself mechanic. When it is possible to perform the job with more commonly available tools, it will be pointed out, but occasionally, a special tool was designed to perform a specific function and should be used. Before substituting another tool, you should be convinced that neither your safety nor the performance of the vehicle will be compromised.

Special tools can usually be purchased from an automotive parts store or from your dealer. In some cases special tools may be available directly from the tool manufacturer.

Electric Power Tools

▶ **See Figures 40 and 41**

Power tools are most often associated with wood working. However, there are a few which are very helpful in automotive work.

The most common and most useful power tool is the bench grinder. You'll need a grinder with a grinding stone on one side and a wire brush wheel on the other. The brush wheel is indispensible for cleaning parts and the stone can be used to remove rough surfaces and for reshaping, where necessary.

Almost as useful as the bench grinder is the drill. Drills can come in very handy when a stripped or broken fastener is encountered. See Chapter 4 for their uses.

Fig. 40 Three types of common power tools useful in your work. Left to right: a hand-held grinder, drill and impact wrench

Fig. 41 The bench grinder may be the most frequently used power tool, since it's used for cleaning just about every part removed from the engine

Power ratchets and impact wrenches can come in very handy. Power ratchets can save a lot of time and muscle when removing and installing long bolts or nuts on long studs, especially where there is little room to swing a manual ratchet. Electric impact wrenches can be invaluable in a lot of automotive work, especially wheel lugs and axle shaft nuts. They don't have much use on engines, though.

Air Tools and Compressors

▶ See Figures 42 and 43

Air-powered tools are not necessary for engine work. They are, however, useful for speeding up many jobs and for general clean-up of parts. If you don't have air tools, and you want them, be prepared for an initial outlay of a lot of money.

The first thing you need is a compressor. Compressors are available in electrically driven and gas engine driven models. As long as you have electricity, you don't need a gas engine driven type.

Fig. 42 This is about the best size and type compressor set for the do-it-yourselfer. It operates off ordinary house current and provides all the air pressure you'll need

The common shop-type air compressor is a pump mounted on a tank. The pump compresses air and forces it into the tank where it is stored until you need it. The compressor automatically turns the pump on when the air pressure in the tank falls below a certain preset level.

There are all kinds of air powered tools, including ratchets, impact wrenches, saws, drills, sprayers, nailers, scrapers, riveters, grinders and sanders. In general, air powered tools are much cheaper than their electric counterparts.

When deciding what size compressor unit you need, you'll be driven by two factors: the psi (pounds per square inch) capacity of the unit and the deliver rate in cfm (cubic feet per minute). For example, most air powered ratchets require 90 psi at 4 to 5 cfm to operate at peak efficiency. Grinders and saws may require up to 7 cfm at 90 psi. So, before buying the compressor unit, decide what types of tools you'll want so that you don't short-change yourself on the compressor purchase.

If you decide that a compressor and air tools isn't for you, you can have the benefit of air pressure rather cheaply. Purchase an air storage tank, available in sizes up to 20 gallons at most retail stores that sell aut products. These stor-

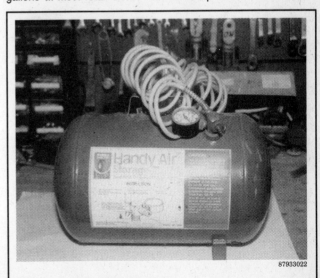

Fig. 43 An air storage tank

age tanks can safely store air pressure up to 125 psi and come with a high pressure nozzle for cleaning things and an air chuck for filling tires. The tank can be filled using the common tire-type air compressor.

Engine Tools

▶ See Figure 44

You're not going to need too many tools that are used just for engine work. Among them, the most used are:
- Piston ring expander
- Piston ring compressor
- Valve spring compressor
- Ridge reamer
- 2-jawed puller
- 3-jawed puller
- slide hammer
- dial indicator
- micrometer
- feeler gauges
- calipers
- compression tester
- vacuum gauge
- vacuum pump

The use of of the piston ring tools will be explained in Chapter 5. Essentially they are absolute necessities for removing and installing the rings.

The ridge reamer is used for removing the ridge in a cylinder caused by excessive wear.

The valve spring compressor grasps the valve face and levers the spring downward allowing the valve spring keepers to be removed.

Pullers and slide hammers are needed for removing gears, bearings, and sprockets from shafts or bores.

Feelers, micrometers, calipers, compression testers, vacuum gauges and vacuum pumps are measuring tools. Their uses will be explained in Chapter 5 and 6.

87933003

Fig. 44 A really handy tool is the nut splitter. When a frozen nut simply won't budge, use on of these

Shop Cranes, Dollies, Jacks and Engine Stands

SHOP CRANES

▶ See Figure 45

Your shop crane should be of at least 1 ton capacity. A crane with adjustable legs is preferable. Adjustable legs allow you to get closer to the vehicle. The further away the base of the crane is, the further out you have to extend the boom, reducing the lifting capacity.

All cranes have booms which adjust in a telescoping fashion. The more adjustable your crane is, the easier the removal or installation will be.

Stands and cranes can be taken apart for storage. They are available at a lot of tool retailers or through tool catalogs.

ENGINE DOLLY

▶ See Figure 46

An engine dolly is a relatively simple device. Most are made of bolted-together lengths of angle iron in a size and shape to support an engine. The device is mounted on heavy swiveling casters to allow you to roll it around the garage. You can easily make one yourself using an old bed frame.

ENGINE STANDS

▶ See Figure 47

You can't do the overhaul without an engine stand. The engine stand holds the engine up off the floor, about waist high, and allows you to rotate the engine 360° for easy access to all parts.

Whatever engine stand you get should be at least of 750 lbs. capacity. The lighter capacity stands have three wheels or 'legs'. The heavier capacity stands have 4 wheels or legs. The 4-wheel stands are less likely to tip over.

JACKS AND JACKSTANDS

▶ See Figures 48 and 49

Your vehicle was supplied with a jack for emergency road repairs. This jack is fine for changing a flat tire or other short term procedures not requiring you to go beneath the vehicle. For any real work, you MUST use a floor jack.

Never place the jack under the radiator, engine or transmission components. Severe and expensive damage will result when the jack is raised. Additionally, never jack under the floorpan or bodywork; the metal will deform.

Whenever you plan to work under the vehicle, you must support it on jackstands or ramps. Never use cinder blocks or stacks of wood to support the vehicle, even if you're only going to be under it for a few minutes. Never crawl under the

Fig. 45 A 4,000 lb. capacity shop crane with adjustable legs and boom

vehicle when it is supported only by the tire-changing jack or other floor jack.

➡**Always position a block of wood or small rubber pad on top of the jack or jackstand to protect the lifting point's finish when lifting or supporting the vehicle.**

Small hydraulic, screw, or scissors jacks are satisfactory for raising the vehicle. Drive-on trestles or ramps are also a handy and safe way to both raise and support the vehicle. Be careful though, some ramps may be too steep to drive your vehicle onto without scraping the front bottom panels. Never support the vehicle on any suspension member (unless specifically instructed to do so by a repair manual) or by an underbody panel.

JACKING PRECAUTIONS

The following safety points cannot be overemphasized:
• Always block the opposite wheel or wheels to keep the vehicle from rolling off the jack.
• When raising the front of the vehicle, firmly apply the parking brake.
• When the drive wheels are to remain on the ground, leave the vehicle in gear to help prevent it from rolling.
• Always use jackstands to support the vehicle when you are working underneath. Place the stands beneath the vehicle's jacking brackets. Before climbing underneath, rock the vehicle a bit to make sure it is firmly supported.

87933572

Fig. 46 A good engine dolly, capable of holding 1,000 lbs.

87935100

Fig. 47 An engine on a workstand, in the shop

87933573

Fig. 48 Floor jacks come in all sizes and capacities. Top is a large 2¼ ton models; underneath is a compact 2 ton model

FASTENERS

▸ **See Figures 50, 51 and 52**

Although there are a great variety of fasteners found in the modern car or truck, the most commonly used retainer is the threaded fastener (nuts, bolts, screws, studs, etc). Most threaded retainers may be reused, provided that they are not damaged in use or during the repair. Some retainers (such as stretch bolts or torque prevailing nuts) are designed to deform when tightened or in use and should not be reinstalled.

Whenever possible, we will note any special retainers which should be replaced during a procedure. But you should always inspect the condition of a retainer when it is removed and replace any that show signs of damage. Check all threads for rust or corrosion which can increase the torque necessary to achieve the desired clamp load for which that fastener was originally selected. Additionally, be sure that the driver surface of the fastener has not been compromised by rounding or other damage. In some cases a driver surface may become only partially rounded, allowing the driver to catch in only one

direction. In many of these occurrences, a fastener may be installed and tightened, but the driver would not be able to grip and loosen the fastener again. (This could lead to frustration down the line should that component ever need to be disassembled again).

If you must replace a fastener, whether due to design or damage, you must ALWAYS be sure to use the proper replacement. In all cases, a retainer of the same design, material and strength should be used. Markings on the heads of most bolts will help determine the proper strength of the fastener. The same material, thread and pitch must be selected to assure proper installation and safe operation of the vehicle afterwards.

Thread gauges are available to help measure a bolt or stud's thread. Most automotive and hardware stores keep gauges available to help you select the proper size. In a pinch, you can use another nut or bolt for a thread gauge. If the bolt you are replacing is not too badly damaged, you can select a

87933510

Fig. 49 Jackstands are necessary for holding your vehicle up off the ground. Top are 6 ton models; bottom are 4 ton models

POZIDRIVE   PHILLIPS RECESS   TORX®   CLUTCH RECESS

INDENTED HEXAGON   HEXAGON TRIMMED   HEXAGON WASHER HEAD

tccs1037

Fig. 50 Here are a few of the most common screw/bolt driver styles

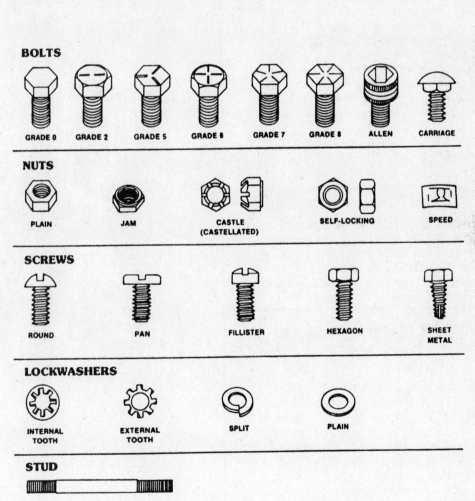

BOLTS

GRADE 0   GRADE 2   GRADE 5   GRADE 6   GRADE 7   GRADE 8   ALLEN   CARRIAGE

NUTS

PLAIN   JAM   CASTLE (CASTELLATED)   SELF-LOCKING   SPEED

SCREWS

ROUND   PAN   FILLISTER   HEXAGON   SHEET METAL

LOCKWASHERS

INTERNAL TOOTH   EXTERNAL TOOTH   SPLIT   PLAIN

STUD

tccs1036

Fig. 51 There are many different types of threaded retainers found on vehicles

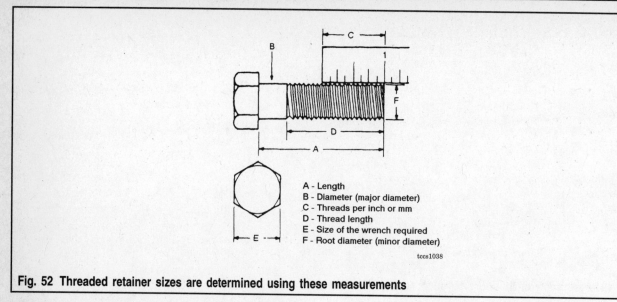

A - Length
B - Diameter (major diameter)
C - Threads per inch or mm
D - Thread length
E - Size of the wrench required
F - Root diameter (minor diameter)

tccs1038

Fig. 52 Threaded retainer sizes are determined using these measurements

match by finding another bolt which will thread in its place. If you find a nut which threads properly onto the damaged bolt, then use that nut to help select the replacement bolt. If however, the bolt you are replacing is so badly damaged (broken or drilled out) that its threads cannot be used as a gauge, you might start by looking for another bolt (from the same assembly or a similar location on your vehicle) which will thread into the damaged bolt's mounting. If so, the other bolt can be used to select a nut; the nut can then be used to select the replacement bolt.

In all cases, be absolutely sure you have selected the proper replacement. Don't be shy, you can always ask the store clerk for help.

✳✳WARNING

Be aware that when you find a bolt with damaged threads, you may also find the nut or drilled hole it was threaded into has also been damaged. If this is the case, you may have to drill and tap the hole, replace the nut or otherwise repair the threads. NEVER try to force a replacement bolt to fit into the damaged threads.

Bolts and Screws

▶ **See Figure 53**

Technically speaking, bolts are hexagon head or cap screws. For the purposes of this book, however, cap screws will be called bolts because that is the common terminology for them. Both bolts and screws are turned into drilled or threaded holes to fasten two parts together. Frequently, bolts require a nut on the other end, but this is not always the case. Screws seldom, if ever, require a nut on the other end.

Screws are supplied with slotted or Phillips heads. For obvious reasons, screws are not generally used where a great deal of torque is required. Most of the screws you will encounter will be used to retain components, such as the camshaft cover or other components, where strength is not a factor. Screw sizes are designated as 8-32, 10-32, or ¼-32. The first number indicates the minor diameter, and the second number indicates the number of threads per inch.

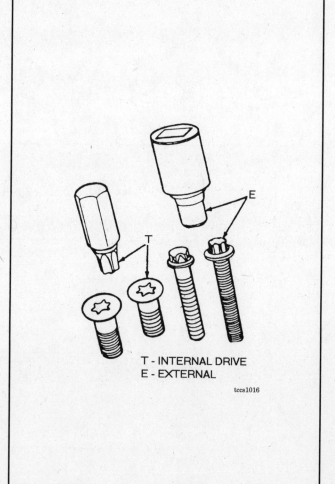

T - INTERNAL DRIVE
E - EXTERNAL

tccs1016

Fig. 53 Special fasteners such as these Torx® head bolts are used by manufacturers to discourage people from working on vehicles without the proper tools

Nuts

▶ **See Figure 54**

Nuts have only one use: they simply hold the other end of the bolt and, thereby, hold the two parts together. There are a variety of nuts used on cars, but a standard hexagon head (six-sided) nut is the most common.

Castellated and slotted nuts are designed for use with a cotter pin and are usually used when it is extremely important that the nuts do not work loose (in wheel bearings, for example). Other nuts are self-locking nuts that have a slot cut in the side.

When the nut is tightened, the separated sections pull together and lock the nut onto the bolt. Interference nuts have a collar of soft metal or fiber. The bolt cuts threads in the soft material which then jams in the threads and prevents the nut and bolt from working loose.

A jam nut is a second hexagon nut that is used to hold the first nut in place. They are usually found where some type of adjustment is needed. valve trains, for instance.

Pawlnuts are single thread nuts that provide some locking action when they have been turned down on the nut.

Speed nuts are simply rectangular bits of sheet metal that are pushed down over a bolt, screw, or stud to provide locking action.

Studs

Studs are simply pieces of threaded rod. They are similar to bolts and screws in their thread configuration, but they have no heads. One end is turned into a threaded hole and the other end is generally secured by same type of nut. Unless the nut is self-locking, a lockwasher or jam nut is generally used underneath it.

Lockwashers

Lockwashers are a form of washer. They may be either split or toothed, and they are always installed between a nut or screwhead and the actual part being held. The split washer is crushed flat and locks the nut in place by spring tension. The toothed washer provides many edges to improve the locking effect and is usually used on smaller bolts and screws.

Screw and Bolt Terminology

Bolts and screws are identified by type, major diameter, minor diameter, pitch or threads per inch, class, length, thread length, and the size of the wrench required.

MAJOR DIAMETER

▶ **See Figure 55**

This is the widest diameter of the bolt as measured from the top of the threads on one side to the top of the threads on the other side.

MINOR DIAMETER

This is the diameter obtained by measuring from the bottom of the threads on one side of the bolt to the bottom of the threads on the other side. In other words, it is the diameter of the bolt if it does not have any threads.

PITCH OR THREADS PER INCH

▶ **See Figure 56**

Thread pitch is the distance between the top of one thread to the top of the next. It is simply the distance between one thread and the next. There are two types of threads in general use today. Unified National Coarse thread, and Unified National Fine. These are usually known simply as either fine or coarse thread.

Anyone who has been working on cars for any length of time can tell the difference between the two simply by looking at the screw, bolt, or nut. The only truly accurate way to determine thread pitch is to use a thread pitch gauge. There are some general rules to remember, however.

Coarse thread screws and bolts are used frequently when they are being threaded into aluminum or cast iron because the finer threads tend to strip more easily in these materials. Also, as a bolt or screw's diameter increases, thread pitch becomes greater.

THREAD CLASS

Thread class is a measure of the operating clearance between the internal nut threads and the external threads of the bolt. There are three classes of fit, 1, 2, or 3. In addition, there are letter designations to designate either internal (class A) or external (class B) threads.

Class 1 threads are a relatively loose fit and are used when ease of assembly and disassembly are of paramount importance.

Class 2 bolts are most commonly encountered in automotive applications and give an accurate, but not an overly tight, fit.

Class 3 threads are used when utmost accuracy is needed. You might find a class 3 bolt and nut combination on an airplane, but you won't encounter them very often on a car.

LENGTH AND THREAD LENGTH

Screw length is the length of the bolt or screw from the bottom of the head to the bottom of the bolt or screw. Thread length is exactly that, the length of the threads. The illustrations show this in greater detail.

Types or Grades of Bolts and Screws

▶ **See Figure 57**

The tensile strength of bolts and screws varies widely. Standards for these fasteners have been established by the Society

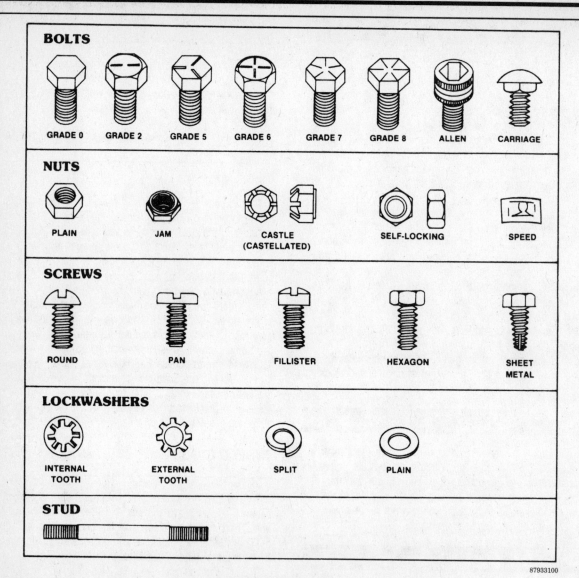

Fig. 54 Various types of fasteners found in automotive applications

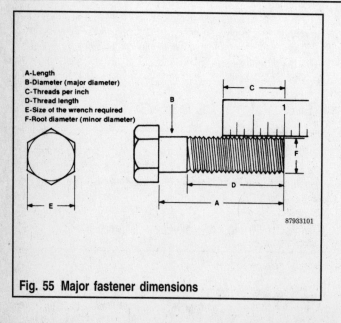

A-Length
B-Diameter (major diameter)
C-Threads per inch
D-Thread length
E-Size of the wrench required
F-Root diameter (minor diameter)

Fig. 55 Major fastener dimensions

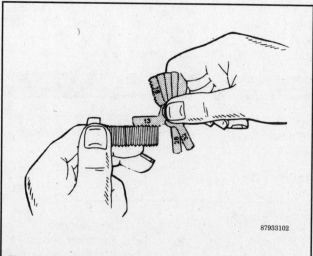

Fig. 56 A thread gauge will quickly identify the thread size

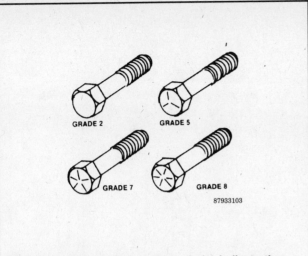

Fig. 57 Markings on U.S. measure bolts indicate the relative strength of the bolt

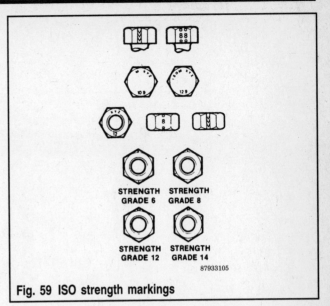

Fig. 59 ISO strength markings

of Automotive Engineers (SAE). Distinctive markings on the head of the bolt will identify its tensile strength.

These outward radiating lines are normally called points. A bolt with no points on the head is a grade 1 or a grade 2 bolt. This type of bolt is suitable for applications in which only a low-strength bolt is necessary.

On the other hand, a grade 5 bolt is found in a number of automotive applications and has double the tensile strength of a grade 2 bolt. A grade 5 bolt will have three embossed lines or points on the head.

Grade 8 bolts are the best and are frequently called aircraft grade bolts. Grade 8 bolts have six points on the head.

METRIC BOLTS
▶ See Figures 58, 59, 60 and 61

While metric bolts may seem to be the same as their U.S. measure counterparts, they definitely are not. The pitch on a metric bolt is different from that of an U.S. measure bolt. It is entirely possible to start a metric bolt into a hole with U.S. measure threads and run it down a few turns. Then it is going to bind. Recognizing the problem at this point is not going to do much good. It is also possible to run a metric nut down on an U.S. measure bolt and find that it is too loose to provide sufficient strength.

Metric bolts are marked in a manner different from that of U.S. measure bolts. Most metric bolts have a number stamped on the head. This metric grade marking won't be an even number, but something like 4.6 or 10.9. The number indicates the relative strength of the bolt. The higher the number, the greater the strength of the bolt. Some metric bolts are also

marked with a single-digit number to indicate the bolt strength. Metric bolt sizes are also identified in a manner different from that of U.S. measure fasteners.

If, for example, a metric bolt were designated 14 x 2, that would mean that the major diameter is 14 mm (.56 in.), and that the thread pitch is 2 mm (.08 in.). More important, metric bolts are not classified by number of threads per inch, but by the distance between the threads, and the distance between threads does not quite correspond to number of threads per inch. For example, 2 mm between threads is about 12.7 threads per inch.

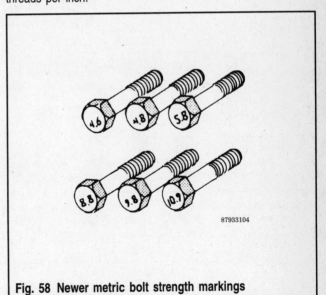

Fig. 58 Newer metric bolt strength markings

	Mark		Class		Mark	Class
Hexagon head bolt	 Bolt head No.	4 — 5 — 6 — 7 — 8 — 9 — 10 — 11 —	4T 5T 6T 7T 8T 9T 10T 11T	Stud bolt	No mark	4T
	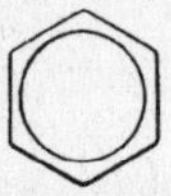 No mark		4T			
Hexagon flange bolt w/ washer hexagon bolt	 No mark		4T		Grooved	6T
Hexagon head bolt	 Two protruding lines		5T			
Hexagon flange bolt w/ washer hexagon bolt	 Two protruding lines		6T	Welded bolt		4T
Hexagon head bolt	 Three protruding lines		7T			
Hexagon head bolt	 Four protruding lines		8T			

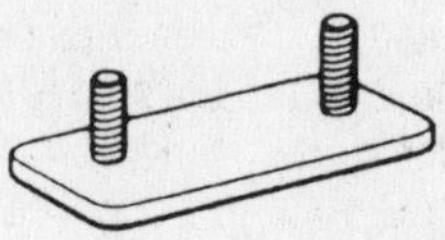

tccs1240

Fig. 60 Metric bolt strength indicator marks

THE HARD WORK STARTS

4

THE
ENGINE

THE HARD WORK STARTS

Before you start the actual hand-on work, let's go over a few work rules.

There are 3 common mistakes in mechanical work:

• Incorrect order of assembly, disassembly or adjustment. When taking something apart or putting it together, doing things in the wrong order usually just cost you extra time; however, it CAN break something. Read the entire procedure before beginning disassembly. Do everything in the order in which the instructions say you should do it, even if you can't immediately see a reason for it. When you're taking apart something that is very intricate (for example, a carburetor), you might want to draw a picture of how it looks when assembled at one point in order to make sure you get everything back in its proper position. (We will supply exploded view whenever possible). When making adjustments, especially tune-up adjustments, do them in order; often, one adjustment affects another, and you cannot expect satisfactory results unless each adjustment is made only when it cannot be changed by any order.

• Overtorquing (or undertorquing). While it is more common for over-torquing to cause damage, undertorquing can cause a fastener to vibrate loose causing serious damage. Especially when dealing with aluminum parts, pay attention to torque specifications and utilize a torque wrench in assembly. If a torque figure is not available, remember that if you are using the right tool to do the job, you will probably not have to strain yourself to get a fastener tight enough. The pitch of most threads is so slight that the tension you put on the wrench will be multiplied many, many times in actual force on what you are tightening. A good example of how critical torque is can be seen in the case of spark plug installation, especially where you are putting the plug into an aluminum cylinder head. Too little torque can fail to crush the gasket, causing leakage of combustion gases and consequent overheating of the plug and engine parts. Too much torque can damage the threads, or distort the plug which changes the spark gap. There are many commercial products available for ensuring that fasteners won't come loose, even if they are not torqued just right (a very common brand is Loctite®). If you're worried about getting something together tight enough to hold, but loose enough to avoid mechanical damage during assembly, one of these products might offer substantial insurance. Read the label on the package and make sure the products is compatible with the materials, fluids, etc. involved before choosing one.

• Crossthreading. This occurs when a part such as a bolt is screwed into a nut or casting at the wrong angle and forced. Cross threading is more likely to occur if access is difficult. It helps to clean and lubricate fasteners, and to start threading with the part to be installed going straight in. Then, start the bolt, spark plug, etc. with your fingers. If you encounter resistance, unscrew the part and start over again at a different angle until it can be inserted and turned several turns without much effort. Keep in mind that many parts, especially spark plugs, used tapered threads so that gentle turning will automatically bring the part you're treading to the proper angle if you don't force it or resist a change in angle. Don't put a wrench on the part until its's been turned a couple of turns by hand. If you suddenly encounter resistance, and the part has not seated fully, don't force it. Pull it back out and make sure it's clean and threading properly.

Always take your time and be patient; the further you go, the more confident you will become.

Storing Parts

Above all, I can't emphasize too strongly the necessity of a neat and orderly disassembly. Even if you are an experienced mechanic, parts can get mislaid, misidentified and just plain lost.

Start with an indelible marker, lots of cans and/or boxes and tags. Each time a part is removed, label it and store it safely. 'Parts' includes all fasteners (bolts, nuts, screws, washers). Bolts and nuts may look alike and not be alike. Similar looking bolts may be different lengths or thread count. Lockwashers may be required in some places and not in others. Everything should go back exactly where it came from.

Engine Overhaul Tips

Most engine overhaul procedures are fairly standard. Examples of standard rebuilding practices are shown and should be used along with specific details concerning your particular engine.

Competent and accurate machine shop services will ensure maximum performance, reliability and engine life. In most instances it is more profitable for the do-it-yourself mechanic to remove, clean and inspect the component, buy the necessary parts and deliver these to a shop for actual machine work.

On the other hand, much of the rebuilding work (crankshaft, block, bearings, piston rods, and other components) is well within the scope of the do-it-yourself mechanic.

TOOLS

The tools required for an engine overhaul or parts replacement will depend on the depth of your involvement. With a few exceptions, they will be the tools found in a mechanic's tool kit. More in-depth work will require any or all of the following:

• a dial indicator (reading in thousandths) mounted on a universal base
• micrometers and telescope gauges
• jaw and screw-type pullers
• scraper
• valve spring compressor
• ring groove cleaner
• piston ring expander and compressor
• ridge reamer
• cylinder hone or glaze breaker
• Plastigage®
• engine stand

The use of most of these tools are illustrated in this Chapter. Many can be rented for a one-time use from a local parts jobber or tool supply house specializing in automotive work.

Occasionally, the use of special tools is called for. See the information on Special Tools and Safety Notice in the front of this book before substituting another tool.

INSPECTION TECHNIQUES

Procedures and specifications are given in this section for inspecting, cleaning and assessing the wear limits of most major components. Other procedures such as Magnaflux® and Zyglo® can be used to locate material flaws and stress cracks. Magnaflux® is a magnetic process applicable only to ferrous materials. The Zyglo® process coats the material with a fluorescent dye penetrant and can be used on any material. Checking for suspected surface cracks can be more readily made using spot check dye. The dye is sprayed onto the suspected area, wiped off and the area sprayed with a developer. Cracks will show up brightly.

OVERHAUL TIPS

Aluminum has become extremely popular for use in engines, due to its low weight. Observe the following precautions when handling aluminum parts:

• Never hot tank aluminum parts (the caustic hot tank solution will eat the aluminum.

• Remove all aluminum parts (identification tag, etc.) from engine parts prior to the tanking.

• Always coat threads lightly with engine oil or anti-seize compounds before installation, to prevent seizure.

• Never overtorque bolts or spark plugs especially in aluminum threads.

Stripped threads in any component can be repaired using any of several commercial repair kits (Heli-Coil®, Microdot®, Keenserts®, etc.).

When assembling the engine, any parts that will be in frictional contact must be prelubed to provide lubrication at initial start-up. Any product specifically formulated for this purpose can be used, but engine oil is not recommended as a prelube.

When semi-permanent (locked, but removable) installation of bolts or nuts is desired, threads should be cleaned and coated with Loctite® or other similar, commercial non-hardening sealant.

FASTENERS

The term fasteners refers to the bolts, nuts, screws, pins, and washers that hold everything together. These components come in all sizes shapes and grades. It is extremely important to have the correct size and grade fastener for the job.

Replacing Fasteners

Whenever you remove a bolt, screw or nut, check its condition. Wipe it off with a shop rag and clean it up with a wire brush or brush wheel. Check the threads for signs of stripping, stretching or breakage. Check the shaft of the bolt or

screw for rust, cracks or pitting. If everything looks okay, the fastener can be used again. If you are at all suspicious of the condition of any part, fasteners included, replace it. When replacing a fastener, always use the exact same size and type.

NEVER use a substitute bolt or screw of a lower grade or unknown grade. Markings on the bolt head will tell you what the grade is. The grading indicates the bolt's strength. See the accompanying chart for a complete explanation of fastener grading.

Often, the length of a particular bolt or screw is critical. Never replace a bolt or screw with one that is longer. A lot of bolts and screw are threaded into blind holes. A bolt that is too long won't secure the part. Worse still, a bolt that is a few threads too long may look or feel tight but actually won't be, resulting in engine trouble later on.

When removing a fastener, consider how long it's been in place. If it's been in there a while it's bound to be rusted and/or seized. Always use a liberal amount of penetrating oil on and around a rusted fastener, or for that matter, all the fasteners from an old engine.

Keep in mind that old, rusted fasteners will probably be hard to remove, even with all your preparation. So, don't get impatient and force something that doesn't want to move. When trying to unscrew a stubborn, old bolt, use the breaker bar and apply gradually increasing force until the bolt or nut begins to move. At this point, apply a little more penetrating oil. The oil can now get under the bolt head and maybe onto the threads. WEAR HEAVY GLOVES for when the bolt or nut breaks free.

➡Before any assembly takes place, always clean up (chase) the threads of any fastener or threaded hole with your tap and die set. This simple procedure makes assembly much easier and reduces the risk of crossthreading, stripping or breakage.

Broken Bolts or Studs

I'm sure this won't happen to you, but if you know anyone who happens to come across a broken bolt or stud or who is unfortunate enough to break one, here's what to do.

There are tools called stud extractors. If, after breakage, the is a piece of the bolt or stud still visible, the stud extractors can grab a hold of it and continue the unscrewing process.

Or, if the shaft of the bolt or stud is thick enough, you can file a notch in the end for a screwdriver.

Or, you may be able to grab the shaft of the bolt or stud with a pair of locking pliers, such as ViseGrips®.

However, if the bolt or stud is broken off flush with the surface of the part, a tool kit called screw extractors or 'Easy-Outs' is available. These tools are coarsely threaded reamers with left-hand threads. To use them, you drill a tap hole down through the shaft of the offending bolt or stud and screw the extractor into it. The extractor tightens in the direction of bolt loosening, turn the bolt out.

If all the above methods don't work, which sometimes happens, your only recourse is to complete drill out the stud or bolt, CAREFULLY! Don't over-drill! Usually when you drill out enough of the bolt or stud the rest will come out easily. What will probably happen as a result of all this drilling is that you'll do some damage to the threads in the hole. If the damage isn't too severe, you can clean up the threads with a tap and die set, using the proper sized tap. If the threads are completely destroyed, go on to the next paragraph.

REPAIRING DAMAGED THREADS

◗ **See Figures 1, 2, 3, 4 and 5**

Several methods of repairing damaged threads are available. Heli-Coil® (shown here), Keenserts® and Microdot® are among the most widely used. All involve basically the same principle — drilling out stripped threads, tapping the hole and installing a prewound insert — making welding, plugging and oversize fasteners unnecessary.

Two types of thread repair inserts are usually supplied: a standard type for most - Inch Coarse, Inch Fine, Metric Course and Metric Fine thread sizes and a spark lug type to fit most spark plug port sizes. Consult the individual manufacturer's catalog to determine exact applications. Typical thread repair kits will contain a selection of prewound threaded inserts, a tap (corresponding to the outside diameter threads of the insert)

Fig. 3 Drill out the damaged threads with specified drill. Drill completely through the hole or to the bottom of a blind hole.

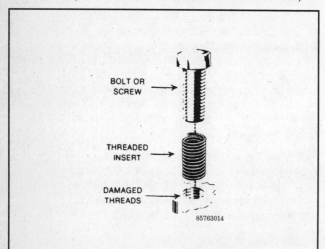

Fig. 1 Damaged bolt holes can be repaired with thread insert kits

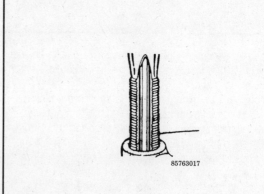

Fig. 4 With the tap supplied, tap the hole to receive the thread insert. Keep the tap well oiled and back it out frequently to avoid clogging the threads.

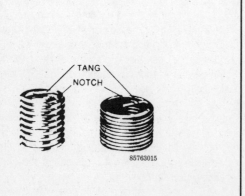

Fig. 2 Standard thread repair insert (left) and spark plug thread insert (right)

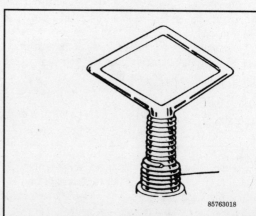

Fig. 5 Screw the threaded insert onto the installation tool until the tang engages the slot. Screw the insert into the tapped hole until it is 1/4-1/2 turn below the top surface. After installation break off the tang with a hammer and punch.

and an installation tool. Spark plug inserts usually differ because they require a tap equipped with pilot threads and a combined reamer/tap section. Most manufacturers also supply blister-packed thread repair inserts separately in addition to a master kit containing a variety of taps and inserts plus installation tools.

Before effecting a repair to a threaded hole, remove any snapped, broken or damaged bolts or studs. Penetrating oil can be used to free frozen threads. The offending item can be removed with locking pliers or with a screw or stud extractor. After the hole is clear, the thread can be repaired, as shown in the series of accompanying illustrations.

Clearing the Way

Before removing the engine, there are a few parts that have to come out. They are:

Carburetor or Throttle Body

The main reason that you'll remove this now is to prevent its being damaged by the lifting chain. To remove the carburetor or throttle body, tag and disconnect the fuel and vacuum lines, and the linkage. Remove the holddown bolts or nuts and lift the unit off. Store it safely on a shelf.

RADIATOR

▶ See Figures 6, 7, 8, 9, 10 and 11

1. Disconnect the negative battery cable and drain the engine cooling system.

✳✳CAUTION

When draining the coolant, keep in mind that cats and dogs are attracted by the ethylene glycol antifreeze, and are quite likely to drink any that is left in an uncovered container or in puddles on the ground. This will prove fatal in sufficient quantity. Always drain the coolant into a sealable container. Coolant should be reused unless it is contaminated or several years old.

2. As necessary, remove the fan, the upper fan shroud and/or the upper support.

➡If the fan is removed on vehicle equipped with a clutch type fan, be sure to keep it in an upright position to prevent the fluid from leaking.

3. Disconnect upper and lower hoses.
4. If equipped with an automatic transmission, disconnect and plug the oil cooler lines. The lines should be plugged to prevent system contamination or excessive fluid loss.
5. Lift radiator straight up and out of the vehicle.

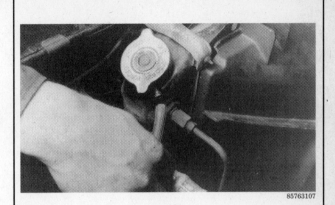

Fig. 6 Removing the overflow hose

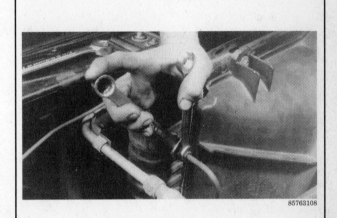

Fig. 7 Loosening the transmission cooler lines

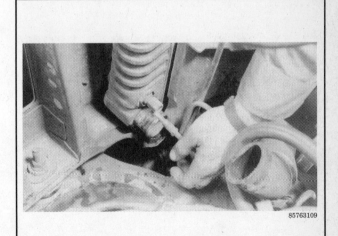

Fig. 8 Disconnecting the transmission cooler lines

Fig. 9 Disconnecting the upper hose from the radiator

Fig. 10 Removing the upper radiator support bolts

Fig. 11 Removing the radiator. It might be a good idea to unbolt the fan shroud from the radiator first

CONDENSER

✳✳CAUTION

Consult your local laws concerning refrigerant discharge and recycling. In many areas it may be illegal for anyone but a certified technician to service the A/C system. Always use an approved recovery station when discharging the air conditioning.

1. Discharge the air conditioning system into a suitable recovery station.
2. Remove the upper radiator shroud.
3. Disconnect the air conditioning lines at the condenser. Plug all openings to prevent system contamination
4. Pull the condenser out from the top.

AIR CONDITIONING COMPRESSOR

1. Remove the drive belt from the compressor.
2. Remove the compressor bracket.
3. Remove the screw attaching the muffler to the compressor support.
4. Remove the hose and muffler assembly from the compressor.
5. Remove the vacuum pump hose from the metal vacuum line.
6. Remove the four nuts and one bolt and spacer from the compressor support.
7. Remove the compressor support by pulling forward.
8. Pull the compressor forward to remove it.

STARTER

Before removing the engine, you'll have to remove the starter. Starter removal on some models may necessitate the removal of the front support which runs from the corner of the frame to the front crossmember. If so, loosen the mounting bolt which attaches the support the frame first, then remove the crossmember bolt and swing the support out of the way.

➡The starters on some engines require the addition of shims to provide proper clearance between the starter pinion gear and the flywheel. These shims are available in 0.015 in. sizes from Chevrolet dealers. Flat washers can be used if shims are unavailable.

1. Disconnect the negative battery cable.
2. Raise and support the vehicle safely using jackstands.

➡If access to the wiring is difficult, the starter may be partially lowered before disconnecting it, but be careful not to stretch or damage the wiring.

3. Disconnect all wiring from the starter solenoid. Replace each nut as the connector is removed, as thread sizes differ from connector to connector. Note or tag the wiring positions for installation purposes.

4. If equipped, remove the front bracket from the starter. On engines with a solenoid heat shield, remove the front bracket upper bolt and detach the bracket from the starter.

5. Remove the starter mounting bolts. If a starter shim tab can be seen protruding out from between the mating surfaces of the starter and the block, remove the outer bolt first, then loosen the inner bolt. With the outer bolt removed and the inner loosened, most shims may be grasped and pulled from the top of the starter at this point. Once the bolts are removed, lower the starter front end first, and remove the unit from the car.

➡If no shim tab could be seen, yet shims or flat washers fall from the starter as it is withdrawn, stop and attempt to determine their locations. If possible, gather the shims for reuse during assembly. Shims without tabs must be positioned on the starter prior to installation, but the bolts may be held through the starter assembly in order to hold the shims in position.

Engine Removal

▶ See Figures 12 and 13

➡Obviously, this section applies only if you are removing an engine for rebuild. If you have purchased an old engine, short block, bare block or whatever, skip it.

We've included engine removal instructions for some of the most popular Ford cars and trucks. If your particular vehicle isn't mentioned here, check the local book stores for a Chilton book that would cover whatever vehicle you have.

Removing an engine from a vehicle could be the hardest part of the whole job. The first thing you should do is remove the hood.

For this job, you'll need a helper. Hoods are heavy and awkward.

The first step in removing the hood it to outline the position of the hinges on the hood with an indelible marker. If you don't do this, you'll have a hard time getting the hood to close properly when you install it. So:

1. Outline the hood positions and slowly start removing the hood-to-hinge retaining bolts. At this point, your helper should be supporting the hood.

2. Remove the bolts evenly, side-to-side, leaving one bolt loosely in place.

3. Now, position yourself at the last bolt, with your helper on the other side. Remove the bolt and lift off the hood.

The best way to store the hood is standing up on its back end. Place wood blocks on the floor and place the hood on the blocks. This will protect the paint and keep the metal out of the wet.

✳✳WARNING

Disconnect the negative battery cable(s) before beginning any work. Always label all disconnected hoses, vacuum lines and wires, to prevent incorrect reassembly.

➡You should be able to remove just about any engine without disconnecting the refrigerant lines. In any event, don't disconnect any air conditioning lines; escaping refrigerant will freeze any surface it contacts, including skin and eyes and is an environmental hazard. If you have to disconnect the refrigerant lines, have the system discharged professionally by someone with a recovery system.

Okay, you have the hood off and safely out of the way, so let's go.

Full-Sized Trucks, through 1987

The factory recommended procedure for engine removal is to remove the engine/transmission as a unit on two wheel drive models. Only the engine should be removed on four wheel drive models.

1. Disconnect the negative battery terminal.
2. Drain the cooling system.

✳✳CAUTION

When draining the coolant, keep in mind that cats and dogs are attracted by the ethylene glycol antifreeze, and are quite likely to drink any that is left in an uncovered container or in puddles on the ground. This will prove fatal in sufficient quantity. Always drain the coolant into a sealable container. Coolant should be reused unless it is contaminated or several years old.

3. Drain the engine oil.
4. Remove the air cleaner and ducts.
5. Scribe alignment marks around the hood hinges, and remove the hood.
6. Remove the radiator and hoses, and the fan shroud if so equipped.
7. Disconnect and label the wires at:
 a. Starter solenoid.
 b. Alternator.
 c. Temperature switch.
 d. Oil pressure switch.
 e. Transmission controlled spark solenoid.
 f. CEC solenoid.
 g. Coil.
 h. Neutral safety switch.
8. Disconnect:
 a. Accelerator linkage. Position away from the engine.
 b. Choke cable at carburetor, if so equipped.
 c. Release the fuel system pressure and disconnect the fuel line to fuel pump.
 d. Heater hoses at engine.
 e. Air conditioning compressor with hoses attached. Do not remove the hoses from the air conditioning compressor. Remove it as a unit and set it aside. Its contents are under pressure, and can freeze body tissue on contact.

➡R-12 refrigerant is a chlorofluorocarbon which, when released into the atmosphere, can contribute to the depletion of the ozone layer in the upper atmosphere. Ozone filters out harmful radiation from the sun. If possible, an approved R-12 Recovery/Recycling machine that meets SAE standards should be employed when discharging the system. Follow the operating instructions provided with the equipment exactly to properly discharge the system.

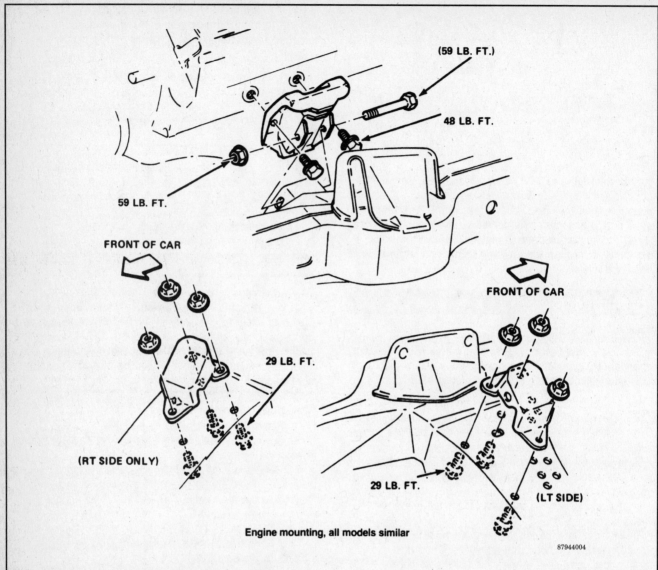

Engine mounting, all models similar

87944004

Fig. 12 Engine front mounts. All models are similar

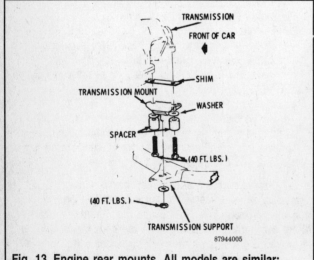

87944005

Fig. 13 Engine rear mounts. All models are similar; some are shimmed

f. Transmission dipstick and tube on automatic transmission models. Plug the tube hole.

g. Oil dipstick and tube. Plug the hole.

h. Vacuum lines.

i. Oil pressure line to gauge, if so equipped.

j. Parking brake cable.

k. Power steering pump. This can be removed as a unit and set aside, without removing any of the hoses.

l. Engine ground straps.

m. Exhaust pipe (support if necessary).

9. Loosen and remove the fan belt, remove the fan blades and pulley. If you have the finned aluminum viscous drive fan clutch, keep it upright in its normal position. If the fluid leaks out, the unit will have to be replaced.

10. Remove the clutch cross-shaft.

11. Attach a lifting device to the engine. You may have to remove the carburetor. Take the engine weight off the engine mounts, and unbolt the mounts. On all models except the gas engine ½ and ¾ ton, support and disconnect the transmission. With automatic transmission, remove the torque converter underpan and starter, unbolt the converter from the flywheel,

detach the throttle linkage and vacuum modulator line, and unbolt the engine from the transmission. Be certain that the converter does not fall out. With manual transmission, unbolt the clutch housing from the engine.

12. On two wheel drive models, remove the driveshaft. Either drain the transmission or plug the driveshaft opening. Disconnect the speedometer cable at the transmission. Disconnect the TCS switch wire, if so equipped. Disconnect the shift linkage or lever, or the clutch linkage. Disconnect the transmission cooler lines, if so equipped. If you have an automatic or a four speed transmission, the rear crossmember must be removed. With the three speed, unbolt the transmission from the crossmember. Raise the engine/transmission assembly and pull it forward.

13. On four wheel drive, raise and pull the engine forward until it is free of the transmission.

14. On all trucks, lift the engine out slowly, making certain as you go that all lines between the engine and the truck have been disconnected.

1988-94 Full-Sized Trucks

5.0L, 5.7L

1. Disconnect the negative battery cable.
2. Remove the hood.
3. Drain the cooling system.

✻✻CAUTION

When draining the coolant, keep in mind that cats and dogs are attracted by the ethylene glycol antifreeze, and are quite likely to drink any that is left in an uncovered container or in puddles on the ground. This will prove fatal in sufficient quantity. Always drain the coolant into a sealable container. Coolant should be reused unless it is contaminated or several years old.

4. Remove the air cleaner.
5. Remove the accessory drive belt, fan and water pump pulley.
6. Remove the radiator and shroud.
7. Disconnect the heater hoses at the engine.
8. Disconnect the accelerator, cruise control and detent linkage if used.
9. Disconnect the air conditioning compressor, if used, and lay aside.
10. Remove the power steering pump, if used, and lay aside.
11. Disconnect the engine wiring from the engine.
12. Disconnect the fuel line.
13. Disconnect the vacuum lines from the intake manifold.
14. Raise the vehicle and support it safely.
15. Drain the engine oil.
16. Disconnect the exhaust pipes from the manifold.
17. Disconnect the strut rods at the engine mountings, if used.

18. Remove the flywheel or torque converter cover.
19. Disconnect the wiring along the oil pan rail.
20. Remove the starter.
21. Disconnect the wire for the fuel gauge.
22. On vehicles equipped with automatic transmission, remove the converter to flex plate bolts.
23. Lower the vehicle and suitably support the transmission. Attach a suitable lifting fixture to the engine.
24. Remove the bell housing to engine bolts.
25. Remove the rear engine mounting to frame bolts and the front through bolts and remove the engine.

7.4L

1. Remove the hood.
2. Disconnect the negative battery cable.
3. Drain the cooling system.

✻✻CAUTION

When draining the coolant, keep in mind that cats and dogs are attracted by the ethylene glycol antifreeze, and are quite likely to drink any that is left in an uncovered container or in puddles on the ground. This will prove fatal in sufficient quantity. Always drain the coolant into a sealable container. Coolant should be reused unless it is contaminated or several years old.

4. Remove the air cleaner.
5. Remove the radiator and fan shroud.
6. Disconnect and tag all necessary engine wiring.
7. Disconnect the accelerator, cruise control and TVS linkage.
8. Disconnect the fuel supply lines.
9. Disconnect all necessary vacuum wires.
10. Disconnect the air conditioning compressor, if used, and lay aside.
11. Dismount the power steering pump and position it out of the way. It's not necessary to disconnect the fluid lines.
12. Raise the vehicle and support it on jackstands.
13. Disconnect the exhaust pipes from the manifold.
14. Remove the starter.
15. Remove the torque converter cover.
16. Remove the converter-to-flex plate bolts.
17. Lower the vehicle and suitably support the transmission. Attach a suitable lifting fixture to the engine.
18. Remove the bellhousing-to-engine bolts.
19. Remove the rear engine mounting-to-frame bolts and the front through bolts and remove the engine.

Full-Sized Vans

5.0L, 5.7L

1. Disconnect the negative battery cable, then the positive battery cable, at the battery.

2. Drain the cooling system.

❋❋CAUTION

When draining the coolant, keep in mind that cats and dogs are attracted by the ethylene glycol antifreeze, and are quite likely to drink any that is left in an uncovered container or in puddles on the ground. This will prove fatal in sufficient quantity. Always drain the coolant into a sealable container. Coolant should be reused unless it is contaminated or several years old.

3. Remove the radiator coolant reservoir bottle.
4. Remove the upper radiator support.
5. Remove the grille and the lower grille valance.

❋❋CAUTION

Discharging the air conditioning refrigerant should only be attempted by those who have the proper tools and training to do so, as serious personal injury may result. The refrigerant will instantly freeze any surface it comes in contact with, including your eyes.

6. Discharge the air conditioning system and remove the air conditioning vacuum reservoir.
7. Remove the air conditioning condenser from in front of the radiator.
8. If the van is equipped with an automatic transmission, remove the fluid cooler lines from the radiator.
9. Disconnect the radiator hoses at the radiator.
10. Remove the radiator support bracket and remove the radiator and the shroud.
11. Remove the engine cover.
12. Remove the air cleaner.
13. Disconnect the accelerator linkage.
14. Disconnect all hoses and wires at the carburetor or TBI unit.
15. Remove the carburetor or TBI unit.
16. Disconnect the engine wiring harness from the firewall connection.
17. Tag and disconnect all vacuum lines.
18. Remove the power steering pump. It's not necessary to disconnect the hoses; just lay it aside.
19. Disconnect the heater hoses at the engine.
20. Remove the thermostat housing.
21. Remove the oil filler tube.
22. Raise and support the van on jackstands.
23. Remove the cruise control servo, servo bracket and transducer.
24. Drain the engine oil.
25. Disconnect the exhaust pipes at the manifolds.
26. Remove the driveshaft and plug the end of the transmission.
27. Disconnect the transmission shift linkage and the speedometer cable.
28. Remove the fuel line from the fuel tank and at the fuel pump.
29. Remove the transmission mounting bolts.
30. Lower the van, support the transmission and engine.
31. Remove the engine mount bracket-to-frame bolts.
32. Remove the engine mount through bolts.

33. Raise the engine slightly and remove the engine mounts. Support the engine with wood between the oil pan and the crossmember.
34. Remove the manual transmission and clutch as follows:
   a. Remove the clutch housing rear bolts.
   b. Remove the bolts attaching the clutch housing to the engine and remove the transmission and clutch as a unit.

➡Support the transmission as the last bolt is being removed to prevent damaging the clutch.

   c. Remove the starter and clutch housing rear cover.
   d. Loosen the clutch mounting bolts a little at a time to prevent distorting the disc until spring pressure is released. Remove all of the bolts, the clutch disc and the pressure plate.
35. Remove the automatic transmission as follows:
   a. Lower the engine and support it on blocks.
   b. Remove the starter and converter housing underpan.
   c. Remove the flywheel-to-converter attaching bolts.
   d. Support the transmission on blocks.
   e. Disconnect the detent cable on the Turbo Hydra-Matic.
   f. Remove the transmission-to-engine mounting bolts.
   g. Remove the blocks from the engine only and glide the engine away from the transmission.

7.4L

1. Disconnect the battery cables.
2. Drain the cooling system.

❋❋CAUTION

When draining the coolant, keep in mind that cats and dogs are attracted by the ethylene glycol antifreeze, and are quite likely to drink any that is left in an uncovered container or in puddles on the ground. This will prove fatal in sufficient quantity. Always drain the coolant into a sealable container. Coolant should be reused unless it is contaminated or several years old.

3. Remove the engine cover.
4. Remove the air cleaner.
5. Remove the cruise control servo, servo bracket and transducer.
6. Remove the grille and the lower grille valance.
7. Remove the upper radiator support.

❋❋CAUTION

Discharging the air conditioning refrigerant should only be attempted by those who have the proper tools and training to do so, as serious personal injury may result. The refrigerant will instantly freeze any surface it comes in contact with, including your eyes.

8. Discharge the air conditioning system and remove the air conditioning vacuum reservoir.
9. Remove the air conditioning condenser from in front of the radiator. Cap all openings at once!
10. Disconnect the radiator hoses at the radiator.
11. Remove the fluid cooler lines from the radiator.
12. Remove the radiator coolant reservoir bottle.

13. Remove the radiator support bracket and remove the radiator and the shroud.

14. Remove the power steering pump.

15. Remove the air conditioning compressor. Cap all openings at once!

16. Disconnect the wiring fuel lines and linkage at the TBI unit.

17. Remove the TBI unit.

18. Disconnect the engine wiring harness from the firewall connection.

19. Disconnect the starter wires.

20. Disconnect the alternator wires.

21. Disconnect the temperature sensor wire.

22. Disconnect the oil pressure sender.

23. Disconnect the distributor and coil wiring.

24. Disconnect and plug the fuel supply and vapor lines.

25. Tag and disconnect all vacuum hoses.

26. Disconnect the heater hoses at the engine.

27. Remove the thermostat housing.

28. Remove the windshield wiper jar and bracket.

29. Remove the oil filler pipe and the engine dipstick tube.

30. Raise and support the van on jackstands.

31. Disconnect the exhaust pipes at the manifolds.

32. Remove the driveshaft and plug the end of the transmission.

33. Disconnect the transmission shift linkage and the speedometer cable.

34. Drain the engine oil.

35. Support the engine with a floor jack. DO NOT position the jack under the oil pan, crankshaft pulley or any sheet metal!

36. Attach an engine crane to the engine and take up its weight.

37. Remove the transmission mounting bolts.

38. Raise the engine slightly and remove the engine mounts. Support the engine with wood between the oil pan and the crossmember.

39. Lower the van.

40. Raise the engine as necessary and maneuver the engine/transmission assembly from the van.

41. Separate the engine and transmission as follows:
    a. Support the engine on blocks.
    b. Remove the starter and converter housing underpan.
    c. Remove the flywheel-to-converter attaching bolts.
    d. Support the transmission on blocks.
    e. Disconnect the detent cable.
    f. Remove the transmission-to-engine mounting bolts.
    g. Remove the blocks from the engine only and guide the engine away from the transmission.

42. Mount the engine on a work stand.

Camaro through 1992

1. Disconnect the negative battery cable.

2. Mark the location of the hood on the hood hinges and remove the hood.

3. Remove the air cleaner.

4. Drain the cooling system.

5. Remove the radiator hoses.

6. Disconnect the transmission cooler lines, the electrical connectors and retaining clips at the fan and remove the fan and shroud.

7. Remove the radiator.

8. Remove the accessory drive belt.

9. Disconnect the throttle cable.

10. Remove the plenum extension screws and the plenum extension, if equipped.

11. Disconnect the spark plug wires at the distributor and remove the distributor.

12. Disconnect the necessary vacuum hoses and wiring.

13. Disconnect the power steering and air conditioning compressors from their respective brackets and lay them aside.

14. Properly relieve the fuel system pressure. Disconnect the fuel lines.

15. Disconnect the negative battery cable at the engine block.

16. Raise and safely support the vehicle.

17. Remove the exhaust pipes at the exhaust manifolds.

18. Remove the flywheel cover and remove the converter to flywheel bolts.

19. Disconnect the starter wires.

20. Remove the bellhousing bolts and the motor mount through bolts.

21. Lower the vehicle.

22. Support the transmission with a suitable jack.

23. Remove the AIR/converter bracket and ground wires from the rear of the cylinder head.

24. Attach a suitable lifting device and remove the engine assembly.

1993-96 Camaro

1. Disconnect the negative battery cable.

2. Mark the location of the hood on the hood hinges and remove the hood.

3. Remove the air cleaner.

4. Drain the cooling system.

5. Remove the radiator hoses.

6. Disconnect the transmission cooler lines, the electrical connectors and retaining clips at the fan and remove the fan and shroud.

7. Remove the radiator.

8. Remove the accessory drive belt.

9. Disconnect the throttle cable.

10. Remove the plenum extension screws and the plenum extension, if equipped.

11. Disconnect the spark plug wires at the distributor and remove the distributor.

12. Disconnect the necessary vacuum hoses and wiring.

13. Disconnect the power steering and air conditioning compressors from their respective brackets and lay them aside.

14. Properly relieve the fuel system pressure. Disconnect the fuel lines.

15. Disconnect the negative battery cable at the engine block.

16. Raise and safely support the vehicle.

17. Remove the exhaust pipes at the exhaust manifolds.

18. Remove the flywheel cover and remove the converter to flywheel bolts.

19. Disconnect the starter wires.

20. Remove the bellhousing bolts and the motor mount through bolts.
21. Lower the vehicle.
22. Support the transmission with a suitable jack.
23. Remove the AIR/converter bracket and ground wires from the rear of the cylinder head.
24. Attach a suitable lifting device and remove the engine assembly.

1964-88 Mid-Sized Cars

1. Scribe alignment marks on hood and remove hood from hinges.
2. Disconnect the negative battery cable.
3. Drain cooling system, then remove the heater hoses and the radiator hoses from the engine.

✳✳CAUTION

When draining the coolant, keep in mind that cats and dogs are attracted by the ethylene glycol antifreeze, and are quite likely to drink any that is left in an uncovered container or in puddles on the ground. This will prove fatal in sufficient quantity. Always drain the coolant into a sealable container. Coolant should be reused unless it is contaminated or several years old.

4. Remove the upper fan shroud and the fan assembly.
5. If equipped with air conditioning and power steering, remove the compressor and the power steering pump from the engine, then position them aside.
6. Disconnect the accelerator and the T.V. cables.
7. Remove the transmission oil cooler lines (if equipped) from the radiator and remove the radiator.
8. Disconnect and label the vacuum hoses and the CCC wiring harness connector(s) from the engine.
9. If equipped, remove the AIR pipe from the converter.
10. Remove the windshield washer bottle.
11. Disconnect and mark the wiring harness and related engine wiring.
12. Remove the distributor cap and the cruise control cable (if equipped).
13. Disconnect the positive battery cable from the battery and, if equipped, the frame straps. Disconnect the negative battery cable from the air conditioning hose/alternator bracket.
14. Raise and support the vehicle on jackstands.
15. Remove the crossover pipe and the catalytic converter as an assembly.
16. If equipped with an automatic transmission, remove the torque converter cover and the torque converter bolts.

➡**Before removing the torque converter bolts, scribe a mark to ensure the relationship between the torque converter and the flex plate.**

17. Remove the engine-to-mount bolts.
18. Disconnect the fuel line from the fuel pump.
19. If equipped with an automatic transmission, disconnect the torque converter clutch wiring from the transmission. Disconnect the transmission oil cooler lines from the clip at the engine oil pan.

20. Remove the engine-to-transmission bolts.
21. Lower the vehicle and support the transmission.
22. Secure a vertical lifting device to the engine and remove the engine from the vehicle. Pause several times while lifting the engine to make sure no components, wires or hoses are caught.

✳✳CAUTION

When removing the engine from the transmission, be careful that the torque converter does not pull out of the transmission.

Full-Sized Cars through 1989

1. Scribe alignment marks on hood and remove hood from hinges.
2. Disconnect the negative battery cable.
3. Drain cooling system, then remove the heater hoses and the radiator hoses from the engine.

✳✳CAUTION

When draining the coolant, keep in mind that cats and dogs are attracted by the ethylene glycol antifreeze, and are quite likely to drink any that is left in an uncovered container or in puddles on the ground. This will prove fatal in sufficient quantity. Always drain the coolant into a sealable container. Coolant should be reused unless it is contaminated or several years old.

4. Remove the upper fan shroud and the fan assembly.
5. If equipped with air conditioning and power steering, remove the compressor and the power steering pump from the engine, then position them aside.
6. Disconnect the accelerator and the T.V. cables.
7. Remove the transmission oil cooler lines from the radiator and remove the radiator.
8. Disconnect and label the vacuum hoses and the ECM wiring harness connector(s) from the engine.
9. If equipped, remove the AIR pipe from the converter.
10. If necessary, remove the windshield washer bottle.
11. Tag and disconnect the wiring harness and related engine wiring.
12. Remove the distributor cap and the cruise control cable (if equipped).
13. Disconnect the positive battery cable from the battery and, if equipped, the frame straps. Disconnect the negative battery cable from the air conditioning hose/alternator bracket.
14. Raise and support the vehicle on jackstands.
15. Disconnect the crossover pipe and the catalytic converter as an assembly.

➡**Before removing the torque converter bolts, scribe a mark to ensure the relationship between the torque converter and the flex plate.**

16. Remove the torque converter cover and the torque converter bolts.
17. Remove the engine-to-mount bolts.
18. Disconnect and plug the fuel line from the fuel pump.

19. Disconnect the torque converter clutch wiring from the transmission, then disconnect the transmission oil cooler lines from the clip at the engine oil pan.

20. Remove the engine-to-transmission bolts.

21. Lower the vehicle and support the transmission.

22. Secure a vertical lifting device to the engine and remove the engine from the vehicle. Pause several times while lifting the engine to make sure no components, wires or hoses are caught.

✳✳CAUTION

When removing the engine from the transmission, be careful that the torque converter does not pull out of the transmission.

1990-93 Caprice

5.0L (VIN Y)

1. Disconnect the negative battery cable.
2. Remove the hood from hinges and mark for reassembly.
3. Drain coolant into a suitable container.
4. Remove the air cleaner assembly and hot air pipe.
5. Remove the radiator hoses and upper fan shroud.
6. Remove the radiator.
7. Remove the engine cooling fan.
8. Disconnect the heater hoses at the engine.
9. Disconnect the power steering pump, air conditioning compressor and brackets, and position out of the way leaving the hoses attached.
10. Disconnect the accelerator, TV, and cruise control cables.
11. Disconnect all necessary vacuum hoses and the fuel hose from the fuel line.
12. Disconnect the ECM wiring harness, the engine wiring harness at the engine bulkhead, engine to bulkhead ground straps and all other wires between body and engine.
13. Set the engine on TDC and remove the distributor.
14. Remove the battery ground-to-cylinder head cable.
15. Raise and support the vehicle safely.
16. Disconnect the battery positive cable and wires at the starter motor.
17. Disconnect the crossover pipe at the manifolds.
18. Remove the flywheel cover and mark the relationship of the torque converter to the flywheel, remove the torque converter bolts.
19. Remove the engine mount through-bolts.
20. Disconnect the front fuel hoses from the front fuel pipes.
21. Disconnect the transmission converter clutch wiring at the transmission and the transmission oil cooler lines at the clip on the oil pan.
22. Disconnect the catalytic converter AIR pipe at the exhaust manifold.
23. Remove the transmission to engine bolts.
24. Lower the vehicle.
25. Support the transmission and connect a suitable lifting device to the engine.
26. Remove the engine.

5.0L (VIN E) and 5.7L

1. Relieve the fuel system pressure and disconnect the negative battery cable.
2. Remove the hood from hinges and mark for reassembly.
3. Drain coolant into a suitable container.
4. Remove the air cleaner assembly.
5. Remove the radiator hoses and upper fan shroud.
6. Remove the radiator.
7. Remove the engine cooling fan.
8. Disconnect the heater hoses at the engine
9. Disconnect the power steering pump and air conditioning compressor brackets, if equipped, and position out of the way.
10. Disconnect the accelerator, TV, and cruise control cables.
11. Disconnect all necessary vacuum hoses.
12. Disconnect the ECM wiring harness, the engine wiring harness at the engine bulkhead, engine to bulkhead ground straps and all other wires between body and engine.
13. Set the engine on TDC and remove the distributor.
14. Remove the wiper motor, MAP sensor and battery negative to cylinder head cable.
15. Raise and support the vehicle safely.
16. Disconnect the battery positive cable and wires at the starter motor.
17. Disconnect the crossover pipe and catalytic converter as an assembly.
18. Remove the flywheel cover and torque converter to flywheel bolts.
19. Remove the engine mount through-bolts.
20. Disconnect the front fuel hoses from the front fuel pipes.
21. Disconnect the transmission converter clutch wiring at the transmission and the transmission oil cooler lines at the clip on the oil pan.
22. Disconnect the catalytic converter AIR pipe at the exhaust manifold.
23. Remove the transmission to engine bolts.
24. Lower the vehicle.
25. Support the transmission and connect a suitable lifting device to the engine.
26. Remove the engine.

Flywheel/Flex Plate and Ring Gear

You'll have to remove the flywheel before mounting the engine on the stand.

➡️**Flex plate is the term for a flywheel mated with an automatic transmission.**

➡️**The ring gear is replaceable only on engines mated with a manual transmission. Engines with automatic transmissions have ring gears which are welded to the flex plate.**

1. Remove the clutch, if equipped, or torque converter from the flywheel. The flywheel bolts should be loosened a little at a time in a cross pattern to avoid warping the flywheel. On cars with manual transmissions, replace the pilot bearing in the end of the crankshaft.

➡️**You're going to have to hold the crankshaft to keep it from turning. This is best done with a breaker bar and socket on the damper nut.**

2. The flywheel should be checked for cracks and glazing. It can be resurfaced by a machine shop.

The Engine Dolly

1. Roll the crane backwards, CAREFULLY, until the engine is clear of the vehicle.
2. Place the engine dolly under the engine.
3. Carefully lower the engine onto the engine dolly. Make sure that the engine is squarely set on the dolly before removing the crane. Wrap a safety chain around the engine and dolly to avoid an accident.
4. Roll the engine into your garage.
5. Remove the mounting head from the engine stand and bolt it to the back of the engine, aligning the mounting arms with the appropriate bellhousing mating holes.
6. Bring the crane inside and lift the engine off the dolly. Position the engine stand behind the engine, align the tube of the mounting head with the stand upright and slide it into the upright. Tighten the set bolt. Remove the crane.
7. Now you can relax! Take a break! Be proud of yourself!

Cleaning The Engine

Break's over. Whether the engine came from your vehicle or a junkyard, it is pretty dirty. You can't work on a dirty engine. It's not safe, either for you or the parts. There are several ways to clean an engine, but none of them are particularly pleasant.

You don't have to get the engine completely spotless, but you really should remove all heavy surface dirt, grease and oil. This can be done with any number of safe, non-flammable solvents available at any good auto parts store. You can begin by placing a large dropcloth on the floor under the engine. Then, scrape off the heaviest stuff with a putty knife and wire brush. You'll be surprised at how much you can remove this way.

Once that's done, apply the solvent to specific areas, working from the top down and, with plenty of shop rags, remove as much as you can.

When you're satisfied, dispose of the dropcloth and dirt. Look the engine over at this point for any signs of damage, obvious leaks, etc. Also, just stand back and get familiar with what the engine looks like. The more familiar you are with the general layout, the easier your job will be.

Next, wire-brush all exposed nuts and bolts. Then, take a penetrating solvent, such as Liquid Wrench® or WD-40® and soak all exposed nuts and bolts. Wipe up the mess.

You can now begin disassembly.

Budgeting Your Time

If, as mentioned before, you're working under a deadline, such as getting your car back on the road as soon as possible, you'll be tempted to rush the job. DON'T! If at all possible, take your time. Hurrying leads to mistakes. Mistakes can cause injury, damage and money, and usually, more time. Don't work until you're over-tired. Tired workers make mistakes.

If the job is a hobby or long term project.....no problem. Take your time, take attention to detail and you'll do a great job!

Before Disassembly

By this time, you should have adequate shelf space, at least one work bench, all your tools in order and plenty of places or containers for removed parts, pieces, fasteners, etc.

Before you begin the actual operation, step back, take a deep breath and organize your thoughts. Okay, get your indelible marker ready and begin.

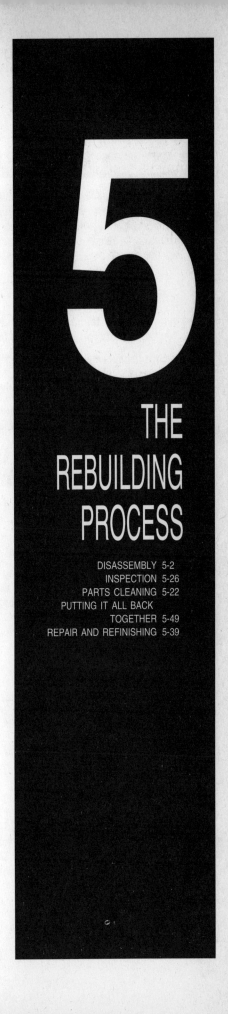

5

THE REBUILDING PROCESS

DISASSEMBLY

▶ **See Figures 1, 2, 3, 4, 5 and 6**

Exhaust Manifold

1. If equipped with AIR (Air Injection Reaction), remove the air injector manifold assembly. The ¼ in. pipe threads in the manifold are straight threads. Do not use a ¼ in. tapered pipe tap to clean the threads.

2. Remove the spark plug wire heat shields. On Mark IV, remove spark plugs.

➡ **The fasteners on the exhaust system are often rusted into place. If you haven't already done it, in order to save your knuckles, spray the fasteners with a penetrating lubricant a few minutes before you attempt to remove them.**

3. Using a hammer and chisel, bend the locktabs and remove the end bolts, then the center bolts. With the retainers removed, carefully pull the manifold from the cylinder head.

➡ **When installing a new manifold on the right side, you must transfer the heat stove from the old manifold to the new one.**

Distributor

Point-Type Ignition

1. Remove the distributor cap.
2. Scribe a mark on the distributor body and the engine block showing their relationship. Mark the distributor housing to show the direction in which the rotor is pointing. Note the positioning of the vacuum advance unit.
3. Remove the hold-down bolt and clamp and remove the distributor.

HEI Distributor

1. Depress and release the 4 distributor cap-to-housing retainers and lift off the cap assembly.
2. Scribe a mark on the distributor body and the engine block showing their relationship. Mark the distributor housing to show the direction in which the rotor is pointing or otherwise matchmark the rotor with the housing.
3. Loosen and remove the distributor hold-down bolt and clamp, then carefully lift the distributor out of the engine. Note the position of the rotor alignment mark on the housing and make a second mark on the housing to align with the rotor. It's a good idea to reinstall the distributor cap in order to protect the internal components from damage.

Alternator

1. Loosen the alternator lower though-bolt, then remove the alternator brace/adjuster bolt.
2. On some vehicles equipped with power steering, it may be necessary to loosen the pump brace and mount nuts, then detach the pump drive belt.
3. Pivot the alternator inward and remove the drive belt from the pulley.
4. Support the alternator and remove the lower mount bolt(s), then remove the unit from the engine.

Sending Units

Coolant Temperature

On most vehicles the coolant temperature sensor is located in the left cylinder head between spark plugs. The coolant sensor may also be found on the opposite cylinder head or even in the intake manifold. For most fuel injected vehicles the coolant sensor is threaded into the front of the intake manifold.

Using a deep 12-point socket, loosen the sensor, then carefully unthread and remove it from the engine.

Oil Pressure

The oil pressure switch is usually threaded into the rear of the intake manifold, just in front of the distributor. If the switch is not there, possible alternate locations include the block, above the starter or the oil filter adapter.

Disengage the sensor electrical connector. Using a deep 12-point socket, loosen the sensor, then carefully unthread and remove it from the engine.

Rocker Arm (Valve) Covers

1. On the right side, if it has one, remove the EGR valve.
2. On the left side, remove the PCV valve from the cover.
3. Remove the rocker arm cover bolts, then remove the rocker cover from the engine. If the cover won't break loose easily, try rapping it sharply with a rubber mallet. If that doesn't work, you're going to have to pry it off, which means that you'll end up bending the flanges. Be sure to straighten them.
4. Using a putty knife or gasket scraper, clean the gasket mounting surfaces.

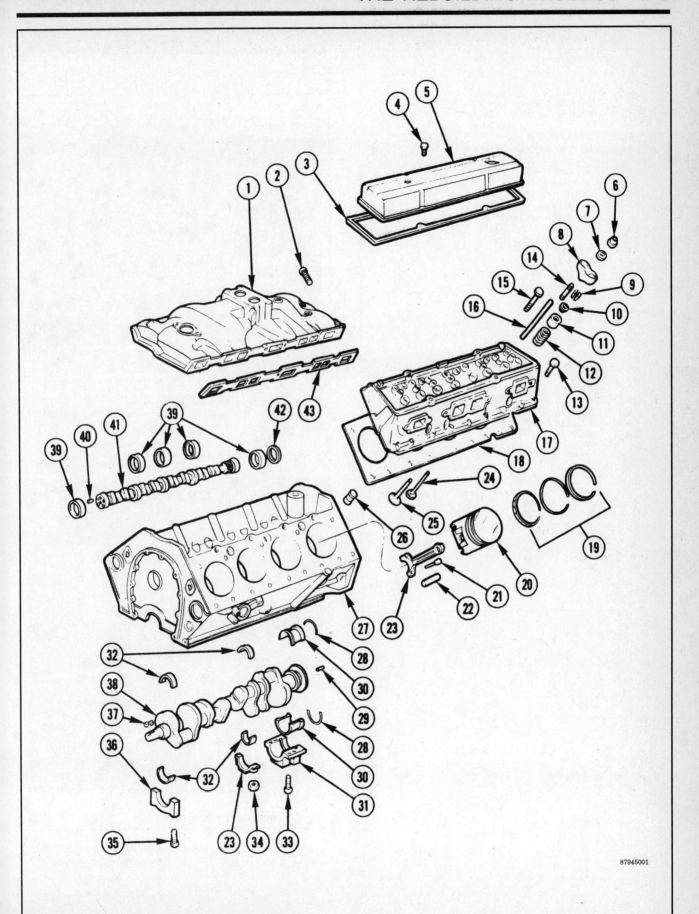

Fig. 1 Small block V8 engine exploded view, part 1

87945001

1. **MANIFOLD ASM,** Intake
2. **BOLT,** Hex (3/8x16x2)
3. **GASKET,** Valve Rocker Arm Cover
4. **BOLT,** Hex (1/4x20x9/16)
5. **COVER,** Valve Rocker Arm
6. **NUT,** Valve Push Rod Adj
7. **BALL,** Valve Rocker Arm
8. **ARM,** Valve Rocker
9. **KEY,** Valve Spring Cap
10. **CAP,** Valve Spring
11. **SHIELD,** Valve Spring Oil
12. **SPRING,** Valve
13. **BOLT,** Hex (7/16x14x1 5/8)
14. **STUD,** Valve Push Rod Adj
15. **BOLT,** Hex (7/16x14x3 11/16)
16. **ROD,** Valve Push
17. **HEAD ASM,** Cylinder
18. **GASKET,** Cylinder Head
19. **RING KIT,** Piston
20. **PISTON ASM,** Engine (Incl #22)
21. **BOLT,** Connecting Rod
22. **PIN,** Piston
23. **ROD ASM,** Eng Connecting
24. **VALVE,** Exhaust
25. **VALVE,** Intake
26. **LIFTER ASM,** Valve
27. **BLOCK,** Eng
28. **SEAL,** Crankshaft Rear Main Brg Oil
29. **PIN,** Eng Flywheel
30. **BEARING KIT,** Crankshaft Rear
31. **CAP,** Crankshaft Rear Main Brg
32. **BEARING KIT,** Crankshaft
33. **BOLT,** Crankshaft Main Bearing Cap
34. **NUT,** Hex (3/8x24)
35. **BOLT,** Hex (7/16x14x3 3/4)
36. **CAP,** Crankshaft Frt Brg
37. **KEY,** Crankshaft Gear (3/16x3/4)
38. **CRANKSHAFT,** Engine
39. **BEARING,** Camshaft
40. **PIN,** Camshaft
41. **CAMSHAFT,** Engine
42. **PLUG,** Camshaft Hole (Exp Cup 2.107 OD)
43. **GASKET,** Intake Manifold

87945002

Fig. 2 Parts list for small block V8 engine exploded view, part 1

Intake Manifold

▶ See Figure 7

Fig. 7 Removing the intake manifold

If you have done so already, disconnect the water pump bypass at the water pump (Mark IV only). Remove the manifold-to-head attaching bolts, then remove the manifold.

Using a putty knife, clean the gasket and seal surfaces of the cylinder heads and manifold.

Rocker Arms and Pushrods

▶ See Figure 8

Fig. 8 Removing the pushrods

Loosen and remove the adjusting nuts and the rocker arm pivots. The rocker arms are then free to be removed from the cylinder head studs. Remove the rockers one at a time, wipe them off with a shop rag and place them on a clean piece of waxed paper. Mark the waxed paper with the number of each rocker, using a magic marker. When they are all off, clean

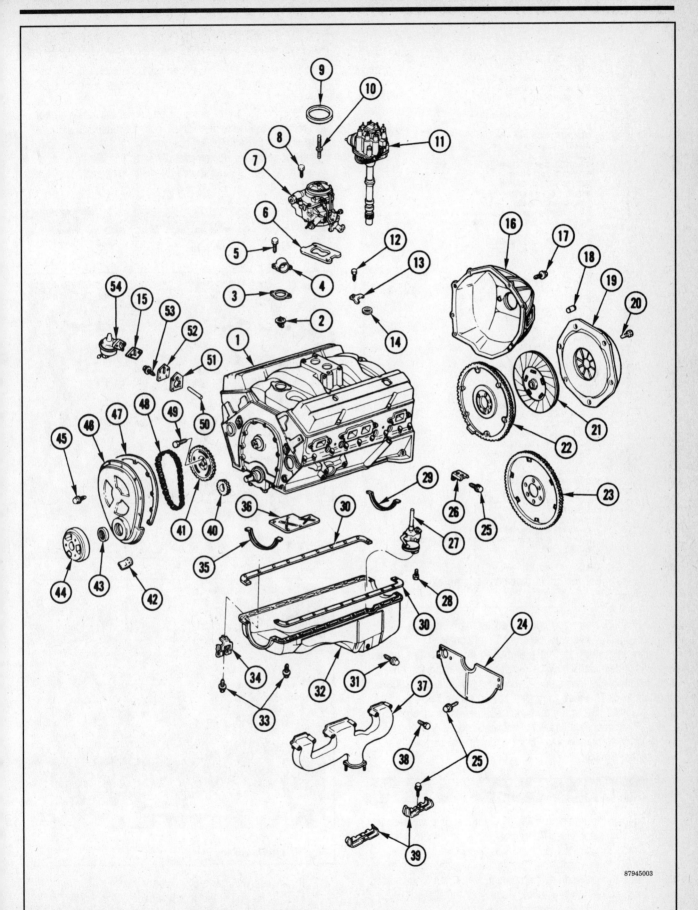

Fig. 3 Small block V8 engine exploded view, part 2

87945003

1.	**BLOCK**, Fitted
2.	**THERMOSTAT**, Eng Water Temp
3.	**GASKET**, Water Outlet
4.	**OUTLET**, Water
5.	**BOLT**, Hex (3/8x16x7/8)
6.	**INSULATOR**, Carb Heat
7.	**CARBURETOR ASM**,
8.	**BOLT**, Hex (5/16x18x1 1/4)
9.	**GASKET**, Air Cleaner to Carb
10.	**STUD**, Air Cleaner to Carb
11.	**DISTRIBUTOR**, Ignition
12.	**BOLT**, Hex (3/8x16x3/4)
13.	**CLAMP**, Dist
14.	**GASKET**, Dist to Block
15.	**GASKET**, Fuel Pump
16.	**HOUSING**, Eng Clutch
17.	**BOLT**, Hex (1/4x20x7/16)
18.	**PIN**, Trans Line Up
19.	**COVER**, W/Plate Asm, Clutch
20.	**BOLT**, Cover W/Plate (5/16x18x3/4)
21.	**PLATE**, Clutch Driven
22.	**FLYWHEEL**, Engine (M/T)
23.	**FLYWHEEL**, Engine (A/T)
24.	**COVER**, Clutch Hsg Lwr
25.	**BOLT**, Hex (1/4x20x7/16)
26.	**BRACKET**, Spark Plug Shield
27.	**PUMP ASM**, Oil
28.	**BOLT**, Hex (7/16x14x2 3/16)
29.	**SEAL**, Oil Pan Rear
30.	**GASKET**, Oil Pan Side
31.	**PLUG**, (1/2x20)
32.	**PAN ASM**, Oil
33.	**BOLT**, Hex (5/16x18x9/16)
34.	**CLIP**, Fluid Line
35.	**SEAL**, Oil Pan Front
36.	**BAFFLE**, Part of #32
37.	**MANIFOLD**, Eng Exh
38.	**BOLT**, Hex (3/8x16x2 3/16)
39.	**SHIELD**, Spark Plug Wire
40.	**SPROCKET**, Crankshaft
41.	**SPROCKET**, Camshaft
42.	**POINTER**, Timing
43.	**SEAL ASM**, Eng Frt
44.	**BALANCER**, Harmonic
45.	**BOLT**, Hex (1/4x20x7/16)
46.	**COVER**, Eng Frt
47.	**GASKET**, Eng Frt Cvr
48.	**CHAIN**, Timing
49.	**BOLT**, Hex (5/16x18x3/4)
50.	**ROD**, Pump Push
51.	**GASKET**, Fuel Pump
52.	**PLATE**, Fuel Pump Mtg
53.	**SCREW**, W/Lock Washer, Fuel Pump Mtg
54.	**PUMP**, Fuel

87945004

Fig. 4 Parts list for small block V8 engine exploded view, part 2

them enough so that you can put an ID mark on them with the marker. That way you can't get them confused.

Rocker arm studs that have damaged threads or are loose in the cylinder heads may be replaced by reaming the bore and installing oversize studs. Oversizes available are 0.003 in. and 0.013 in. The bore may also be tapped and screw-in studs installed. Several aftermarket companies produce complete rocker arm stud kits with installation tools. Mark IV and late high performance small block engines use screw-in studs and pushrod guide plates.

Thermostat

1. Loosen the retaining bolts, then remove the water outlet elbow (thermostat housing) assembly from the engine.
2. Grasp the top of the thermostat and pull it from the bore. If necessary, use a pair of pliers to grip the top of the thermostat and pull it from the opening. Note the direction that the thermostat was facing in the engine for installation purposes.

Water Pump

1. Remove the fan and water pump pulley.
2. If you haven't already done so, remove the power steering pump.
3. Support the water pump and remove the retaining bolts, then remove the pump from the block. Because the water pump is held by bolts of various lengths, the bolt positions should be noted during removal. Draw a little diagram on a piece of paper and keep it with the bolts. That way you won't forget.

Cylinder Head

♦ See Figures 9, 10 and 11

87945104

Fig. 9 Removing the head bolts

87945106

Fig. 10 Lifting off the head

1. If necessary, remove the diverter valve.
2. Rotate the engine so that the head being worked on is up. It makes it easier to handle that way.

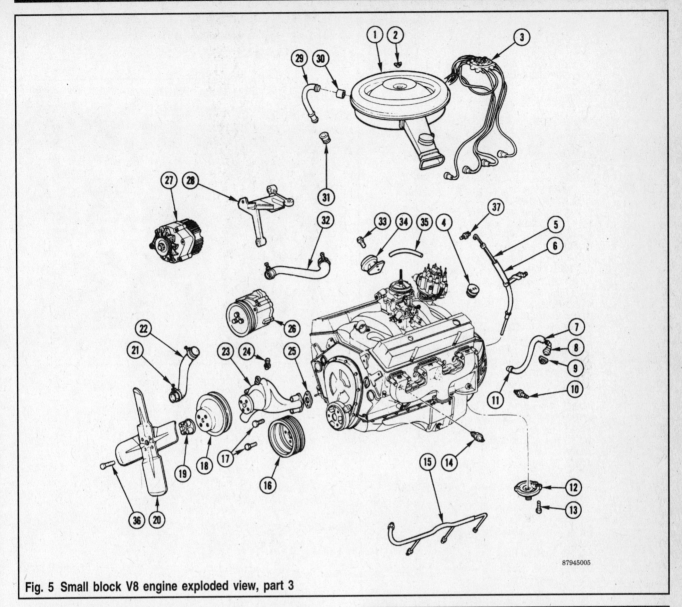

Fig. 5 Small block V8 engine exploded view, part 3

3. Gradually loosen and remove the cylinder head bolts, then remove the cylinder heads from the engine block. If necessary, a prybar may be used to gently loosen the gasket seal, but be VERY careful not to damage the sealing surfaces or the engine or cylinder head. Always protect surfaces being pried, using wood or cloth.

4. Using a putty knife, clean the gasket mounting surfaces.

Fig. 11 Scraping the block deck

1.	**AIR CLEANER,**
2.	**NUT,** Wing
3.	**WIRE,** Spark Plug
4.	**CAP,** C/Case Oil Filler
5.	**INDICATOR,** Oil Level
6.	**TUBE,** Oil Level Indicator
7.	**HOSE** (3/8)
8.	**VALVE,** C/Case Vent
9.	**GROMMET,** C/Case Vent Hose
10.	**PLUG,** Spark
11.	**CLAMP** (5/8)
12.	**ADAPTER,** Oil Filter
13.	**BOLT,** Adapter
14.	**SWITCH,** Water Temp
15.	**PIPE,** Air Inj
16.	**PULLEY,** Crankshaft
17.	**BOLT,** Hex (7/16x20x13/16)
18.	**PULLEY,** Water Pump W/Fan
19.	**SPACER,** Eng Fan
20.	**FAN,** Engine
21.	**CLAMP,** Hose
22.	**HOSE,** Rad Outlet
23.	**PUMP,** Eng Coolant
24.	**NIPPLE,** By-Pass Hose
25.	**GASKET,** Coolant Pump to Eng
26.	**PUMP,** Air Inj Reactor
27.	**GENERATOR,**
28.	**BRACKET,** Gen Mtg
29.	**PIPE,** C/Case Vent
30.	**HOSE,** (Cut as Req)
31.	**GROMMET,** C/Case Vent
32.	**HOSE,** Rad Inlet
33.	**BOLT,** Hex (5/16x16x1 5/8)
34.	**VALVE,** EGR
35.	**HOSE,** EGR Valve (Cut as Req)
36.	**BOLT,** Hex
37.	**SWITCH,** Aux Fan Engine Temp (W/C60)

87945006

Fig. 6 Parts list for small block V8 engine exploded view, part 3

Valve Lifters

▶ See Figures 12, 13, 14 and 15

87945112

Fig. 12 Spray the lifters with WD-40

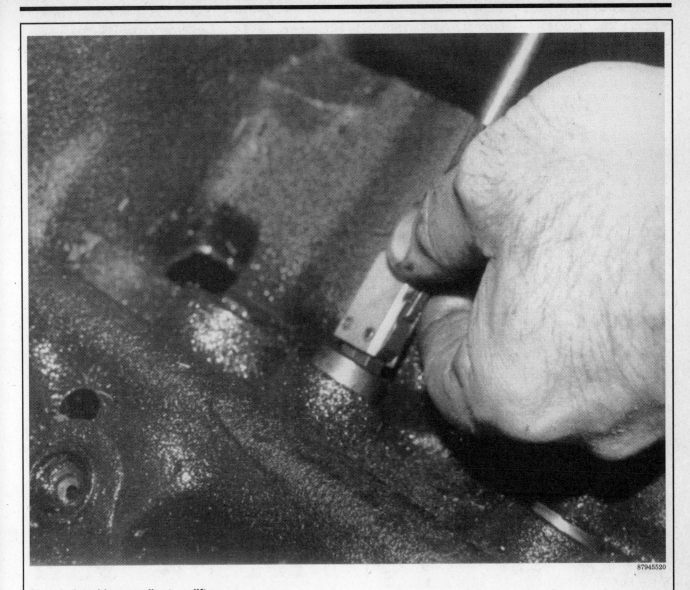

Fig. 13 Attaching a puller to a lifter

Fig. 14 Yanking a lifter. Most of them will stick badly. If they do, don't break the lifter puller. Wait until the lower end is out, then drive the stuck lifters out from below with a brass drift

Fig. 15 Removing a lifter. On this engine, 2 of 16 came out using the puller

➡If you intend to reuse the lifters, keep them marked and in order so they can be reinstalled in their original position. Some engines will have both standard size and 0.010 in. oversize valve lifters as original equipment. The oversize lifters are etched with an O on their sides; the cylinder block will also be marked with an O if the oversize lifter is used.

1. On 1988 and later engines (roller lifters), remove the valve lifter retainer and restricter.

2. Using a lifter puller, remove the lifters. Most of them probably won't come out, even with the puller. The ones that won't will have to be driven out from below with a hammer and brass drift. Do this after the crankshaft is out.

3. If the lifters are coated with varnish, apply carburetor cleaning solvent to the lifter body. The solvent should dissolve the varnish in about 10 minutes.

Oil Pan

▶ **See Figures 16, 17 and 18**

Fig. 17 Removing the oil pan

Fig. 16 Removing the oil pan bolts

Fig. 18 Removing the oil filter adapter bolts

Invert the engine. Remove the oil pan retaining bolts, then remove the pan from the engine block.

Oil Pump

▶ See Figures 19 and 20

Fig. 19 Removing the oil pump bolt

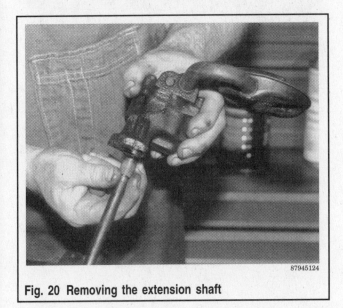

Fig. 20 Removing the extension shaft

Remove the pump-to-rear main bearing cap bolt and remove the pump and extension shaft.

Crankshaft Damper

▶ See Figures 21 and 22

Fig. 21 Attaching the puller to the damper

Fig. 22 Removing the damper

➡Some early model vehicles are equipped with press fit pulleys and/or dampers. For a press fit component there is no retaining bolt to removed before using a puller to remove it from the crankshaft.

1. If separate from the damper, remove the mounting bolts, then remove the crankshaft pulley from the damper.

2. Spray the damper bolt with penetrating oil and allow it to soak in for at least a few minutes. If you have an impact wrench, use it to remove the bolt. If you don't, thread a couple of flywheel bolts back into place and wedge a prybar through them and against the engine stand. This will keep the crank from turning while you loosen the bolt.

3. Remove the damper from the end of the crankshaft using a threaded damper puller, NOT a jawed-type puller which would most likely destroy the damper.

✳✳WARNING

The use of any other type of puller, such as a universal claw type which pulls on the outside of the hub, can destroy the balancer. The outside ring of the balancer is bonded in rubber to the hub. Pulling on the outside will break the bond.

Timing Cover

▶ See Figure 23

Fig. 23 Removing the timing cover bolts

Remove the retaining bolts, the carefully remove the timing cover from the front of the engine block.

Timing Cover Oil Seal

Using a small pry bar, carefully remove the oil seal from the timing cover.

Timing Chain

▶ See Figure 24

Fig. 24 The timing chain and sprockets

CHECKING TIMING CHAIN DEFLECTION

▶ **See Figure 25**

87945519

Fig. 25 Checking timing chain deflection

To measure timing chain deflection, rotate the crankshaft clockwise to take up slack on the left side of chain. Choose a reference point and measure the distance from this point and the chain. Rotate the crankshaft in the opposite direction to take up slack on the right side of the chain. Force the left (slack) side of the chain out and measure the distance to the reference point chosen earlier. The difference between the two measurements is the deflection.

The deflection measurement should not exceed ½ in. (13mm). The timing chain should be replaced if the deflection measurement exceeded the specified limit.

REMOVAL

▶ See Figures 26, 27 and 28

87945110

Fig. 26 Removing the camshaft sprocket bolts

87945111

Fig. 27 Remove the camshaft sprocket and chain. The crankshaft sprocket will have to be removed with a puller

87945150

Fig. 28 Removing the crankshaft sprocket with a puller

1. Turn the crankshaft until the mark on the camshaft sprocket aligns with the mark on the crankshaft sprocket.
2. Remove the camshaft sprocket bolts, then remove the camshaft sprocket and timing chain assembly. You'll need a puller to remove the crankshaft sprocket.

Camshaft

▶ See Figure 29

87945116

Fig. 29 Removing the camshaft

Install a long ⁵/₁₆-18 bolt in the camshaft nose and carefully pull it from the front of the engine while rotating it back and forth.

➡**When removing or replacing the camshaft, be careful not to damage the camshaft bearings.**

Camshaft Bearings

➡ **You'll need a special tool for this job. Rent one from your local automotive retailer. The front and rear bearings should be removed last, and installed first. Those bearings act as guides for the other bearings and pilot.**

1. Drive the camshaft rear plug from the block.
2. Assemble a removal puller with its shoulder on the bearing to be removed. Gradually tighten the puller nut until the bearing is removed.
3. Remove the remaining bearings, leaving the front and rear for last. To remove these, reverse the position of the puller, so as to pull the bearings towards the center of the block.

Pistons and Connecting Rods

▶ **See Figures 30, 31, 32, 34 and 33**

Before removing the pistons, the top of the cylinder bore must be examined for a ridge. A ridge at the top of the bore is the result of normal cylinder wear, caused by the piston rings only traveling so far up the bore in the course of the piston stroke. The ridge can be felt by hand; it must be removed before the pistons are removed.

87945521

Fig. 30 A typical cylinder wear ridge

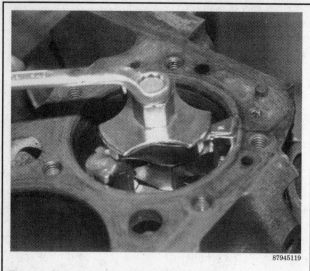

Fig. 31 Tightening the ridge reamer screw

Fig. 32 Turning the reamer in the cylinder

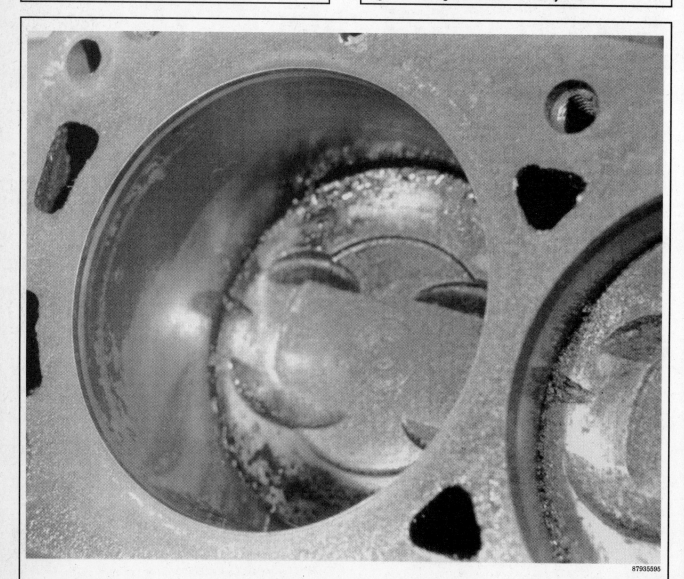

Fig. 33 A view of the cylinder with the ridge removed

A ridge reamer is necessary for this operation. Place the piston at the bottom of its stroke, and cover it with a rag. Cut the ridge away with the ridge reamer, using extreme care to avoid cutting too deeply. Remove the rag, and remove the cuttings that remain on the piston with a magnet and a rag soaked in clean oil. Make sure the piston top and cylinder bore are absolutely clean before moving the piston.

Fig. 34 Matchmarking the rod and cap

➡Starting at the front of the left bank the cylinders are numbered 1-3-5-7 and from the front of the right bank cylinders are 2-4-6-8.

1. Matchmark the connecting rod cap to the connecting rod with a scribe; each cap must be reinstalled on its proper rod in the proper direction. Remove the connecting rod bearing cap and the rod bearing. You'll have to tap the caps loose with a mallet. The rod studs have probably spread, so you'll have to wiggle the cap back and forth to remove it. Take your time. Number the top of each piston with paint or a felt-tip pen for later assembly.

2. Cut lengths of ⅜ in. diameter host to use as rod bolt guides. Install the hose over the threads of the rod bolts, to prevent the bolt threads from damaging the crankshaft journals and cylinder walls when the piston is removed.

3. Squirt some WD-40 onto the cylinder wall from above, until the wall is coated. Carefully push the piston and rod assembly up and out of the cylinder by tapping on the bottom of the connecting rod with a wooden hammer handle.

4. Place the rod bearing and cap back on the connecting rod, and install the nuts temporarily.

5. Remove the remaining pistons in a similar manner.

Rear Main Oil Seal

➡For engines with a 2-piece seal (through 1985), the rear main seal is removed with the rear main bearing cap.

1986-88 (One Piece Seal)

Using the notches provided in the rear seal retainer, carefully pry out the seal using a small tool.

➡**Extreme care should be taken when removing the seal so as not to nick and damage the crankshaft sealing surface.**

ONE PIECE SEAL RETAINER AND GASKET

1. Remove the retainer and seal assembly.
2. Remove the gasket and seal from the retainer assembly.

➡**Whenever the retainer is removed a new retainer gasket and rear main seal must be installed.**

Crankshaft and Main Bearings

▶ **See Figures 35, 36, 37, 38, 39, 40, 41 and 42**

Fig. 35 Removing the rear main cap bolts

Fig. 36 Removing the rear main cap

Fig. 37 Removing the other main caps

Fig. 38 Lifting out the crankshaft

Fig. 39 Dislodging the rear main upper bearing shell

87945131

Fig. 40 Removing the rear main upper bearing shell

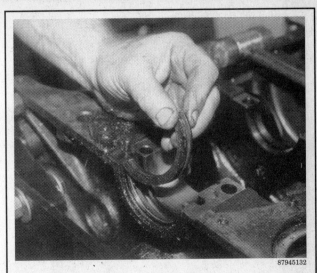

87945132

Fig. 41 Removing the rear main upper seal half

87945523

Fig. 42 The bottom end parts removed and identified. Not bad! Take a break

1. Mark the main bearing caps with a punch so that they can be reinstalled in their original positions.

2. Remove all main bearing caps bolts. Tap each cap loose with a mallet and lift it off.

3. Carefully lift the crankshaft out of the block.

4. Remove the upper and lower bearing shells.

Core (Freeze) Plugs

▶ **See Figures 43, 44, 45, 46, 47, 48 and 49**

Fig. 43 A leaking block core plug

Fig. 44 Drilling the core plug

Fig. 45 Yanking the core plug with a slidehammer

Fig. 46 The core plug bore

Fig. 47 Drilling an oil gallery plug

Fig. 48 Removing the gallery plug with a slidehammer

1. Drill or center-punch a hole in the plug. For large plugs, drill a ½ in. hole; for small plugs, drill a ¼ in. hole.
2. For large plugs, using a slide-hammer, thread a machine screw adapter or insert 2-jawed puller adapter into the hole in the plug. Pull the plug from the block; for small plugs, pry the plug out with a pin punch.

Fig. 49 Removing a threaded gallery plug

PARTS CLEANING

➡️**You really don't have to have the engine parts professionally cleaned. You can do the job adequately yourself if you have the time, patience and plenty of rags.**

Don't worry about absolute cleanliness at this time because machine work still has to be done. After that has been completed, the time for that extra special cleaning job will be at hand. If the block is to be hot tanked, take the head(s) along. Hot tanking will remove grease, corrosion, and scale from the surfaces and water passages. Heads that are to be hot tanked should have the freeze plugs removed so the solution can reach as many places in the water passages as possible.

Some machine shops offer glass bead cleaning. This does a good job, and the part comes back looking like new.

Parts cleaning can be handled in several different ways, depending on the part and the cleaning equipment available. The basic methods of cleaning parts are:
1. Hand scrubbing and scraping
2. Cold spraying
3. Hot tank immersion
4. Cold tank immersion
5. Steam cleaning
6. Glass bead cleaning

Hand Cleaning

Many parts of the engine block and cylinder head are cleaned best by hand. Carbon deposits are usually scraped by hand scrapers or with a wire brush. Soft metal parts, such as bearings, should be washed in a cleaning solvent. Aluminum should be cleaned by hand with a safe solvent.

As each part and fastener is removed you should a least wipe it off with a shop rag before storing it. Once the engine is completely disassembled you'll be ready for mass cleaning.

All parts should be cleaned in a safe, non-flammable solvent. NEVER USE GASOLINE!! Inhaling gasoline vapors is harmful; gasoline wrecks your skin; gasoline vapors are extremely flammable!

Some of the major components that require special attention are:

Cold Spraying

In this method, a cleaning solvent is sprayed over the part to be cleaned. The chemical softens the dirt and helps loosen the bond. The grime and grease are flushed off with water. If the grime and grease are stubborn, a heavier application of spray and some working in with a cleaning brush and strong water pressure will help remove it. Several coats of spray and some soaking time also help to remove stubborn deposits.

Hot Tank Immersion

A hot tank immersion is one of the most efficient and economical means of cleaning parts. The work is placed in the hot solution and agitation takes place making cleaning more efficient. The parts are rinsed off with a high-pressure water hose after cleaning. Remember, never have aluminum parts hot

tanked. Cam bearings immersed in a hot tank will have to be replaced.

Cold Tank Immersion

Cold tanks are generally used for cleaning small parts; however, they are usually big enough to take a cylinder head or a disassembled engine block. Some cold tanks have a sliding tray near the top to put parts on and a pump that circulates the cleaning solvent through an adjustable nozzle to help clean and wash the parts.

Steam Cleaning

Steam cleaners get their name from the fact that steam is used to generate pressure and is also the by-product of heating the cleaning solution. The steam itself has little cleaning power. However, the cleaning solution, when heated and under pressure, does a reasonable job of cleaning.

Valves

▶ See Figures 50 and 51

Fig. 50 Cleaning the valve faces and combustion chambers

1. Use an electric drill and rotary wire brush to clean the intake and exhaust valve ports, combustion chamber and valve seats. In some cases, the carbon will need to be chipped away. Use a blunt pointed drift for carbon chipping. Be careful around the valve seat areas.

2. Use a wire valve guide cleaning brush and safe solvent to clean the valve guides.

3. Clean the valves with a revolving wire brush. Heavy carbon deposits may be removed with the blunt drift.

➡️**When using a wire brush to clean carbon on the valve ports, valves etc., be sure that the deposits are actually removed, rather than burnished.**

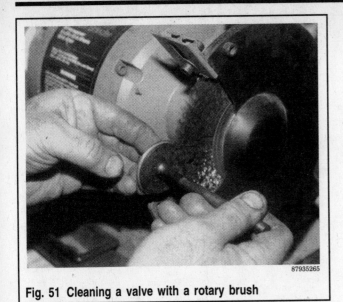

Fig. 51 Cleaning a valve with a rotary brush

4. Wash and clean all valve springs, keepers, retaining caps etc., in safe solvent.

Cylinder Head and Block

▶ See Figures 52, 54 and 53

Fig. 52 Cleaning the valve ports

Fig. 53 Cleaning the block with a drill-mounted wire brush

87945526

Fig. 54 Cleaning the oil and water galleries with a cleaning rod and brush. This particular rod and brush is a cleaning rod for a .30 cal. rifle

1. With the valves installed to protect the valve seats, remove deposits from the combustion chambers and valve heads with a scraper and a wire brush. Be careful not to damage the cylinder head gasket surface. After the valves are removed, clean the valve guide bores with a valve guide cleaning tool. Using cleaning solvent to remove dirt, grease and other deposits, clean all bolts holes; be sure the oil passage is clean.

2. Remove all deposits from the valves with a fine wire brush or buffing wheel.

Pistons and Rods

♦ See Figure 55

Thoroughly clean all carbon and varnish from the piston with solvent.

❊❊WARNING

Do not use a wire brush or caustic solvent (acids, etc.) on aluminum pistons.

Fig. 55 Cleaning the upper ring groove

Crankshaft

▶ See Figure 56

Fig. 56 Burnishing the crankshaft journals with crocus cloth

INSPECTION

Once everything is cleaned and sorted, inspect each part. Fasteners should be inspected of cracks, bad or stripped threads, rounded corners, rust, etc. Anything that appears at all suspect should be replaced. When replacing bolts, make sure that they are of equal grade. That's the markings on the bolt head.

Parts that require special attention are:

➥Handle the crankshaft carefully to avoid damage to the finish surfaces.

1. Clean the crankshaft with solvent, and blow out all oil passages with compressed air. Clean the oil seal contact surface at the rear of the crankshaft with solvent to remove any corrosion, sludge or varnish deposits.
2. Polish the main and rod journals with crocus cloth.
3. Use crocus cloth to remove any sharp edges, burrs or other imperfections which might damage the oil seal during installation or cause premature seal wear.

➥Do not polish the seal surfaces. A finely polished surface may produce poor sealing or cause premature seal wear.

Main Bearings

Clean the bearing inserts and caps thoroughly in solvent, and dry them with compressed air.

Cylinder Head

▶ See Figures 57 and 58

Fig. 57 Placing a straightedge on the head

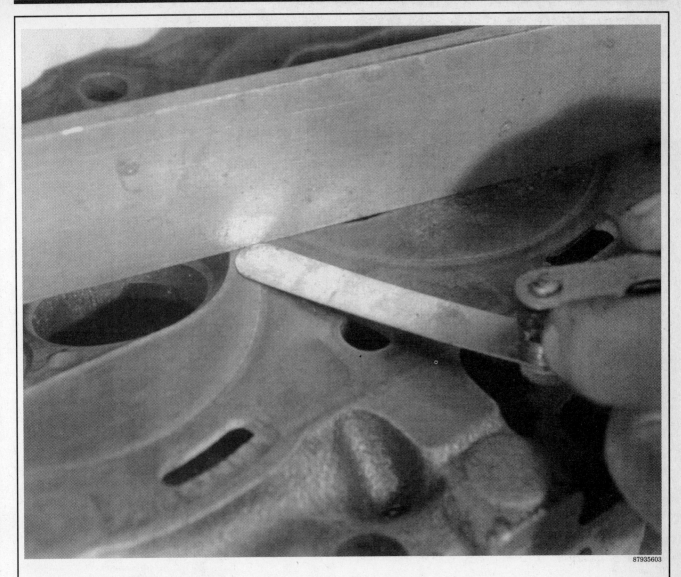

87935603

Fig. 58 Checking the head for flatness

1. Check the head for cracks. Cracks in the cylinder head usually start around an exhaust valve seat because it is the hottest part of the combustion chamber. If a crack is suspected but cannot be detected visually have the area checked with dye penetrant or similar method, by the machine shop.

2. Inspect the cylinder heads for cracks or excessively burned areas in the exhaust outlet ports.

3. On cylinder heads that incorporate valve seat inserts, check the inserts for excessive wear, cracks, or looseness.

Valves

▶ See Figure 59

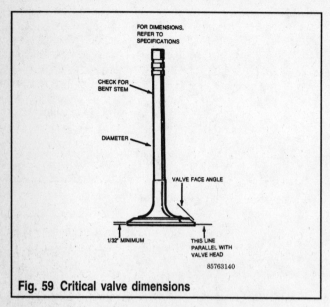

Fig. 59 Critical valve dimensions

After all cylinder head parts are reasonably clean, check the valve stem-to-guide clearance. If a dial indicator is not on hand, a visual inspection can give you a fairly good idea if the guide, valve stem or both are worn.

Insert the valve into the guide until slight away from the valve seat. Wiggle the valve sideways. A small amount of wobble is normal, excessive wobble means a worn guide or valve stem. If a dial indicator is on hand, mount the indicator so that the stem of the valve is at 90 degrees to the valve stem, as close to the valve guide as possible. Move the valve off the seat, and measure the valve guide-to-stem clearance by rocking the stem back and forth to actuate the dial indicator. Measure the valve stem using a micrometer and compare to the chart to determine whether stem or guide wear is causing excessive clearance.

Check the valve stems using a 0-1 in. micrometer. Check the unworn part of the stem (below or above the valve guide travel) against the worn part. A 0.001 in. wear is usually all right, but up to 0.002 in. is borderline. New 'standard' valves should be used if the stem wear is greater than 0.002 in.

Next inspect the cleaned valve faces. Deeply grooved faces may not clean enough, or if they do, will not have enough existing metal for good heat control. Burnt valves (usually exhaust) must be replaced. Some light burning might be cleaned up by refacing.

Check the valve stem tips and keeper grooves. If the tip has been hammered by the rocker arm and worn to within 1/16 in. of the keeper retainer, replace the valve.

The valve guide, if worn, must be repaired before the valve seats can be resurfaced. Ford supplies valves with oversize stems to fit valve guides that are reamed to oversize for repair. The machine shop will be able to handle the guide reaming for you. In some cases, if the guide is not too badly worn, knurling may be all that is required.

VALVE SPRINGS

▶ See Figures 60 and 61

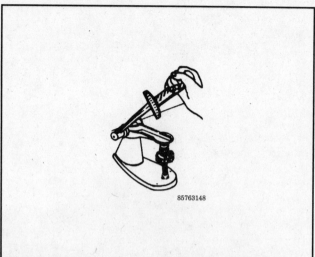

Fig. 60 Have the valve spring pressure checked at a machine shop. Make sure the readings are correct

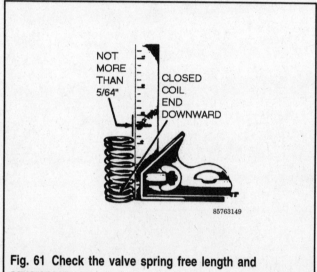

Fig. 61 Check the valve spring free length and squareness

Place the valve spring on a flat surface next to a carpenter's square. Measure the height of the spring, and rotate the spring against the edge of the square to measure distortion. If the spring height varies (by comparison) by more than 1/16 in. (1.6mm) or if the distortion exceeds 1/16 in. (1.6mm), replace the spring.

Have the valve springs tested for spring pressure at the installed and compressed (installed height minus valve lift) height using a valve spring tester. Springs should be within one pound, plus or minus each other. Replace springs as necessary.

VALVE SPRING INSTALLED HEIGHT

After installing the valve spring, measure the distance between the spring mounting pad and the lower edge of the spring retainer. Compare the measurement to chart. If the installed height is incorrect, add shim washers between the spring mounting pad and the spring. Use only washers designed for valve springs, available at most parts houses.

VALVE STEM-TO-GUIDE CLEARANCE

Valve stem-to-guide clearance should be checked upon assembling the cylinder head, and is especially necessary if the valve guides have been reamed or knurled, or if oversized valves have been installed. Excessive oil consumption often is a result of too much clearance between the valve guide and valve stem.

1. Clean the valve stem with lacquer thinner or a similar solvent to remove all gum and varnish. Clean the valve guides using solvent and an expanding wire-type valve guide cleaner (a rifle cleaning brush works well here).

2. Mount a dial indicator so that the stem is 90 degrees to the valve stem and as close to the valve guide as possible.

3. Move the valve off its seat, and measure the valve guide-to-stem clearance by rocking the stem back and forth to actuate the dial indicator. Measure the valve stems using a micrometer and compare to the chart to determine whether stem or guide wear is responsible for excessive clearance.

HYDRAULIC VALVE LIFTER

▶ See Figures 62 and 63

87945524

Fig. 62 Honing the lifter bores with a wheel cylinder hone

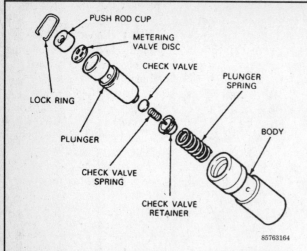

Fig. 63 Exploded view of a lifter used in all gasoline engines

Remove the lifters from their bores and remove any gum and varnish with safe solvent. Check the lifters for concave wear. If the bottom of the lifter is worn concave or flat, replace the lifter. Lifters are built with a convex bottom, flatness indicates wear. If a worn lifter is detected, carefully check the camshaft for wear.

To test lifter leak down, submerge the lifter in a container of kerosene. Chuck a used pushrod or its equivalent into a drill press. Position the container of kerosene so the pushrod acts on the lifter plunger. Pump the lifter with the drill press until resistance increases. Pump several more times to bleed any air from the lifter. Apply very firm, constant pressure to the lifter and observe the rate which fluid bleeds out of the lifter. If the lifter bleeds down very quickly (less than 15 seconds), the lifter should be replaced. If the time exceeds 60 seconds, the lifter is sticking and should be cleaned or replaced. If the lifter is operating properly (leak down time 15-60 seconds) and not worn, lubricate and reinstall in engine.

➡**Always inspect the valve pushrods for wear, straightness and oil blockage. Damaged pushrods will cause erratic valve operation.**

Camshaft

CHECKING CAMSHAFT

◗ **See Figure 64**

Check each camshaft journal with a micrometer. Check the readings against the figure in the chart at the end of this section.

Pistons and Connecting Rods

Inspect the pistons for scuffing, scoring, cracks, pitting, or excessive ring groove wear. If these are evident, the piston must be replaced.

The piston should also be checked in relation to the cylinder diameter. Using a telescoping gauge and micrometer, or a dial gauge, measure the cylinder bore diameter perpendicular (90 degrees) to the piston pin, $2\frac{1}{2}$ in. (64mm) below the cylinder block deck (surface where the block mates with the heads). Then, with the micrometer, measure the piston, perpendicular to its wrist pin on the skirt. the difference between the two measurements is the piston clearance. If the clearance is correct or slightly below (after the cylinders have been bored or hones), finish honing is all that is necessary. If the clearance is excessive, try to obtain a slightly larger piston to bring clearance to within the correct range. If this is not possible, obtain the first oversize piston and hone (or if necessary, bore) the cylinder to size. Generally, if the cylinder bore is tapered 0.005 in. (0.127mm) or more or is out-of-round 0.003 in. (0.076mm) or more, it is advisable to rebore for the smallest possible oversize piston and rings.

➡**Cylinder boring should be performed by a reputable, professional mechanic with the proper equipment.**

PISTON RING END GAP

◗ **See Figures 65, 66 and 67**

Fig. 65 Placing a ring in a cylinder bore

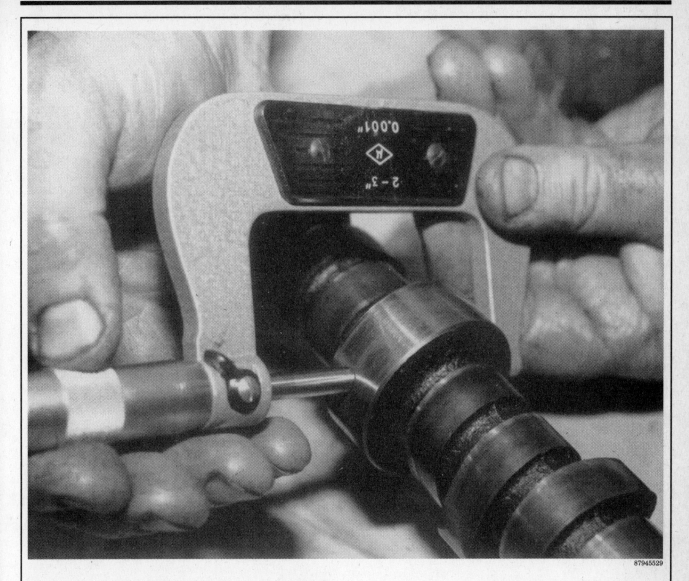

87945529

Fig. 64 Checking the camshaft journals with a micrometer

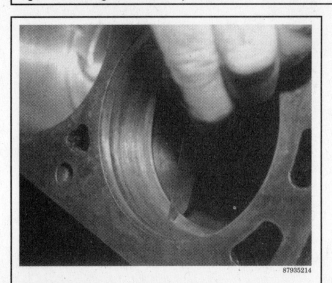

87935214

Fig. 66 Measuring the ring end gap

Piston ring end gap should be checked while the rings are removed from the pistons. Incorrect end gap indicates that the wrong size rings are being used; ring breakage could occur.

Compress the piston rings to be used in a cylinder, one at a time, into that cylinder. Squirt clean oil into the cylinder, so that the rings and the top 2 in. (51mm) of cylinder wall are coated. Using an inverted piston, press the rings approximately 1 in. (25mm) below the deck of the block. Measure the ring end gap with the feeler gauge, and compare it to the ring gap listed in the chart at the end of this chapter. Carefully pull the ring out of the cylinder and file the ends squarely with a fine file to obtain the proper clearance.

87935591

Fig. 67 Pushing the ring into the bore with a clean piston

PISTON RING SIDE CLEARANCE CHECK

Check the pistons to see that the ring grooves and oil return holes have been properly cleaned. Slide a piston ring into its groove, and check the side clearance with a feeler gauge. Make sure you insert the gauge between the ring and its lower land (lower edge of the groove), because any wear that occurs forms a step at the inner portion of the lower land. If the piston grooves have worn to the extent that relatively high steps exist on the lower land, the piston should be replaced, because these will interfere with the operation of the new rings and ring clearance will be excessive. Piston rings are not furnished in oversize widths to compensate for ring groove wear.

MEASURING THE OLD PISTONS

◢ See Figures 68, 69 and 70

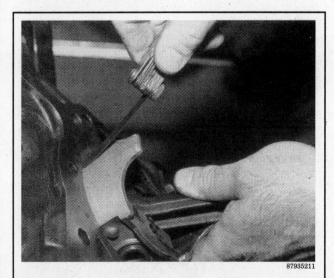

Fig. 68 Measuring piston-to-bore clearance

Fig. 70 Measure the piston's outer diameter using a micrometer

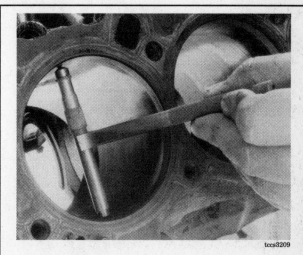

Fig. 69 A telescoping gauge may be used to measure the cylinder bore diameter

Check used piston-to-cylinder bore clearance as follows:

1. Measure the cylinder bore diameter with a telescope gauge.

2. Measure the piston diameter. When measuring the pistons for size or taper, measurements must be made with the piston pin removed.

3. Subtract the piston diameter from the cylinder bore diameter to determine piston-to-bore clearance.

4. Compare the piston-to-bore clearances obtained with those clearances recommended. Determine if the piston-to-bore clearance is in the acceptable range.

5. When measuring taper, the largest reading must be at the bottom of the skirt.

Selecting New Pistons

▶ **See Figure 71**

87945557

Fig. 71 A piston with damaged lands

1. If the used piston is not acceptable, check the service piston size and determine if a new piston can be selected. Service pistons are available in standard, high limit and standard oversize.

2. If the cylinder bore must be reconditioned, measure the new piston diameter, then hone the cylinder bore to obtain the preferred clearance.

3. Select a new piston and mark the piston to identify the cylinder for which it was fitted. Oversize pistons are available. These pistons will be 0.010 in. (0.254mm) oversize.

CONNECTING ROD BEARING INSPECTION

➡ **Make sure connecting rods and their caps are kept together, so that the caps are installed in the proper direction.**

When the shells are placed in position, the ends extend slightly beyond the rod and cap surfaces so that with the rod bolts torqued the shells will be clamped tightly in place to insure positive seating and to prevent turning. A tang holds the shells in place.

➡ **The ends of the bearing shells must never be filed flush with the mating surfaces of the rod and cap.**

If a rod bearing becomes noisy or is worn so that its clearance on the crank journal is sloppy, a new bearing of the correct undersize must be selected and installed since there is no provision for adjustment.

Under no circumstances should the rod end or cap be filed to adjust the bearing clearance, nor should shims of any kind be used.

Inspect the rod bearings while the rod assemblies are out of the engine. If the shells are scored or show flaking, they should be replaced. If they are in good shape, check for proper clearance on the crank journal (see below). Any scoring or ridges on the crank journal means the crankshaft must be reground and fitted with undersized bearings, or replaced.

Replacement bearings are available in standard size, and in undersizes for reground crankshafts. Connecting rod-to-crankshaft bearing clearance is checked using Plastigage® at either the top or bottom of each crank journal. Plastigage® has a range of 0 to 0.003 in. (0.076mm).

1. Remove the rod cap with the bearing shell. Completely clean the bearing shell and the crank journal, and blow any oil from the oil hole in the crankshaft.

➡The journal surfaces and bearing shells must be completely free of oil, because Plastigage® is soluble in oil.

2. Place a strip of Plastigage® lengthwise along the bottom center of the lower bearing shell, then install the cap with shell and torque the bolt or nuts to the correct torque. DO NOT TURN the crankshaft with the Plastigage® installed in the bearing.

3. Remove the bearing cap with the shell. The flattened Plastigage® will be found sticking to either the bearing shell or crank journal. Do not remove it yet.

4. Use the printed scale on the Plastigage® envelope to measure the flattened material at its widest point. The number within the scale which most closely corresponds to the width of the Plastigage® indicated bearing clearance in thousandths of an inch.

5. Check the chart at the back of this chapter for the desired clearance. It is advisable to install a new bearing if clearance exceeds 0.003 in. (0.076mm); however, if the bearing is in good condition and is not being checked because of bearing noise, bearing replacement is not necessary.

6. If you are installing new bearings, try a standard size, then each undersize in order until one is found that is within the specified limits when checked for clearance with Plastigage®. Each under size has its size stamped on it.

Crankshaft

▶ See Figure 72

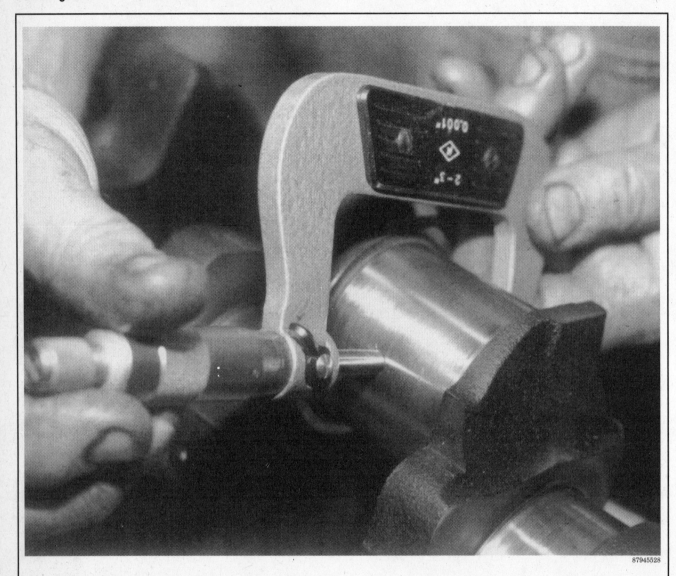

Fig. 72 Checking the rod journals with a micrometer

1. Inspect the main and connecting rod journals for cracks, scratches, grooves or scores.

2. Measure the diameter of each journal at least four places to determine out-of-round, taper or undersize condition.

3. On an engine with a manual transmission, check the fit of the clutch pilot bearing in the bore of the crankshaft. A needle roller bearing and adapter assembly is used as a clutch pilot bearing. It is inserted directly into the engine crankshaft. The bearing and adapter assembly cannot be serviced separately. A new bearing must be installed whenever a bearing is removed.

4. Inspect the pilot bearing, when used, for roughness, evidence of overheating or loss of lubricant. Replace if any of these conditions are found.

5. Inspect the rear oil seal surface of the crankshaft for deep grooves, nicks, burrs, porosity, or scratches which could damage the oil seal lip during installation. Remove all nicks and burrs with crocus cloth.

If the crankshaft is in bad shape, it's probably best to purchase what is called a crank kit. A crank kit is a new or remanufactured crankshaft with a complete set of matched bearings. You can't go wrong with a crank kit. It will save money and time.

Main Bearings

▶ See Figures 73, 74 and 75

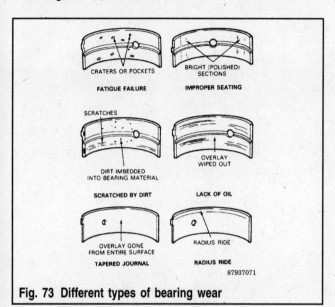

Fig. 73 Different types of bearing wear

Fig. 74 A dial gauge may also be used to check crankshaft runout

1. Inspect each bearing carefully. Bearings that have a scored, chipped, or worn surface should be replaced.

2. The copper-lead bearing base may be visible through the bearing overlay in small localized areas. This may not mean that the bearing is excessively worn. It is not necessary to replace the bearing if the bearing clearance is correct.

3. Check the clearance of bearings that appear to be satisfactory with Plastigage® or its equivalent. If the clearance are not within the correct range have the journals reground.

4. Regrind the journals to give the proper clearance with the next undersize bearing. If the journal will not clean up to maximum undersize bearing available, replace the crankshaft.

5. Always reproduce the same journal shoulder radius that existed originally. Too small a radius will result in fatigue failure of the crankshaft. Too large a radius will result in bearing failure due to radius ride of the bearing.

6. After regrinding the journals, chamfer the oil holes, then polish the journals with a #320 grit polishing cloth and engine oil. Crocus cloth may also be used as a polishing agent.

CHECKING MAIN BEARING CLEARANCES

▶ See Figures 76, 77 and 78

Fig. 75 Mounting a dial gauge to read crankshaft runout

Fig. 76 Plastigage on a main bearing journal before crushing

Fig. 77 Torquing the main cap

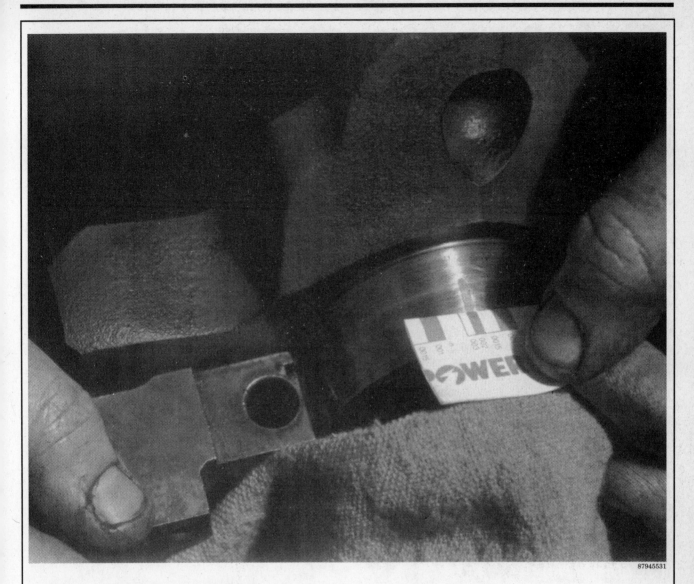

Fig. 78 Measuring the crushed Plastigage

Check the clearance of each main bearing by using the following procedure:

1. Place a piece of Plastigage® or its equivalent, on bearing surface across full width of bearing cap and about ¼ in. (6mm) off center.

2. Install the cap and tighten the bolts to the proper torque. Do not turn the crankshaft while the Plastigage® is in place.

3. Remove the cap. Using the Plastigage® scale, check the width of Plastigage® at its widest point to get the mini-

mum clearance. Check at narrowest point to get maximum clearance. The difference between the readings is the taper of the journal.

4. If the clearance exceeds specified limits, try a 0.001 in. (0.0254mm) or 0.002 in. (0.051mm) undersize bearing in combination with the standard bearing. The bearing clearance must be within specified limits. If the undersize bearings do not bring the clearance within desired limits, refinish the crankshaft journal, then install undersize bearings.

REPAIR AND REFINISHING

Many parts can be reused when repaired or refinished. Among them are:

Valves and Seats

After the valve faces and stems are cleaned, the next step is to resurface the valve face. If the valve guides have been

machined to accept an oversize valve stem, new valves will be used.

The valves are refaced in a specialized piece of equipment called a valve grinder. It consists of a motor driven chuck used to hold and rotate the valve face against a rotating grinding wheel. The chuck is adjustable to the correct angle required by the valve face. A cooling fluid is fed over the wheel and valve face while the valve is being ground. The wheel grinds the face of the valve, removing all burned spots and pits.

Always check the angle before grinding the valves. The face angle is not always identical to the valve seat angle. A minimum margin of 1/32 in. should remain at the edge of the valve after grinding. The valve stem top should always be dressed. This is done by placing the stem in the V-block of the grinder and rotating the valve stem while pressing lightly against the grinding wheel.

Sodium-filled exhaust valves must not be refaced on a machine. If the face is not too badly worn or burnt, the valve should be hand lapped. Valves that are in bad shape should be replaced.

If you you have access to head reconditioning machines and will do the job yourself, read on. The valve seats should be a true 45° angle. Remove only enough material to clean up any pits or grooves. Be sure the valve seat is not too wide or narrow. Use a 60° grinding wheel to remove material from the bottom of the seat for raising and a 30° grinding wheel to remove material from the top of the seat to narrow.

After the valves are refaced by machine, hand lap them to the valve seat. Clean the grinding compound off and check the position of face-to-seat contact. Contact should be close to the center of the valve face. If contact is close to the top edge of the valve, narrow the seat; if too close to the bottom edge, raise the seat.

Valves should be refaced to a true angle of 44°. Remove only enough metal to clean up the valve face or to correct runout. If the edge of a valve head, after machining, is 1/32 inch; (0.8mm) or less, replace the valve. The tip of the valve stem should also be dressed on the valve grinding machine, however, do not remove more than 0.010 inch.

After all valve and valve seats have been machined, check the remaining valve train parts (springs, retainers, keepers, etc.) for wear. Check the valve springs for straightness and tension.

CYLINDER HEAD

CRACK REPAIR

Cracks in a cylinder head or block can usually be repaired, although it usually is less expensive, in the long run, to pick up a good used head or block and recondition it. A crack under a valve seat can be repaired by inserting a series of tapered threaded pins all along the crack and across the valve seat. The valve seat area is then machined to receive a valve seat insert.

If a crack is to be repaired on a cast iron head, the tapered threaded pin repair is not possible because of the fine thread line left. However, a repair is possible using tapered drive-in plugs that can be ground smooth. Check with your local machine shop and ask their advice.

If a crack is repaired in either the head or the engine block, always add a can of heavy-duty ceramic sealer to the cooling system.

HEAD RESURFACING

▶ **See Figures 79 and 80**

87935296

Fig. 79 Rebuilt cylinder heads stacked in the machine shop

87935303

Fig. 80 A cylinder head being resurfaced at a machine shop

Check the flatness of the cylinder head gasket surfaces.

1. Place a straightedge across the gasket surface of the cylinder head. Using feeler gauges, determine the clearance at the center of the straightedge.

2. If warpage exceeds 0.003 inch in a 6 inch span, or 0.006 inch over the total length, the cylinder head must be resurfaced.

3. If necessary to refinish the cylinder head gasket surface, do not plane or grind off more than 0.010 inch from the original gasket surface.

➡**When milling the cylinder heads, the intake manifold mounting position is altered, and must be corrected by milling the manifold flange a proportionate amount. Consult an experienced machinist about this.**

VALVE SEATS

Valve seats may be resurfaced either by reaming or by grinding. Valve seats in cast iron heads may be reamed, while hardened valve seat inserts must be ground. A reamed seat must be lapped with valve grinding compound and the refaced or new valve that will be installed. It is not a bad idea to hand lap any valve when installing it in a newly machined seat.

Reaming the Valve Seat
▶ See Figures 81, 82 and 83

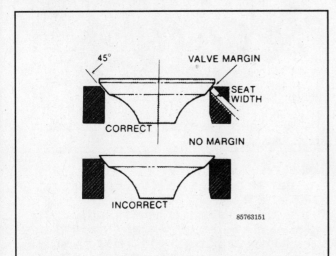

Fig. 81 Valve seat width and centering after proper reaming

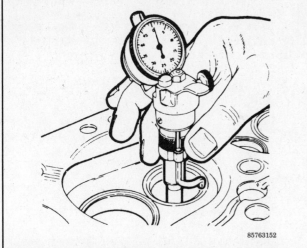

Fig. 82 Checking valve seat concentricity with a dial gauge

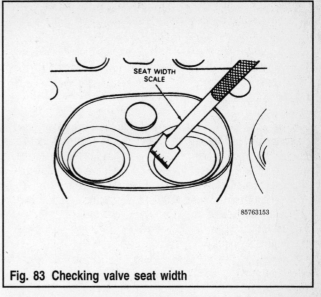

Fig. 83 Checking valve seat width

Select a reamer of the correct seat angle, slightly larger than the diameter of the valve seat, and assemble it with the pilot of the correct size. Install the pilot in the valve guide and using steady pressure, turn the reamer clockwise (never turn the reamer counterclockwise, the cutters and the valve seat can be damaged). Remove only enough material to clean the seat.

Check the concentricity (roundness) of the valve seat. This can be done by using Prussian blue dye. Coat the face of the valve that is to be installed with the dye. Install and rotate the valve on the valve seat. Using the dye marked area as a centering guide, center and narrow the valve seat to the proper angle with correction cutters. If the numbers are not available, minimum seat width for exhaust valves should be $5/64$ in.; intake valves $1/16$ in. After making any correction cuts, recheck with the seats and valves with the dye.

Refacing Valve Seats with a Grinder
▶ See Figure 84

Fig. 84 A valve ready to be refaced at a machine shop

A high-speed grinder, driving a grinding stone mounted on a holder and riding on a valve-guide-mounted pilot probably is used more than any other method to reface valve seats.

The finish on the valve seat depends on what grinding stone is used. By the correct use of various angle stones, the seat may be narrowed, stepped, or centered.

Checking Valve Seat Concentricity

Always check the concentricity of the valve seat after grinding either by the Prussian dye method (see Reaming the Valve Seat) or by using a dial indicator. Install the dial indicator pilot into the valve guide, rest the arm on the valve seat, and zero the gauge. Rotate the arm around the center of the seat. The run-out should not exceed. 0.002 in. Refinish the seat if the run-out is over 0.002. in.

Stepped Valve Seat Angles
▶ See Figure 85

87935301

Fig. 85 Valve seats being reground. This machine cuts compound angles

Many miles on an automobile engine can cause 'sunken' valve seats; that is, seats that are very wide after grinding. To prevent too large a diameter seat or one that is too deep in the head, the top and bottom of the seat are cut at different angles, and then the center. For example, a normal 45 degree seat would have the top portion at 30 degrees, the center at 45 degrees and the bottom at 60 degrees. Not only does this method of grinding center the valve contact point, it also prevents the restriction of air flow.

If the stepped method of valve seat grinding is used, the width of the seat must be measured. If measurement is impossible, check the valve contact width by using the Prussian dye method. If the contact point is too wide or too narrow, a correction to the valve seat must be made or valve burning and face recession can occur.

VALVE LAPPING

▶ See Figures 86, 87 and 88

Fig. 86 Applying lapping compound to the valve seat

87945189

Fig. 87 Lower the valve into position and twist with a lapping tool

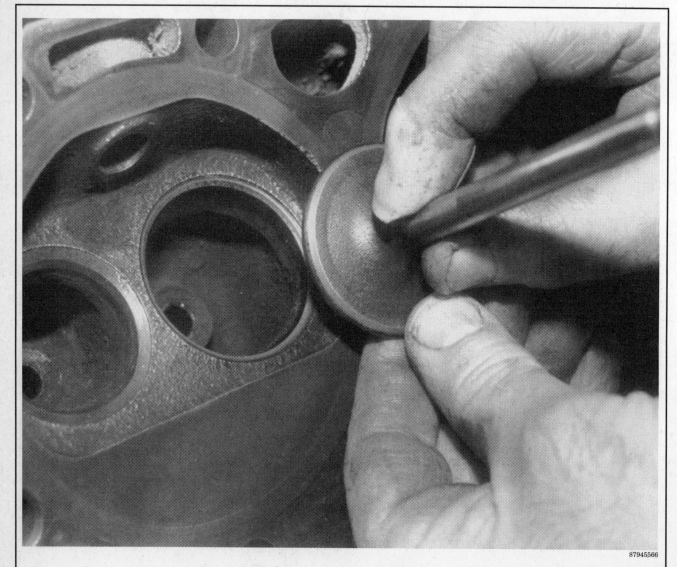

87945566

Fig. 88 After wiping off the lapping compound, check the contact surfaces

The valves must be lapped into their seats after resurfacing, to ensure proper sealing. Even if the valves have not been refaced, they should be lapped into the head before they are installed.

Set the cylinder head on the workbench, combustion chamber side up. Rest the head on wooden blocks on either end, so there is 2-3 inches between the tops of the valve guides and the bench.

1. Lightly lube the valve stem with clean engine oil. Coat the valve seat completely with valve grinding compound. Use just enough compound so that the full width and circumference of the seat are covered.

2. Install the valve in its proper location in the head. Attach the suction cup end of the valve lapping tool to the valve head. It usually helps to put a small amount of saliva into the suction cup to aid it sticking to the valve.

3. Rotate the tool between the palms, changing position and lifting the tool often to prevent grooving. Lap the valve in until a smooth, evenly polished seat and valve face are evident.

4. Remove the valve from the head. Wipe away all traces of grinding compound from the valve face and seat. Wipe out the port with a solvent soaked rag, and swab out the valve guide with a piece of solvent soaked rag to make sure there are no traces of compound grit inside the guide. This cleaning is very important, as engine scoring and damage will result if any grit is remaining when started.

5. Proceed through the remaining valves, one at a time. Make sure the valve faces, seats, cylinder ports and valve guides are clean before reassembling the valve train.

Valve Guides

Worn valve guides can, in most cases, be reamed to accept a valve with an oversized stem. Valve guides that are not excessively worn or distorted may, in some cases, be knurled rather than reamed. However, if the valve stem is worn, reaming for an oversized valve stem is the answer since a new valve would be required anyway.

Knurling is a process in which metal is displaced and raised, thereby reducing clearance. Knurling also produces excellent oil control. The possibility of knurling instead of reaming the valve guides should be discussed with a machinist.

Reaming the Guides

▶ **See Figure 89**

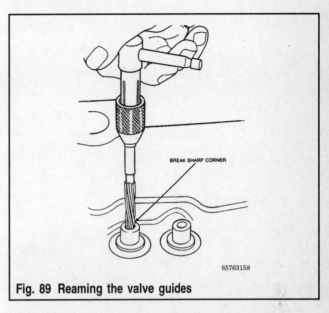

Fig. 89 Reaming the valve guides

If it becomes necessary to ream a valve guide to install a valve with an oversized stem, a reaming kit is available which contains an oversize reamers and pilot tools.

When replacing a standard size valve with an oversized valve always use the reamer in sequence (smallest oversize first, then next smallest, etc.) so as not to overload the reamers. Always reface the valve seat after the valve guide has been reamed, and use a suitable scraper to brake the sharp corner at the top of the valve guide.

Knurling

▶ **See Figure 90**

Fig. 90 Knurling a guide

Valve guides which are not excessively worn or distorted may, in some cases, be knurled rather than reamed. Knurling is a process in which metal inside the valve guide bore is displaced and raised (forming a very fine cross-hatch pattern), thereby reducing clearance. Knurling also provides for excellent oil control. The possibility of knurling rather than reaming the guides should be discussed with a machinist.

Valve Guide Inserts

▶ See Figure 91

Fig. 91 Valve guide inserts being installed

A coil insert can be installed in the valve guide. The guide is tapped and a bronze insert installed. The insert is then reamed to size.

A second type of guide insert, and probably the best way of repairing the cast iron valve guide is the thin-walled bronze insert. The guide is reamed slightly oversize and a split-sleeve thin-walled insert is installed. A special tool is run through the guide bore which expands the insert into the cast guide. The guide is reamed to standard size.

Replacement Guides

It is possible to have the old cast iron guide bored oversize and a replacement guide pressed into the enlarged hole. This is not a bad idea, but the thin-walled bronze insert is a better method.

Rocker Studs

▶ See Figures 92, 93 and 94

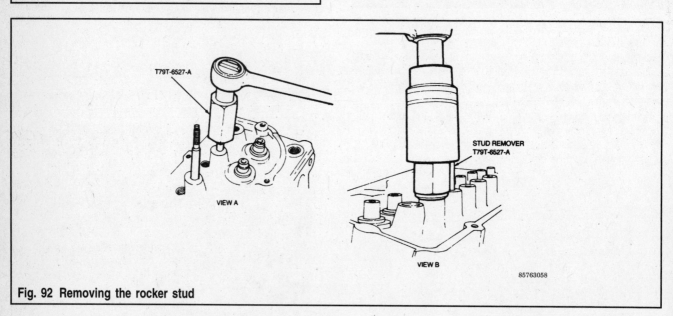

Fig. 92 Removing the rocker stud

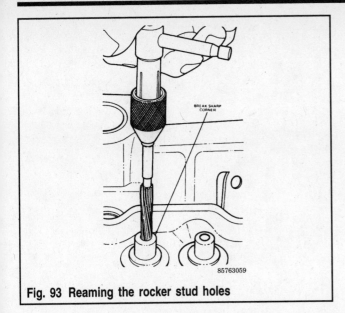

Fig. 93 Reaming the rocker stud holes

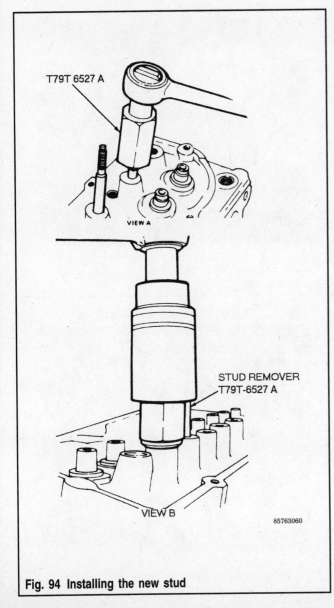

Fig. 94 Installing the new stud

Rocker arm studs which are broken or have damaged threads may be replaced with standard studs. Studs which are loose in the cylinder head must be replaced with oversize studs which are available for service. The amount of oversize and diameter of the studs are as follows:

- 0.006 in. (0.152mm) oversize: 0.3774-0.3781 in. (9.586-9.604mm)
- 0.010 in. (0.254mm) oversize: 0.3814-0.3821 in. (9.688-9.705mm)
- 0.015 in. (0.381mm) oversize: 0.3864-0.3871 in. (9.815-9.832mm)

Tool kits for replacing the rocker studs are available and contain a stud remover and two or three oversize reamers: 0.006 in., 0.010 in., and 0.015 in. oversize studs. To press the replacement studs into the cylinder head, use the stud replacer tool. Use the smaller reamer tool first when boring the hole for oversize studs.

1. Position the sleeve of the rocker arm stud remover over the stud with the bearing end down. Thread the puller into the sleeve and over the stud until it is fully bottomed. Hold the sleeve with a wrench and rotate the puller clockwise to remove the stud.

An alternate method of removing the rocker studs without the special tool is to put spacers over the stud until just enough threads are left showing at the top, so a nut can be screwed onto the top of the rocker arm stud and get a full bite. Turn the nut clockwise until the stud is removed, adding spacers under the nut as necessary.

➡ **If the rocker stud was broken off flush with the stud boss, use a screw extractor to remove the broken-off part of the stud from the cylinder head.**

2. If a loose rocker arm stud is being replaced, ream the stud bore for the selected oversize stud.

➡ **Keep all metal particles away from the valves.**

3. Coat the end of the stud with Lubriplate® or equivalent. Align the stud and installer with the stud bore and top the sliding driver until it bottoms. When the installer contacts the stud boss, the stud is installed to its correct height.

Oil Pump

1. Wash all parts in solvent and dry them thoroughly with compressed air. Use a brush to clean the inside of the pump housing and the pressure relief valve chamber. Be sure all dirt and metal particles are removed.
2. Check the inside of the pump housing and the outer race and rotor for damage or excessive wear or scoring.
3. Check the mating surface of the pump cover for wear. If the cover mating surface is worn, scored, or grooved, replace the pump.
4. Measure the inner rotor tip clearance.
5. With the rotor assembly installed in the housing, place a straight edge over the rotor assembly and the housing. Measure the clearance (rotor end play) between the straight edge and the rotor and the outer race.
6. Check the drive shaft to housing bearing clearance by measuring the OD of the shaft and the ID of the housing bearing.

7. Inspect the relief valve spring to see if it is collapsed or worn.

8. Check the relief valve piston for scores and free operation in the bore.

9. Components of the oil pump are not serviceable. If any part of the pump requires replacement, replace the complete pump assembly.

Block

CYLINDER HONING

▶ **See Figures 95, 96, 97, 98, 99 and 100**

Fig. 95 A cylinder block being bored oversize at a machine shop

Fig. 96 A cylinder block ready to be resurfaced at a machine shop

Fig. 97 Honing the cylinders

Fig. 98 Crankshaft journals being reground at the machine shop

Fig. 99 Crankshafts refinished ready to go at the machine shop

1. When cylinders are being honed, follow the manufacturer's recommendations for the use of the hone.

2. Occasionally, during the honing operation, the cylinder bore should be thoroughly cleaned and checked for correct fit with the selected piston.

3. When finish-honing a cylinder bore, the hone should be moved up and down at a sufficient speed to obtain a very fine uniform surface finish in a cross-hatch pattern of approximately 45-65 degrees included angle. The finish marks should be clean but not sharp, free from imbedded particles and torn or folded metal.

❊❊WARNING

Handle the pistons with care. Do not attempt to force the pistons through the cylinders until the cylinders have been honed to the correct size. Pistons can be distorted through careless handling.

Fig. 100 Clean the bores thoroughly with hot, soapy water

4. Thoroughly clean the bores with hot water and detergent. Scrub them well with a stiff bristle brush and rinse thoroughly with hot water. It is extremely essential that a good cleaning operation be performed. If any of the abrasive material is allowed to remain in the cylinder bores, it will rapidly wear the new rings and cylinder bores. The bores should be swabbed several times with light engine oil and a clean cloth and then wiped with a clean dry cloth. CYLINDERS SHOULD NOT BE CLEANED WITH KEROSENE OR GASOLINE! Clean the remainder of the cylinder block to remove the excess material that got spread around during the honing operation.

PUTTING IT ALL BACK TOGETHER

By now, you should be pretty sure of yourself. After all, you've disassembled, cleaned and inspected an entire V8 engine! Putting it back together should be no problem. Right? Right! If you thought cleanliness, care and attention to detail were important before, they are of supreme importance now! Let's get started.

Painting

At this point you can do the fun part and paint the engine. It's up to you to decide what color or colors you'd like. Traditionalists would paint the engine Chevy Orange. That's fine. But, it's your engine now! You can paint it whatever you'd like! There are a lot of different colors of engine enamel on the market. Just make sure that you use a good quality, high-temperature engine paint. Also, remember that paint doesn't adhere to oily or greasy surfaces. That includes nice, clean oily surfaces. So, if you've applied oil or grease to any part, you'll have to thorough clean it before painting.

➡Be careful! Don't get paint on gasket mating surfaces!

Core (Freeze) Plugs

▶ See Figures 101, 102 and 103

Fig. 101 Cleaning the core plug bore

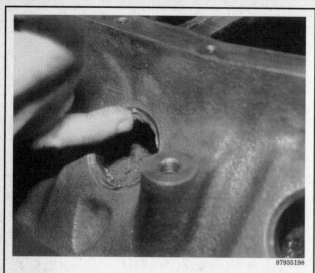

Fig. 102 Coat the bore with RTV silicone sealant

Fig. 103 Hammering in the new plug

Thoroughly clean the opening in the block, using steel wool or emery paper to polish the hole rim.

Coat the outer diameter of the new plug with sealer and place it in the hole.

For cup-type core plugs: these plugs are installed with the flanged end outward. The maximum diameter of this type of plug is located at the outer edge of the flange. Carefully and evenly, drive the new plug into place.

For expansion-type plugs: these plugs are installed with the flanged end inward. The maximum diameter of this type of plug is located at the base of the flange. It is imperative that the correct type of installation tool is used with this type of plug. Under no circumstances is this type of plug to be driven in using a tool that contacts the crowned portion of the plug. Driving in this plug incorrectly will cause the plug to expand prior to installation. When installed, the trailing (maximum) diameter of the plug MUST be below the chamfered edge of the bore to create an effective seal. If the core plug replacing tool has a depth seating surface, do not seat the tool against a non-machined (casting) surface.

Crankshaft and Main Bearings

▶ See Figures 104, 105, 106, 107, 108, 109, 110, 111, 112, 113 and 114

➡Factory-undersized crankshafts are marked, sometimes with a '9'' and/or a large spot of light green paint; the bearing caps also will have the paint on each side of the undersized journal.

Fig. 104 Chasing the main cap bolt holes

Fig. 105 Installing the upper main bearing shells

Fig. 106 Installing the rear main bearing upper shell

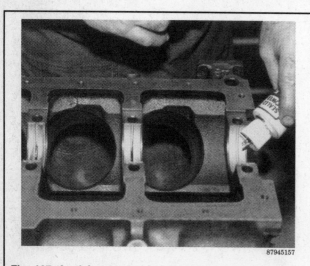

Fig. 107 Applying assembly lube to the upper bearing half

Fig. 108 Lowering the crankshaft into position

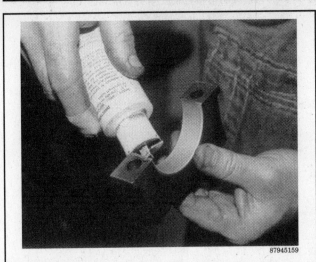

Fig. 109 Applying assembly lube to the lower main bearing shells

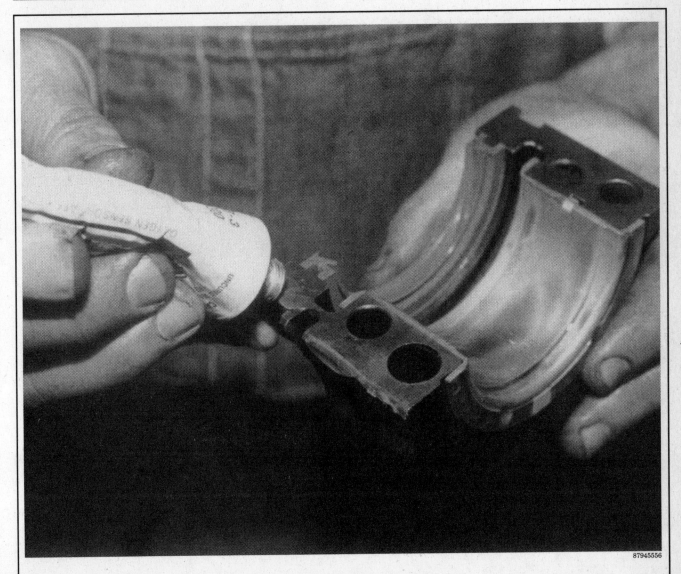

Fig. 110 Applying RTV to the rear main bearing cap beveled edge and seal surface — but not to the seal itself

Fig. 111 **Torquing the main bearing cap bolts**

1. For engines with a 2-piece rear main seal, install the upper main seal half in the groove in the block. Place the lower main seal half in the rear main cap. Follow the instructions that are provided with the seal kit for the use of sealer on the cap.

2. Coat the bearing surfaces of the new, correct size main bearings with assembly lube and install them in the bearing saddles in the block and in the main bearing caps.

Carefully lower the crankshaft into position and install the main bearing caps.

Dip all main bearing cap bolts in clean oil, and torque all main bearings caps, excluding the thrust bearing cap, to the correct torque. Tighten the thrust bearing bolts finger-tight. To align the thrust bearing, pry the crankshaft to the extent of it axial travel several times, holding the last movement toward the front of the engine. Add thrust washers if required for proper alignment. Torque the thrust bearing cap.

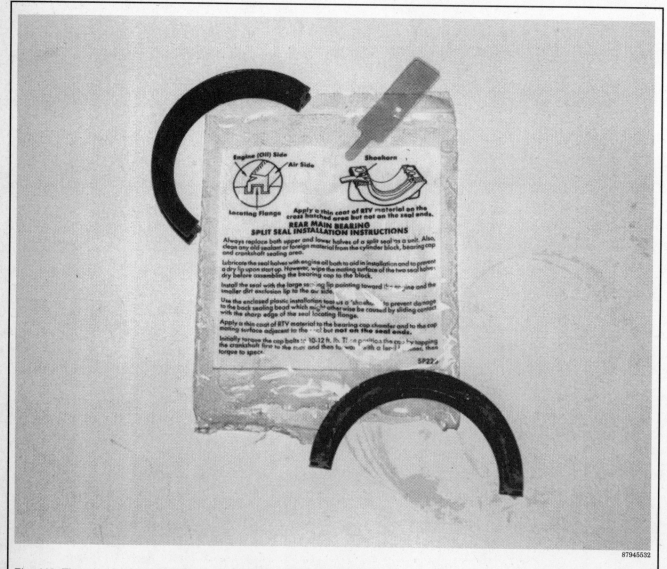

Fig. 112 **The new rear main seal halves with the supplied installation tool**

Fig. 113 Installing the upper rear main seal half

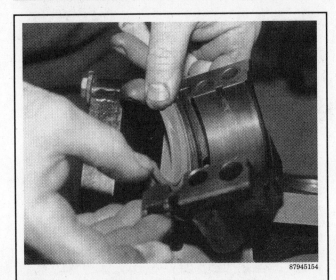

Fig. 114 Installing the lower rear main seal half

To check crankshaft end-play, pry the crankshaft to the extreme rear of its axial travel, then to the extreme front of its travel. Using a feeler gauge, measure the end-play at the front of the rear main bearing. End-play may also be measured at the thrust bearing. Install a new rear main bearing oil seal in the cylinder block and main bearing cap.

Rear Main Oil Seal

1986-88 (One Piece Seal)

1. Before installation lubricate the new seal with clean engine oil.
2. Install the seal on a seal installation tool. Thread the tool into the rear of the crankshaft and tighten the screws snugly, this is to insure that the seal will be installed squarely over the crankshaft. With the tool properly positioned, tighten the tool wing nut until it bottoms.
3. Remove the tool from the crankshaft.

4. Install the transmission assembly to the vehicle.

ONE PIECE SEAL RETAINER AND GASKET

1. Thoroughly clean the gasket mating surfaces.
2. Position a new gasket, then install and secure the seal retainer.
3. Install a new one piece seal to the retainer using a suitable installation tool.

Pistons and Connecting Rods

▶ See Figures 115, 116, 117, 118 and 119

On all engines, the notch on the piston will face the front of the engine for assembly. The chamfered corners of the bearing caps should face toward the front of the left bank and toward the rear of the right bank, and the boss on the connecting rod should face toward the front of the engine for the right bank and to the rear of the engine on the left.

Follow the instructions with the new ring kit for proper ring positioning.

87935217

Fig. 115 Everything you need to install new rings

87945560

Fig. 116 Installing the oil control ring

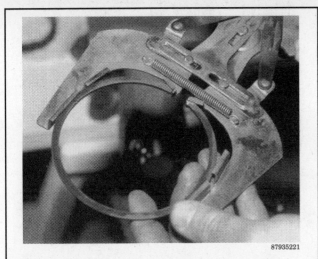

87935221

Fig. 117 Placing the 2nd compression ring on the expander

87945561

Fig. 118 Installing the 2nd compression ring

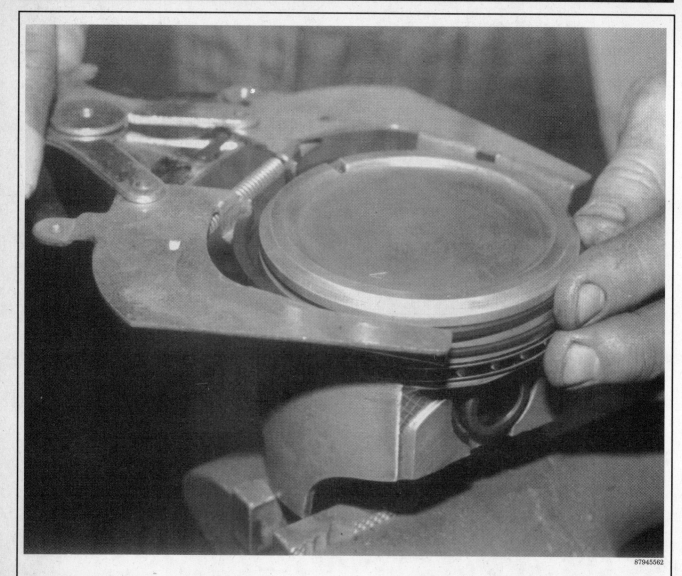

Fig. 119 Installing the upper compression ring

Install the rings on the piston, lowest ring first, using a piston ring expander. There is a high risk of breaking or distorting the rings, or scratching the piston, if the rings are installed by hand or other means. The envelopes that the rings come in have illustrations and instructions showing proper installation techniques.

Position the rings on the piston; spacing of the various piston ring gaps is crucial to proper oil retention and even cylinder wear. When installing new rings, refer to the installation diagram furnished with the new parts.

PISTON AND CONNECTING ROD ASSEMBLY AND INSTALLATION

▶ See Figures 120, 121, 122, 123, 124 and 125

If you have purchased matched pistons and rod, skip this paragraph. If rods and pistons were purchased separately, attach the connecting rod to the piston making sure piston installation notches and any marks on the rod are in proper relation to one another. Lubricate the wrist pin with clean engine oil and install the pin into the rod and piston assembly by using an arbor press as required. Install the wrist pin snaprings if equipped, and rotate them in their grooves to make sure they are seated. To install the piston and rod assemblies:

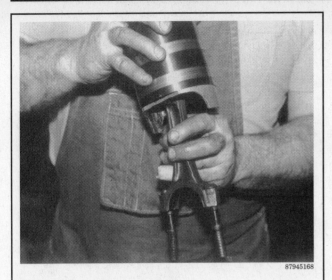

Fig. 120 Compressing the rings

Fig. 122 Pushing the piston in with a hammer handle

Fig. 121 Applying assembly lube to the upper rod bearing shell

Fig. 123 The hose pieces protect the journals

Fig. 124 Installing a rod cap

Fig. 125 Tightening the rod cap nuts

1. Fit pieces of rubber hose over the connecting rod bolt to protect the crankshaft journals.

2. Using a ring compressor, insert the piston assembly into the cylinder so that the notch in the top of the piston faces the front of the engine.

Turn the engine over.

3. Coat each crank journal with assembly lube. Pull the connecting rod, with the new bearing shell in place, into position against the crank journal.

4. Remove the rubber hoses. Install the bearing cap and cap nuts and torque to the correct tighten value.

➡️**The connecting rod cap attaching nuts should only be tightened enough to keep each rod in position until all have been installed. This will ease the installation of the remaining piston assemblies. Once all the piston/rod assemblies are installed, torque the cap nuts.**

5. Check the clearance between the sides of the connecting rods and the crankshaft using a feeler gauge. Spread the rods slightly with a screwdriver to insert the gauge. If clearance is below the minimum tolerance, the rod may be machined to provide adequate clearance.

Camshaft Bearings

1. With the tool in position, pilot the new front and rear bearings on the installer, and pull them into position.

2. Return the puller to its original position and pull the remaining bearings into position.

➡️**Ensure that the oil holes align when install the bearings. This is very important! You can make a simple tool out of the piece of ⁵⁄₃₂ in. brass rod to check alignment.**

3. Replace the camshaft rear plug, and stake it into position.

Camshaft

▶ **See Figure 126**

Fig. 126 Installing the camshaft

Coat the camshaft journals and lobes with assembly lube and carefully guide the camshaft into the engine block and through the bearings.

Timing Chain

▶ **See Figures 127 and 128**

Fig. 127 Installing the camshaft sprocket bolts

Fig. 128 Aligning the timing marks

1. Coat the nose of the crankshaft with anti-seize compound and install the crankshaft sprocket. You'll have to drive it into position with a mallet and brass drift. Rotate the crankshaft so that the timing mark on the sprocket faces up (12 o'clock position). The No.1 piston should be at the top of its stroke.

2. Insert the camshaft timing sprocket into the timing chain so the mark on the sprocket is facing downward.

3. Install the bottom of the chain under the crankshaft sprocket as you install the camshaft sprocket to the end of the shaft. Make sure the sprockets are properly installed and seated, then make sure the timing marks are properly aligned.

4. Install and tighten the camshaft sprocket retaining bolts to 13-23 ft. lbs. (18-31 Nm).

Timing Cover Oil Seal

1. Lubricate the new seal with a light coat of clean engine oil.

2. Support the cover on blocks, place the new seal's open end toward the inside of the cover, then drive the seal into position using the a seal driver.

Timing Gear Cover

▶ **See Figures 129 and 130**

Fig. 129 Installing the timing cover gasket

Fig. 130 Installing the timing cover

1. Thoroughly clean the gasket mating surfaces.
2. Install the front cover on the engine using a new gasket. Apply a ⅛ in. bead of silicone rubber sealer to the oil pan and cylinder block joint faces. Lightly coat the bottom of the seal with engine oil.

Crankshaft Damper

▶ **See Figure 131**

Fig. 131 Installing the damper

1. If removal of the damper was difficult, check the damper inner diameter and the crankshaft outer diameter for corrosion. A small amount of corrosion may be removed using steel wool. Coat the nose of the crankshaft with anti-seize compound.

2. Coat the front cover seal contact edge of the damper lightly with clean engine oil, then install the damper on the end of the crankshaft. Do not hammer the damper into position. Instead, use the bolt to force it into position. Be careful that enough of the threads are in contact to prevent stripping the bolt or crankshaft.

3. Once the damper is fully seated, tighten the retaining bolt to the correct torque.

4. If separate, install and secure the damper pulley.

Oil Pump

▶ **See Figures 132 and 133**

If a new pump is being installed, the pickup from the old pump must be transferred. The pickup is a press fit. Before removing it, matchmark the tube and pump body and put a corresponding mark on the new pump's body. The pickup can then be installed at the same attitude as on the original pump. This is necessary to maintain the screen level and at the right height. Getting it out without crunching it is usually the hardest part. Try driving it out by using a blunt driver against the rib on the tube. If that doesn't work, try a pipe wrench or anything else you can think of.

To install the tube on the new pump, coat the end of the tube with RTV sealer, align the matchmarks and carefully drive the tube into position in the new pump. MAKE SURE that the matchmarks align.

There are special tools available to make the job easier. Among them is an excellent tool made by the Old Car Company, PO Box 244, Elverson, PA 19520.

Lower the pump and pickup assembly into position. Make sure that the driveshaft enters the correct hole in the block. Position the pump on the rear main cap and install the bolt.

87945175

Fig. 132 Installing the oil pump

87945563

Fig. 133 Lowering the shaft into position

Oil Pan

▶ See Figures 134, 135, 136, 137, 138, 139 and 140

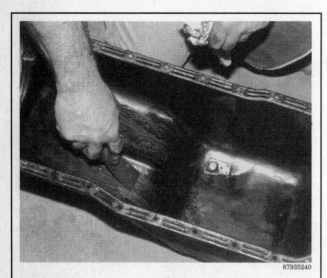

Fig. 134 Cleaning the sludge from the pan

Fig. 135 Cleaning the oil pan gasket rail

Fig. 136 Front oil pan seal installed

Fig. 137 Rear oil pan seal installed

Fig. 138 Oil pan gaskets and seals in place

Fig. 139 Lowering the pan into position

Fig. 140 Installing the pan bolts

➡The gasket kit will have instructions for installing their particular brand of gasket and seals. Follow them to the letter.

Position the front and rear seals in their grooves and position the side gaskets on the block. The block surfaces should be coated with sealer. Coat the pan surfaces with sealer and lower it into position. Use an awl to line up the holes in the gasket with the holes in the pan and block. Install and tighten the pan bolts.

Valve Lifters, Rocker Arms and Pushrods

▶ See Figures 141, 142, 143 and 144

Turn the engine right side up.

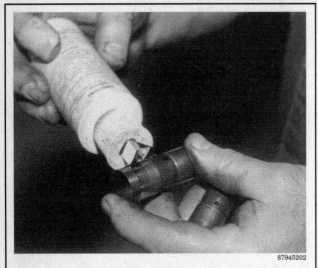

Fig. 141 Applying assembly lube to the lifters

Fig. 143 Installing the pushrods

Fig. 142 Installing the lifters

Fig. 144 Tighten the rocker arm nuts until the pushrod just stops turning

1. New lifters must be primed before installation, as dry lifters will seize when the engine is started. Submerge the lifters in SAE 10 oil, which is very thin. Carefully insert the end of a ⅛ in. (3mm) drift or an old pushrod into the lifter and push down on the plunger. Hold the plunger down while the lifter is still submerged; do not pump the plunger. Release the plunger and the lifter is now primed.

2. Coat the bottoms of the lifters with assembly lube before installation. Install the lifters (old lifters in their original order).

➡An additive containing EP lube, such as EOS, can be added to crankcase oil for break-in when new lifters or a new camshaft is installed. This additive is generally available in automotive parts stores.

Valves

▶ See Figures 145, 146, 147, 148 and 149

87945567

Fig. 145 Installing the valve springs

87945192

Fig. 146 Installing the rotator and cap

87945193

Fig. 148 Compressing the valve springs

87945195

Fig. 147 Attaching the spring compressor

Fig. 149 Installing the keepers

✳✳CAUTION

Keep the first aid kit handy. This the job that will most like cause cuts or scrapes. The valve spring compressor can be difficult to operate.

➡ Remember that when installing valve seals, a small amount of oil is able to pass the seal to lubricate the valve guides; otherwise, excessive wear will result.

1. Lubricate the valve stems with clean engine oil.
2. Install the valves in the cylinder head, one at a time, as numbered.
3. Lubricate and position the seals and valve springs, again a valve at a time.
4. Install the spring caps, and compress the springs.
5. With the valve key groove exposed above the compressed valve spring, wipe some light grease around the groove. This will retain the keys as you release the spring compressor.
6. Using needle nose pliers (or your fingers), place the keys in the key grooves. The grease should hold the keys in place. Slowly release the spring compressor; the valve cap or rotator will raise up as the compressor is released, retaining the key.
7. Once all the valves are assembled, upright the head and tap the end of each valve stem sharply with a plastic or rubber mallet. This will expose any keeper that wasn't fully seated.

Cylinder Head

▶ See Figures 150, 151, 152, 153, 154, 155 and 156

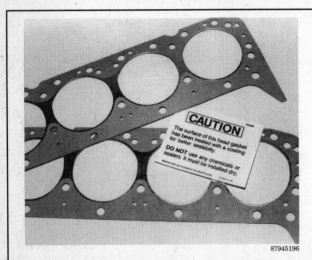

Fig. 150 The head gaskets and the warning label concerning the use of sealer

Fig. 151 Installing a head gasket. Sometimes the gaskets are marked 'up' or 'front'

Fig. 152 A head gasket in position

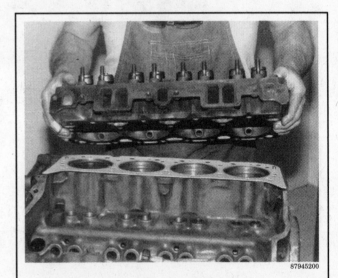

Fig. 153 Lowering a head into position

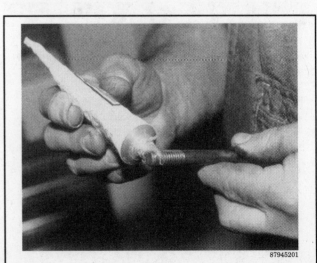

Fig. 154 Coat the bottom third of the threads on each head bolt with RTV silicone sealer

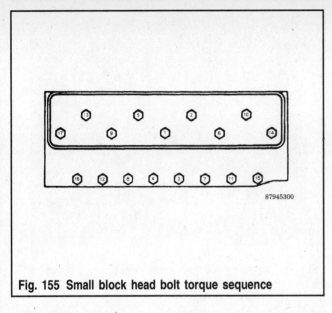

Fig. 155 Small block head bolt torque sequence

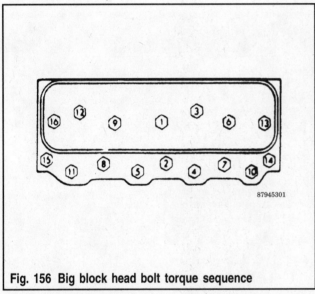

Fig. 156 Big block head bolt torque sequence

➡Follow the instructions that come with the gasket kit regarding the use of sealer. Also, depending on the maker, gaskets may be marked 'up' or 'front'.

1. Position a new cylinder head gasket on the block, then carefully lower the cylinder head assembly into position.
2. Install and finger-tighten the cylinder head retaining bolts, then tighten them to the correct torque value using the proper torque sequence.

3. Install the pushrods.

Intake Manifold

▶ See Figures 157, 158, 159, 160, 161, 162, 163, 163, 165, 166 and 167

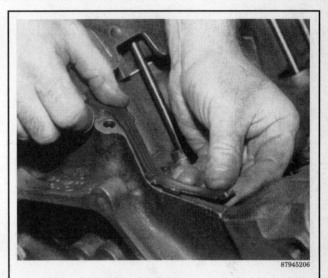

Fig. 157 Installing the end seals

Fig. 158 Applying RTV sealer around the middle water ports

Fig. 159 Applying RTV sealer around the front water ports

Fig. 160 Applying RTV sealer around the rear water ports

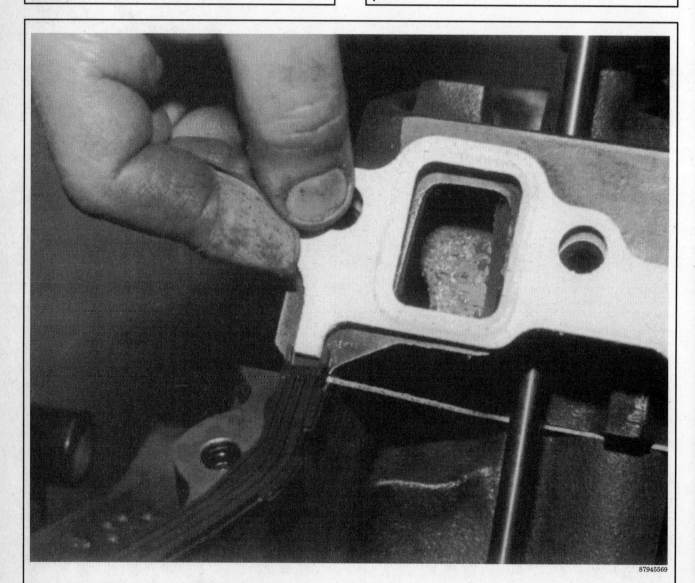

Fig. 161 Installing the intake manifold gaskets

Fig. 162 The intake gaskets and seals ready for manifold installation

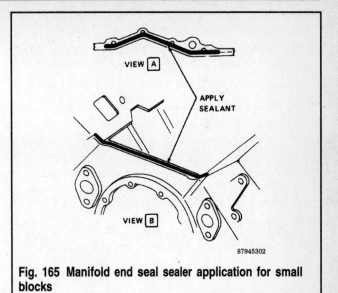
Fig. 165 Manifold end seal sealer application for small blocks

Fig. 163 Lowering the manifold into position

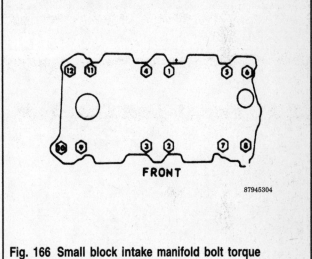
Fig. 166 Small block intake manifold bolt torque sequence

Fig. 164 Torquing the intake manifold bolts

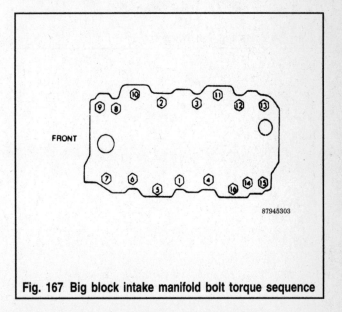
Fig. 167 Big block intake manifold bolt torque sequence

1. Apply a 1/8 in. (3mm) bead of silicone-rubber RTV sealant at the points shown in the accompanying diagram.

❊❊WARNING

Do not apply sealer to the waffle portions of the seals as the sealer will rupture the end seal material.

2. Position new seals on the block.

3. Your gasket kit may have an instruction sheet showing a change in the sealer application for the sealer application. RTV silicone sealer is to be used around the water passages, while non-hardening gasket sealer is to be used everywhere else.

4. Position the gaskets. Be sure gasket holes align with head holes.

5. Carefully lower the manifold into position. Run your finger around the front and rear seals to make sure they are in position. If not, remove the manifold and reposition them.

6. Install the manifold nuts and bolts. Following the tightening sequence, tighten all fasteners.

Rocker Covers

▶ **See Figure 168**

Fig. 168 Installing the rocker covers

1. Make sure the cover flanges are straight and clean.

2. Coat both mating surfaces with gasket sealer and place the new gasket on the head.

3. Place the cover on the head making sure the gasket is evenly seated. Install the bolts and torque them to the figure shown in the torque charts.

Water Pump

1. Be sure to remove all traces of gasket or sealer material from the gasket mating surfaces.

2. Position the pump on the block using new gaskets. The gaskets may be held in place using small amount of RTV sealer or bolts may be held through the pump mounting holes in order to correctly position the gaskets.

➡**Use an anti-seize compound on the water pump bolt threads.**

3. Install all of the water pump bolts and torque to 30 ft. lbs. (41 Nm).

Engine Mechanical Specifications

COMPONENT	U.S.	METRIC
Camshaft End-Play		
All	0.0040 - 0.0120 in.	0.0010 - 0.0030mm
Camshaft Journal-to-Bearing Clearance		
All	0.0010 - 0.0030 in.	0.0254 - 0.0762mm
Camshaft Journal Diameter		
305/350	1.8682 - 1.8692 in.	47.4523 - 47.4777mm
454	1.9482 - 1.9492 in.	49.4843 - 49.5097mm
Camshaft Lobe Lift		
305		
Intake	0.2484 in.	6.3094mm
Exhaust	0.2667 in.	6.7742mm
350		
Intake	0.2600 in.	6.6040mm
Exhaust	0.2733 in.	6.9418mm
454		
Intake	0.2343 in.	5.9512mm
Exhaust	0.2530 in.	6.4262mm
Connecting Rod Bend (max.)		
All	0.0120 in.	0.0406mm
Connecting Rod Lower End Bearing Clearance		
305/350	0.0013 - 0.0035 in.	0.0330 - 0.0889mm
454	0.0009 - 0.0025 in.	0.0229 - 0.0635mm
Connecting Rod-to-Crankshaft Side Clearance		
305/350	0.0080 - 0.0140 in.	0.203 - 0.3556mm
454	0.0130 - 0.0230 in.	0.3302 - 0.5842mm
Connecting Rod Journal Diameter		
305/350	2.0988 - 2.0998 in.	53.3095 - 53.3349mm
454	2.1990 - 2.2000 in.	55.8546 - 55.8800mm
Connecting Rod Journal Taper (max.) (2)		
All	0.0005 in.	0.0127mm
Connecting Rod Twist (max.)		
All	0.0240 in.	0.6096mm
Crankshaft End-play		
305/350	0.0020 - 0.0060 in.	0.0508 - 0.1524mm
454	0.0060 - 0.0100 in.	0.1524 - 0.2540mm
Cylinder Block Head Gasket Surface Flatness (in any 6 inch/152mm span)		
All	0.0030 in.	0.0762mm
Cylinder Bore Diameter		
305	3.7350 - 3.7385 in.	94.8690 - 94.9579mm
350	4.0005 - 4.0025 in.	101.6127 - 101.6635mm
454	4.2495 - 4.2525 in.	107.9373 - 108.0135mm
Cylinder Bore Maximum Taper		
All	0.0010 in.	0.0254mm
Cylinder Bore Out-of-Round (max.)		
All	0.0020 in.	0.0508mm
Cylinder Head Gasket Surface Flatness (in any 6 inch/152mm span)		
All	0.0030 in.	0.0762mm

87945c01

Engine Mechanical Specifications

COMPONENT	U.S.	METRIC
Main Bearing Clearance		
305/350		
No. 1	0.0001 - 0.0015 in.	0.0025 - 0.0381mm
Nos. 2, 3, 4	0.0001 - 0.0025 in.	0.0025 - 0.0635mm
No. 5	0.0025 - 0.0035 in.	0.0635 - 0.0889mm
454		
Nos. 1, 2, 3, 4	0.0010 - 0.0025 in.	0.0254 - 0.0635mm
No. 5	0.0024 - 0.0040 in.	0.0610 - 0.1016mm
Main Bearing Journal Diameter		
305/350		
No. 1	2.4484 - 2.4493 in.	62.1894 - 62.2122mm
Nos. 2, 3, 4	2.4481 - 2.4490 in.	62.1817 - 62.2046mm
No. 5	2.4479 - 2.4488 in.	62.1766 - 62.1995mm
454		
Nos. 1, 2, 3, 4	2.7481 - 2.7490 in.	69.8017 - 69.8246mm
No. 5	2.7476 - 2.7486 in.	69.7890 - 69.8144mm
Main Bearing Journal Runout (max.)		
All	0.0010 in.	0.0254mm
Main Bearing Journal Taper (max.)		
All	0.002 in.	0.0508mm
Piston-to-Bore Clearance		
305/350	0.0007 - 0.0017 in.	0.0178 - 0.0431mm
454	0.0030 - 0.0040 in.	0.0762 - 0.1016mm
Piston Pin Diameter		
305/350	0.9270 - 0.9273 in.	23.5458 - 23.5534mm
454	0.9895 - 0.9898 in.	25.1333 - 25.1409mm
Piston Pin-to-Piston Clearance		
All	0.00025 - 0.00035 in.	0.0064 - 0.0089mm
Piston Pin-to-Rod Clearance		
305/350	0.0008 - 0.0016 in.	0.0203 - 0.0406mm
454	0.0025 - 0.0035 in.	0.0635 - 0.0089mm
Piston Ring End Gap		
305/350		
Top	0.0100 - 0.0200 in.	0.2540 - 0.5080mm
Middle	0.0100 - 0.0250 in.	0.2540 - 0.6350mm
Oil	0.0150 - 0.0550 in.	0.3810 - 1.3970mm
454		
Top	0.0100 - 0.0200 in.	0.2540 - 0.5080mm
Middle	0.0100 - 0.0200 in.	0.2540 - 0.5080mm
Oil	0.0150 - 0.0550 in.	0.3810 - 1.3970mm
Piston Ring Side Clearance		
305/350		
Top	0.0012 - 0.0032 in.	0.0305 - 0.0813mm
Middle	0.0012 - 0.0032 in.	0.0012 - 0.0813mm
Oil	0.0020 - 0.0027 in.	0.0508 - 0.0686mm
454		
Top	0.0017 - 0.0032 in.	0.0432 - 0.0813mm
Middle	0.0017 - 0.0032 in.	0.0432 - 0.0813mm
Oil	0.0050 - 0.0065 in.	0.0050 - 0.0065mm

87945c02

Engine Mechanical Specifications

COMPONENT	U.S.	METRIC
Rocker Arm Lift Ratio		
305/350	1.50:1	
454	1.70:1	
Timing Chain Deflection (max.)		
All	0.5000 in.	12.7000mm
Valve Face Angle		
All	45 degrees	
Valve Face Minimum Margin		
All	0.0625 in.	1.5875mm
Valve Face Runout (max.)		
All	0.0020 in.	0.0508mm
Valve Seat Angle		
All	46 degrees	
Valve Seat Runout (max.)		
All	0.0020 in.	0.0500mm
Valve Seat Width		
All		
Intake	0.0312 - 0.0625 in.	0.7925 - 1.5875mm
Exhaust	0.0625 - 0.0938 in.	1.5875 - 2.3825mm
Valve Spring Compression Pressure (outer)		
305/350		
Intake	194-206 lbs. @ 1.250 in.	88-93kg @ 31.75mm
Exhaust	194-206 lbs. @ 1.160 in.	88-93kg @ 29.46mm
454		
All	210-230 lbs. @ 1.400 in.	95-104kg @ 35.56mm
Valve Spring Free Length (outer)		
305/350		
All	2.0300 in.	51.5620mm
454		
All	2.1200 in.	53.8480mm
Valve Spring Installed Height		
305/350		
Intake	1.7188 in.	43.6575mm
Exhaust	1.5938 in.	40.4825mm
454		
Intake & Exhaust	1.7969 in.	45.6413mm
Valve Spring Out-of-Square (max.)		
All	0.0783 in.	1.9844mm
Valve Stem-to-Guide Clearance		
305/3503		
Intake & Exhaust	0.0010 - 0.0027 in.	0.0254 - 0.0686mm
454		
Intake	0.0010 - 0.0027 in.	0.0254 - 0.0686mm
Exhaust	0.0019 - 0.0029 in.	0.0483 - 0.0737mm

87945c03

Torque Specifications

COMPONENT	U.S.	METRIC
Auxillary Cooling Fan		
All Engines	53 ft. lbs.	72 Nm
Camshaft Sprocket Bolts		
5.0L and 5.7L	18 ft. lbs.	24 Nm
7.4L	20 ft. lbs.	26 Nm
Connecting Rod Cap Nuts		
5.0L and 5.7L	45 ft. lbs.	60 Nm
7.4L	48 ft. lbs.	66 Nm
Flywheel Housing Bolts		
5.0L and 5.7L	32 ft. lbs.	44 Nm
Front Cover to Block Bolts		
5.0L and 5.7L	100 inch lbs.	11.3 Nm
7.4L	96 inch lbs.	10.8 Nm
Front Cover Bolts to Oil Pan		
7.4L	70 inch lbs.	7.9 Nm
Main Bearing Cap bolts		
5.0L and 5.7L		
Outer Bolts 2, 3, and 4	70 ft. lbs.	95 Nm
5.0L and 5.7L		
Inner Bolts	80 ft. lbs.	110 Nm
7.4L	110 ft. lbs.	150 Nm
Oil Pan		
5.0L and 5.7L Nuts	200 inch lbs.	22 Nm
5.0L and 5.7L Bolts	11 inch lbs.	1.2 Nm
7.4L	160 inch lbs.	18.1 Nm
Oil Pump		
5.0L, 5.7L, and 7.4L	65 ft. lbs.	90 Nm
Oil Pump Cover		
5.0L and 5.7L	80 inch lbs.	9.0 Nm
Rocker Arm Cover		
5.0L and 5.7L Studs	15 inch lbs.	1.7 NM
5.0L and 5.7L Carburated	65 inch lbs.	7.3 NM
5.0L and 5.7L TBI	11 inch lbs.	1.2 NM
7.4L	115 inch lbs.	13 NM
Starter		
All Engines	28 Ft. lbs.	38 Nm
Torsional Damper Bolt		
5.0L and 5.7L	70 ft. lbs.	95 Nm
7.4L	85 ft. lbs.	115 Nm
Water Outlet		
5.0L and 5.7L	21 ft. lbs.	28 Nm
7.4L	30 ft. lbs.	40 Nm
Water Pump		
5.0L, 5.7L and 7.4L	30 ft. lbs.	40 Nm

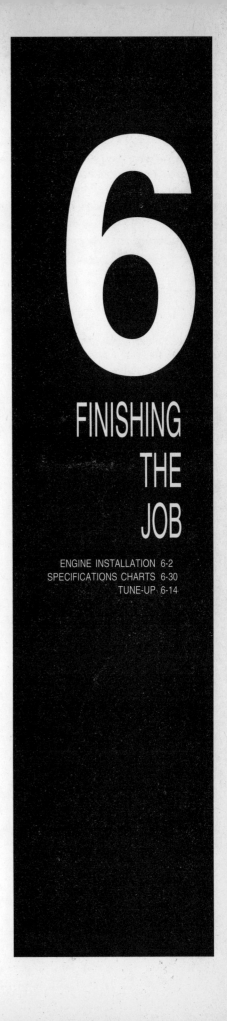

6

FINISHING THE JOB

ENGINE INSTALLATION

Attach the crane to the engine and remove it from the stand with the mounting head attached. Lower it onto the dolly and remove the mounting head. Roll the engine out of the garage and up to a convenient point in front of the vehicle. Attach the crane and lift the engine from the dolly.

Now, using the appropriate procedure found below, install the engine.

Full-Sized Trucks through 1987

1. On four wheel drive, lower the engine into place and align it with the transmission. Push the engine back gently and turn the crankshaft until the manual transmission shaft and clutch engage. Bolt the transmission to the engine. With automatic transmission, align the converter with the flywheel, bolt the transmission to the engine, bolt the converter to the flywheel, replace the underpan and starter, and connect the throttle linkage and vacuum modulator line.

2. On two wheel drive, lower the engine/transmission unit into place. Replace the rear crossmember if removed. Bolt the three speed transmission back to the crossmember. Replace the driveshaft.

3. Install the engine mounts.
4. Remove the transmission support.
5. Install the converter to flex bolts and torque to 35 ft. lbs.
6. Install the fuel gauge wiring and starter.
7. Install the flywheel or torque converter cover.
8. Connect the strut rods at the engine mountings, if used.
9. Install the exhaust pipes at the manifold.
10. Lower the vehicle.
11. Connect the vacuum lines to the intake manifold.
12. Install the fuel line.
13. Connect the engine wiring harness.
14. Install the power steering pump, if used.
15. Connect the air conditioning compressor, if used.
16. Connect the accelerator, cruise control and detent linkage.
17. Connect the heater hoses.
18. Install the radiator and shroud.
19. Install the accessory drive belts.
20. Install the hood.
21. Install the proper quantity and grade of coolant and engine oil.
22. Connect the negative battery cable.

1988-96 Full-Sized Trucks

▶ See Figures 1, 2, 3, 4, 5, 6, 7, 8, 9, 10, 11 and 12

5.0L, 5.7L

1. Raise the vehicle and support it safely.
2. Lower the engine and install the engine mounting bolts. Torque the rear engine mounting to frame bolts or nuts to 45 ft. lbs., the front through-bolts to 70 ft. lbs. and the front nuts to 50 ft. lbs.

3. Install the bell housing to engine bolts and torque to 35 ft. lbs.
4. Remove the transmission support.
5. Install the converter to flex bolts and torque to 35 ft. lbs.
6. Install the fuel gauge wiring and starter.
7. Install the flywheel or torque converter cover.
8. Connect the strut rods at the engine mountings, if used.
9. Install the exhaust pipes at the manifold.
10. Lower the vehicle.
11. Connect the vacuum lines to the intake manifold.
12. Install the fuel line.
13. Connect the engine wiring harness.
14. Install the power steering pump, if used.
15. Connect the air conditioning compressor, if used.
16. Connect the accelerator, cruise control and detent linkage.
17. Connect the heater hoses.
18. Install the radiator and shroud.
19. Install the accessory drive belts.
20. Install the hood.
21. Install the proper quantity and grade of coolant and engine oil.
22. Connect the negative battery cable.

7.4L

▶ See Figures 13, 14, 15, 16, 17, 18, 19 and 20

1. Lower the engine and install the engine mounting bolts. Torque the rear engine mounting-to-frame bolts or nuts to 45 ft. lbs., the front through bolts to 70 ft. lbs. and the front nuts to 50 ft. lbs.

2. Install the bellhousing-to-engine bolts and torque to 35 ft. lbs.
3. Remove the engine lifting fixture and transmission jack.
4. Raise the vehicle and support it on jackstands.
5. Install the converter-to-flex plate bolts and torque them to 35 ft. lbs.
6. Install the fuel gauge wiring and starter.
7. Install the torque converter cover.
8. Install the starter.
9. Install the exhaust pipes at the manifold.
10. Lower the vehicle.
11. Install the power steering pump.
12. Install the air conditioning compressor.
13. Install all vacuum hoses.
14. Install the fuel supply line.
15. Connect the accelerator, cruise control and TVS linkage.
16. Connect the engine wiring.
17. Install the radiator and fan shroud.
18. Install the air cleaner.
19. Install the hood.
20. Connect the negative battery cable.
21. Install the proper quantity and grade of coolant.

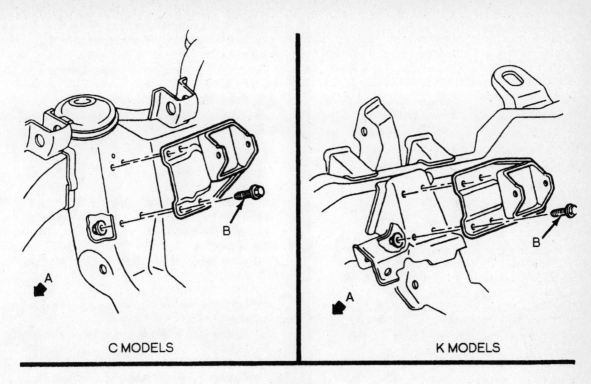

C MODELS

K MODELS

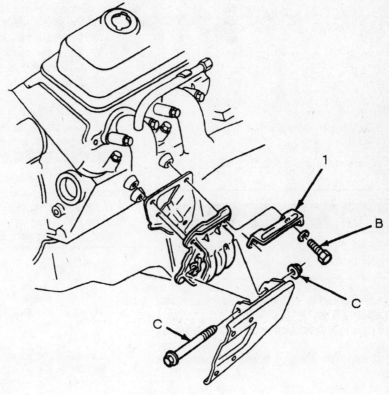

A. Forward
B. 60 Nm (45 ft. lbs.)
C. Torque bolt to 95 Nm (70 ft. lbs.) or. torque nut to 70 Nm (50 ft. lbs.)
1. Bracket (C15 models)

87948100

Fig. 1 Front engine mounts — 5.0, 5.7L engine, C/K series

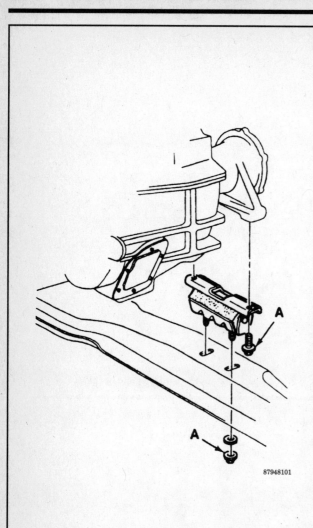

Fig. 2 Rear engine mounts — 5.0L/5.7L engines, K series

Full-Sized Vans

5.0L, 5.7L

1. Raise the engine slightly and install the engine mounts. Torque the bolts to 40 ft. lbs.
2. Install the manual transmission and clutch as follows:
  a. Install the clutch disc and the pressure plate. Tighten the clutch mounting bolts a little at a time to prevent distorting the disc.
  b. Install the starter and clutch housing rear cover.
  c. Install the bolts attaching the clutch housing to the engine and install the transmission and clutch as a unit. Torque the bolts to 40 ft. lbs.
  d. Install the clutch housing rear bolts.
3. Install the automatic transmission as follows:
  a. Position the transmission.
  b. Install the transmission-to-engine mounting bolts.
  c. Connect the throttle linkage and detent cable.

  d. Install the flywheel-to-converter attaching bolts. Torque the bolts to 40 ft. lbs.
  e. Install the starter and converter housing underpan.
4. Install the engine mount through bolts. Torque the bolts to 40 ft. lbs.
5. Install the engine mount bracket-to-frame bolts. Torque the bolts to 40 ft. lbs.
6. Install the clutch cross-shaft.
7. Install the transmission mounting bolts. Torque the bolts to 40 ft. lbs.
8. Connect the transmission shift linkage and the speedometer cable.
9. Install the driveshaft.
10. Install the condenser.
11. Install the hood latch support.
12. Install the lower fan shroud and filler panel.
13. Install the transmission dipstick tube and the accelerator cable at the tube.
14. Install the coolant hose at the intake manifold and the PCV valve.
15. Install the distributor cap.
16. Install the cruise control servo, servo bracket and transducer.
17. Install the oil filler pipe and the engine dipstick tube.
18. Install the thermostat housing.
19. Connect the heater hoses at the engine.
20. Connect the engine wiring harness from the firewall connection.
21. Install the radiator and the shroud.
22. Install the radiator support bracket.
23. Install the carburetor or TBI unit.
24. Connect the accelerator linkage.
25. Install the windshield wiper jar and bracket.
26. Install the air conditioning condenser.
27. Install the air conditioning vacuum reservoir.
28. Charge the air conditioning system.

❈❈CAUTION

Charging the air conditioning refrigerant should only be attempted by those who have the proper tools and training to do so, as serious personal injury may result. The refrigerant will instantly freeze any surface it comes in contact with, including your eyes.

29. If the van is equipped with an automatic transmission, install the fluid cooler lines at the radiator.
30. Install the radiator coolant reservoir bottle.
31. Connect the radiator hoses at the radiator.
32. Install the upper radiator support the grille and the lower grille valance.
33. Install the air cleaner.
34. Install the air stove pipe.
35. Install the engine cover.
36. Fill the cooling system.
37. Connect the battery cables.

7.4L

1. Install the automatic transmission as follows:
  a. Position the transmission.

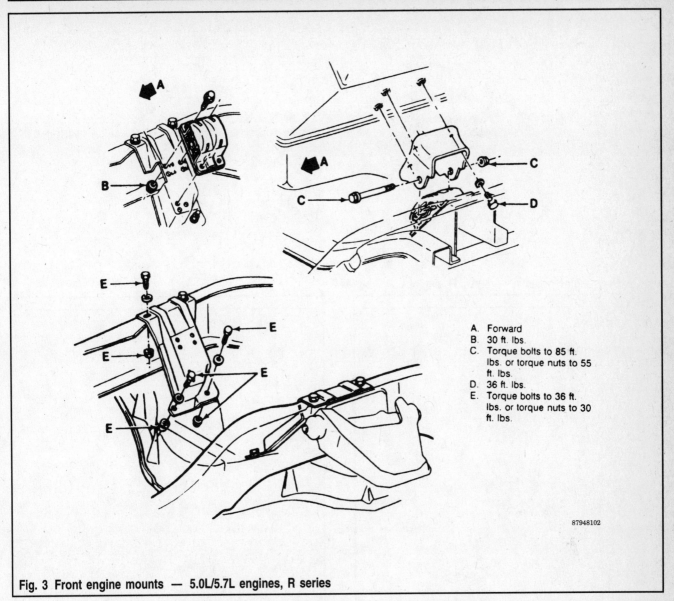

A. Forward
B. 30 ft. lbs.
C. Torque bolts to 85 ft. lbs. or torque nuts to 55 ft. lbs.
D. 36 ft. lbs.
E. Torque bolts to 36 ft. lbs. or torque nuts to 30 ft. lbs.

87948102

Fig. 3 Front engine mounts — 5.0L/5.7L engines, R series

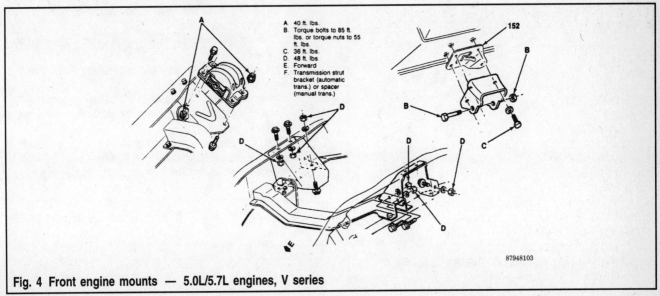

A. 40 ft. lbs.
B. Torque bolts to 85 ft. lbs. or torque nuts to 55 ft. lbs.
C. 36 ft. lbs.
D. 48 ft. lbs.
E. Forward
F. Transmission strut bracket (automatic trans.) or spacer (manual trans.)

87948103

Fig. 4 Front engine mounts — 5.0L/5.7L engines, V series

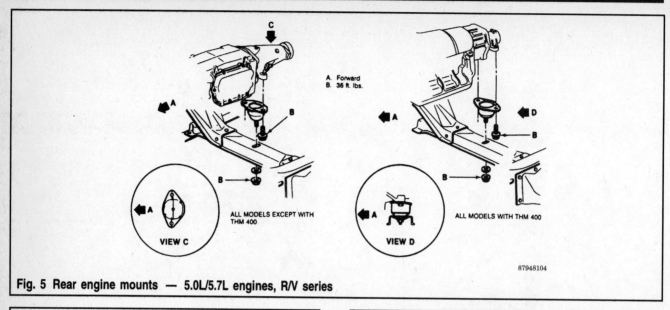

A. Forward
B. 36 ft. lbs.

ALL MODELS EXCEPT WITH THM 400

VIEW C

ALL MODELS WITH THM 400

VIEW D

87948104

Fig. 5 Rear engine mounts — 5.0L/5.7L engines, R/V series

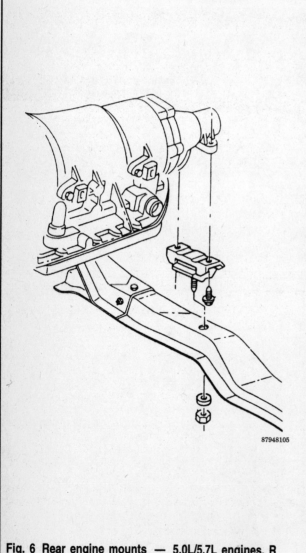

87948105

Fig. 6 Rear engine mounts — 5.0L/5.7L engines, R series

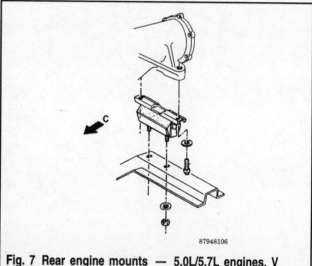

87948106

Fig. 7 Rear engine mounts — 5.0L/5.7L engines, V series

b. Install the transmission-to-engine mounting bolts. Torque the bolts to 40 ft. lbs.

c. Connect the throttle linkage detent cable on the Turbo Hydra-Matic.

d. Install the flywheel-to-converter attaching bolts. Torque the bolts to 40 ft. lbs.

e. Install the starter and converter housing underpan.

2. Raise the engine/transmission and guide the assembly into position in the van.

3. Raise the engine slightly and install the engine mounts. Torque the mount-to-block bolts to 36 ft. lbs.

4. Install the engine mount through bolts. Torque the bolts to 75 ft. lbs.

5. Install the engine mount bracket-to-frame bolts. Torque the front mount bolts to 30 ft. lbs.; the rear mount bolts to 40 ft. lbs.

6. Install the transmission mounting bolts. Torque the nuts to 36 ft. lbs.

7. Connect the transmission shift linkage and the speedometer cable.

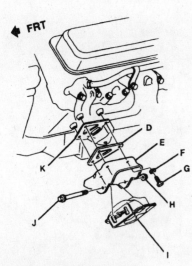

D. SPACER, ENGINE MOUNT BRACKET
E. BRACKET, ENGINE MOUNT
F. WASHER, ENGINE MOUNT BRACKET
G. BOLT, 51 N·m (38 Ft. Lbs.)
H. NUT, 68 N·m (50 Ft. Lbs.)
I. MOUNT, ENGINE
J. BOLT, 95 N·m (70 Ft. Lbs.)
K. BRACKET, TRANSMISSION STRUT

87948107

Fig. 8 Front engine mounts-to-brackets — 5.0L/5.7L engines, C/K series

8. Install the driveshaft.
9. Connect the exhaust pipes at the manifolds.
10. Install the oil filler pipe and the engine dipstick tube.
11. Install the windshield wiper jar and bracket.
12. Install the thermostat housing.
13. Connect the heater hoses at the engine.
14. Connect all vacuum hoses.
15. Connect the fuel supply and vapor lines.
16. Connect the distributor and coil wiring.
17. Connect the oil pressure sender.
18. Connect the temperature sensor wire.
19. Connect the alternator wires.
20. Connect the starter wires.
21. Connect the engine wiring harness at the firewall connection.
22. Install the TBI unit.
23. Connect the wiring, fuel lines and linkage at the TBI unit.
24. Install the air conditioning compressor.
25. Install the power steering pump.
26. Install the radiator and the shroud.

27. Install the radiator support bracket.
28. Install the radiator coolant reservoir bottle.
29. Install the fluid cooler lines at the radiator.
30. Connect the radiator hoses at the radiator.
31. Install the air conditioning condenser.
32. Install the air conditioning vacuum reservoir.
33. Charge the air conditioning system.

✳✳CAUTION

Charging the air conditioning refrigerant should only be attempted by those who have the proper tools and training to do so, as serious personal injury may result! The refrigerant will instantly freeze any surface it comes in contact with, including your eyes!

34. Install the upper radiator support.
35. Connect the radiator hoses at the radiator.
36. Install the grille and the lower grille valance.
37. Install the cruise control servo, servo bracket and transducer.
38. Fill the crankcase.
39. Install the air cleaner.
40. Install the engine cover.
41. Fill the cooling system.
42. Connect the battery cables.

Camaro through 1992

1. Position the engine assembly in the vehicle.
2. Attach the motor mount to engine brackets and lower the engine into place.
3. Remove the engine lifting device and the transmission jack.
4. Raise and safely support the vehicle.
5. Install the motor mount through bolts and tighten to 50 ft. lbs. (68 (Nm).
6. Install the bellhousing bolts and tighten to 35 ft. lbs. (47 Nm).
7. On vehicles with automatic transmission, install the converter to flywheel bolts. Tighten the bolts to 46 ft. lbs. (63 Nm). Install the flywheel cover.
8. Connect the starter wires and the fuel lines.
9. Connect the exhaust pipe at the exhaust manifold.
10. Lower the vehicle.
11. Connect the necessary wires and hoses.
12. Install the power steering pump and air conditioning compressor in their respective brackets.
13. Install the radiator, fan and fan shroud, radiator hoses and heater hoses.
14. Connect the transmission cooler lines and cooling fan electrical connectors.
15. Install the distributor.
16. Install the plenum extension, if equipped.
17. Fill the cooling system with the proper type and quantity of coolant and the crankcase with the proper type of oil to the correct level.
18. Install the air cleaner and the hood.
19. Connect the negative battery cable, start the engine, check for leaks and check timing.

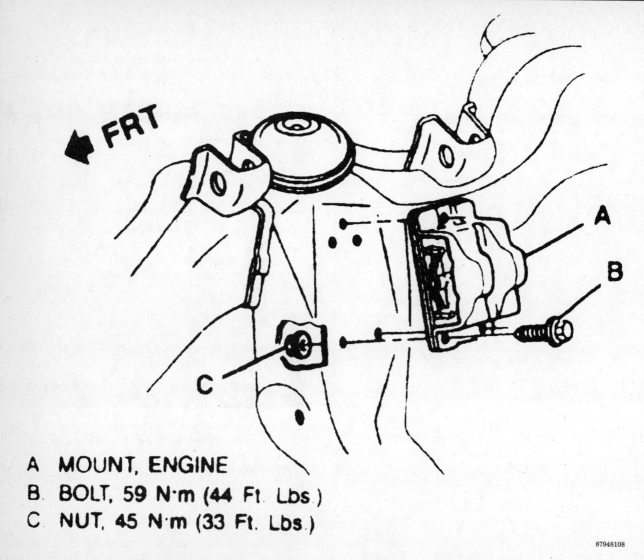

A MOUNT, ENGINE
B. BOLT, 59 N·m (44 Ft. Lbs.)
C. NUT, 45 N·m (33 Ft. Lbs.)

87948108

Fig. 9 Front engine mount brackets-to-frame — 5.0L/5.7L engines, C series

1993-96 Camaro

1. Position the engine assembly in the vehicle.
2. Attach the motor mount to engine brackets and lower the engine into place.
3. Remove the engine lifting device and the transmission jack.
4. Raise and safely support the vehicle.
5. Install the motor mount through bolts and tighten to 50 ft. lbs. (68 (Nm).
6. Install the bellhousing bolts and tighten to 35 ft. lbs. (47 Nm).
7. On vehicles with automatic transmission, install the converter to flywheel bolts. Tighten the bolts to 46 ft. lbs. (63 Nm). Install the flywheel cover.
8. Connect the starter wires and the fuel lines.
9. Connect the exhaust pipe at the exhaust manifold.
10. Lower the vehicle.
11. Connect the necessary wires and hoses.

12. Install the power steering pump and air conditioning compressor in their respective brackets.
13. Install the radiator, fan and fan shroud, radiator hoses and heater hoses.
14. Connect the transmission cooler lines and cooling fan electrical connectors.
15. Install the distributor.
16. Install the plenum extension, if equipped.
17. Fill the cooling system with the proper type and quantity of coolant and the crankcase with the proper type of oil to the correct level.
18. Install the air cleaner and the hood.
19. Connect the negative battery cable, start the engine, check for leaks and check timing.

1964-88 Mid-Sized Cars

1. Secure a vertical lifting device to the engine and install the engine to the vehicle.
2. Support the transmission.
3. Install the engine-to-transmission bolts.

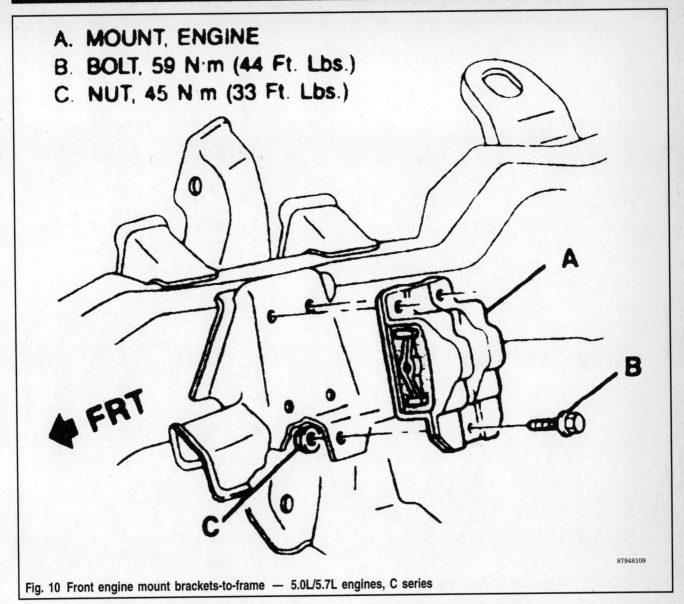

A. MOUNT, ENGINE
B. BOLT, 59 N·m (44 Ft. Lbs.)
C. NUT, 45 N·m (33 Ft. Lbs.)

FRT

87948109

Fig. 10 Front engine mount brackets-to-frame — 5.0L/5.7L engines, C series

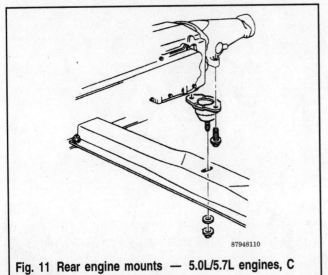

87948110

Fig. 11 Rear engine mounts — 5.0L/5.7L engines, C series

4. If equipped with an automatic transmission, connect the torque converter clutch wiring to the transmission. Connect the transmission oil cooler lines to the clip at the engine oil pan.

5. Connect the fuel line to the fuel pump.

6. Install the engine-to-mount bolts.

7. If equipped with an automatic transmission, install the torque converter bolts and the torque converter cover.

8. Install the crossover pipe and the catalytic converter as an assembly.

9. Lower the vehicle.

10. Connect the positive battery cable to the battery and, if applicable, to the frame straps. Connect the negative battery cable to the air conditioning hose/alternator bracket.

11. Install the distributor cap and, if equipped, the cruise control cable.

12. Engage the wiring harness and related engine wiring connectors.

13. Install the windshield washer bottle.

14. If equipped, install the AIR pipe to the converter.

15. Connect the vacuum hoses and the CCC wiring harness connector(s) to the engine.

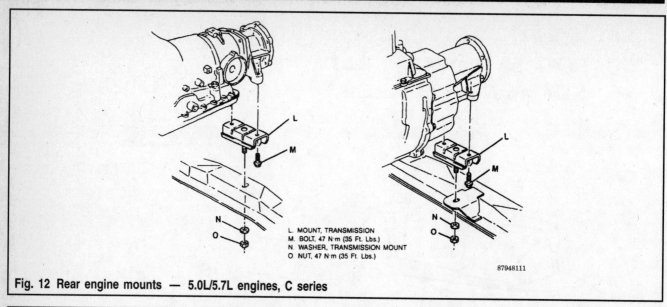

L. MOUNT, TRANSMISSION
M. BOLT, 47 N·m (35 Ft. Lbs.)
N. WASHER, TRANSMISSION MOUNT
O. NUT, 47 N·m (35 Ft. Lbs.)

87948111

Fig. 12 Rear engine mounts — 5.0L/5.7L engines, C series

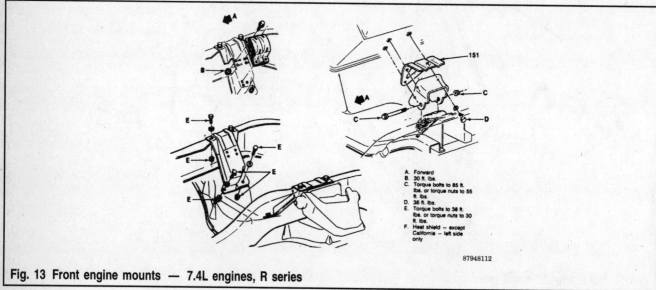

A. Forward
B. 30 ft. lbs.
C. Torque bolts to 85 ft. lbs. or torque nuts to 55 ft. lbs.
D. 36 ft. lbs.
E. Torque bolts to 36 ft. lbs. or torque nuts to 30 ft. lbs.
F. Heat shield — except California — left side only

87948112

Fig. 13 Front engine mounts — 7.4L engines, R series

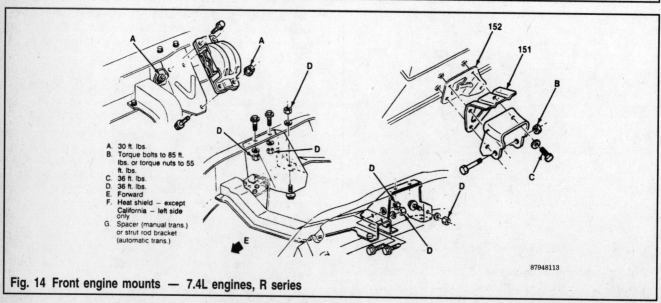

A. 30 ft. lbs.
B. Torque bolts to 85 ft. lbs. or torque nuts to 55 ft. lbs.
C. 36 ft. lbs.
D. 36 ft. lbs.
E. Forward
F. Heat shield — except California — left side only
G. Spacer (manual trans.) or strut rod bracket (automatic trans.)

87948113

Fig. 14 Front engine mounts — 7.4L engines, R series

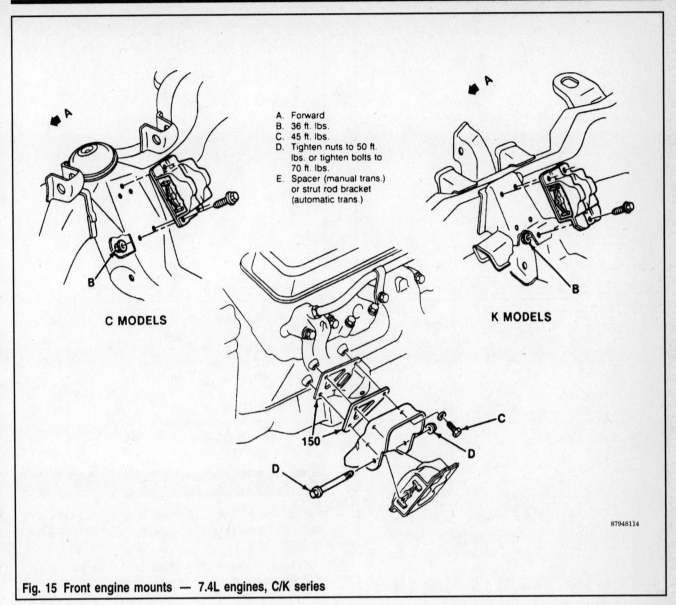

A. Forward
B. 36 ft. lbs.
C. 45 ft. lbs.
D. Tighten nuts to 50 ft. lbs. or tighten bolts to 70 ft. lbs.
E. Spacer (manual trans.) or strut rod bracket (automatic trans.)

C MODELS

K MODELS

150

87948114

Fig. 15 Front engine mounts — 7.4L engines, C/K series

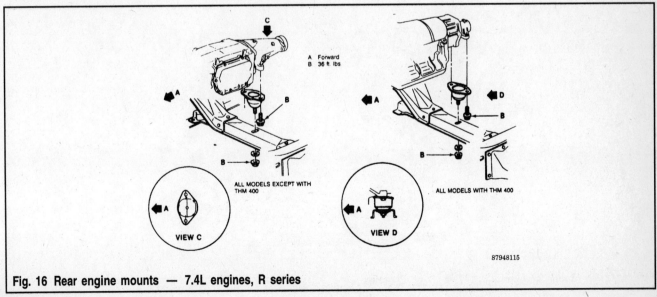

A Forward
B 36 ft lbs

ALL MODELS EXCEPT WITH THM 400

ALL MODELS WITH THM 400

VIEW C

VIEW D

87948115

Fig. 16 Rear engine mounts — 7.4L engines, R series

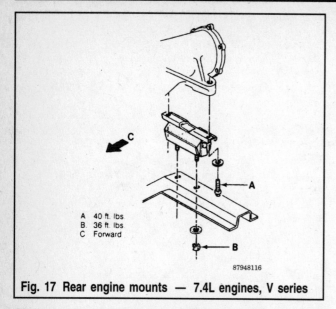

A. 40 ft. lbs
B. 36 ft. lbs
C. Forward

87948116

Fig. 17 Rear engine mounts — 7.4L engines, V series

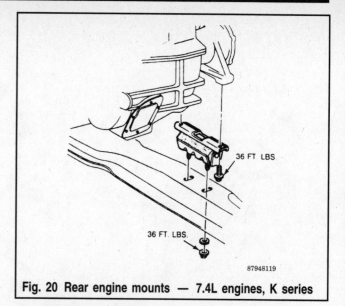

36 FT. LBS.

36 FT. LBS.

87948119

Fig. 20 Rear engine mounts — 7.4L engines, K series

16. Install the transmission oil cooler lines (if equipped) to the radiator and install the radiator.

17. Connect the accelerator and the T.V. cables.

18. As applicable, reposition and secure the compressor and/or the power steering pump.

19. Install the upper fan shroud and the fan assembly.

20. Install the heater hoses and the radiator hoses to the engine, then fill the cooling system.

21. Connect the negative battery cable.

22. Install the hood.

Full-Sized Cars through 1989

➡ **Make sure the torque converter bolts are aligned with the mounting holes on the flexplate, before attaching bell housing to engine.**

1. Secure a vertical lifting device to the engine and install the engine to the vehicle, then carefully install the engine-to-transmission bolts.

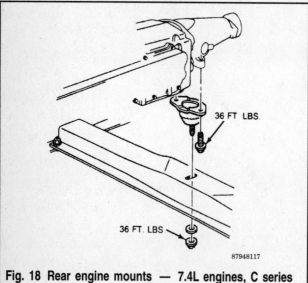

36 FT. LBS.

36 FT. LBS.

87948117

Fig. 18 Rear engine mounts — 7.4L engines, C series

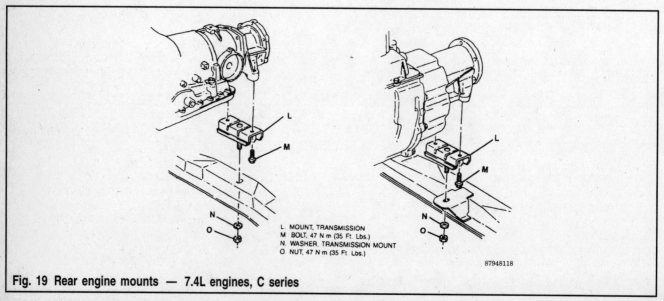

L

M

N

O

L. MOUNT, TRANSMISSION
M. BOLT, 47 N·m (35 Ft. Lbs.)
N. WASHER, TRANSMISSION MOUNT
O. NUT, 47 N·m (35 Ft. Lbs.)

L

M

N

O

87948118

Fig. 19 Rear engine mounts — 7.4L engines, C series

2. Connect the torque converter clutch wiring to the transmission and the transmission oil cooler lines to the clip at the engine oil pan.

3. Connect the fuel line to the fuel pump.

4. Install the engine-to-mount bolts.

5. Install the torque converter bolts and the torque converter cover.

6. Install the crossover pipe and the catalytic converter as an assembly.

7. Lower the vehicle.

8. Connect the positive battery cable to the battery and, if applicable, to the frame straps. Connect the negative battery cable to the air conditioning hose/alternator bracket.

9. Install the distributor cap and, if equipped, the cruise control cable.

10. Engage the wiring harness and related engine wiring connectors.

11. If removed, install the windshield washer bottle.

12. If equipped, install the AIR pipe to the converter.

13. Connect the vacuum hoses and the ECM wiring harness connector(s) to the engine.

14. Install the transmission oil cooler lines to the radiator and install the radiator.

15. Connect the accelerator and the T.V. cables.

16. As applicable, reposition and secure the compressor and/or the power steering pump.

17. Install the upper fan shroud and the fan assembly.

18. Install the heater hoses and the radiator hoses to the engine, then fill the cooling system.

19. Connect the negative battery cable.

20. Install the hood.

1990-93 Caprice

5.0L (VIN Y) ENGINE

1. With the engine safely supported, lower into position with the lifting device and align with the motor mounts and transmission.

2. Install motor mount through-bolts and the transmission to engine bolts. Tighten the transmission to engine bolts to 35 ft. lbs. (47 Nm).

3. Raise and support the vehicle safely.

4. Connect the catalytic converter AIR pipe to the exhaust manifold.

5. Connect the transmission converter clutch wiring to the transmission and the transmission oil cooler lines to the clip on the oil pan.

6. Connect the front fuel hoses to the front fuel pipes.

7. Install the torque converter to flywheel bolts and the flywheel housing cover.

8. Connect the crossover pipe to the exhaust manifolds.

9. Connect the battery positive cable and wires to the starter motor.

10. Lower vehicle.

11. Connect the battery ground to cylinder head cable.

12. Set the engine on TDC and install the distributor.

13. Connect the ECM wiring harness, the engine wiring harness at the engine bulkhead, engine to bulkhead ground straps and all other wires between body and engine.

14. Connect all necessary vacuum hoses.

15. Connect the accelerator, TV and cruise control cables.

16. Connect the power steering pump and air conditioning compressor brackets, if equipped.

17. Connect the heater hoses to the engine.

18. Install the engine cooling fan.

19. Install the radiator, hoses and fan shroud.

20. Install the air cleaner assembly.

21. Install the hood, aligning the marks made during removal.

22. Connect the negative battery cable.

23. Fill the cooling system to the proper level.

24. Inspect vehicle fluid levels, specifications and verify there are no fluid leaks.

5.0L (VIN E) AND 5.7L ENGINES

1. With the engine safely supported, lower into position with the lifting device and align with the motor mounts and transmission.

2. Install motor mount through-bolts and the transmission to engine bolts. Tighten the transmission to engine bolts to 35 ft. lbs. (47 Nm).

3. Raise and support the vehicle safely.

4. Connect the catalytic converter AIR pipe to the exhaust manifold.

5. Connect the transmission converter clutch wiring to the transmission and the transmission oil cooler lines to the clip on the oil pan.

6. Connect the front fuel hoses to the front fuel pipes.

7. Install the torque converter to flywheel bolts and the flywheel housing cover.

8. Connect the crossover pipe and catalytic converter assembly.

9. Connect the battery positive cable and wires to the starter motor.

10. Lower vehicle.

11. Install the wiper motor, MAP sensor and the negative battery to cylinder head cable.

12. Set the engine on TDC and install the distributor.

13. Connect the ECM wiring harness, the engine wiring harness at the engine bulkhead, engine to bulkhead ground straps and all other wires between body and engine.

14. Connect all necessary vacuum hoses.

15. Connect the accelerator, TV and cruise control cables.

16. Connect the power steering pump and air conditioning compressor brackets, if equipped.

17. Connect the heater hoses to the engine.

18. Install the engine cooling fan.

19. Install the radiator, hoses and fan shroud.

20. Install the air cleaner assembly.

21. Install the hood, aligning the marks made during removal.

22. Connect the negative battery cable.

23. Fill the cooling system to the proper level.

24. Inspect vehicle fluid levels, specifications and verify there are no fluid leaks.

Valve Lash Adjustment

SOLID LIFTERS

Engine Running

1. Set the parking brake and block the drive wheels, then start and run the engine until it reaches normal operating temperature.

2. Remove the valve covers retainers, then remove the covers and gaskets by tapping the end of the cover rearward to break the seal. Do not attempt to pry the cover off.

➡Until you are thoroughly familiar with the technique, it may take some time to adjust the valves. It is likely that while you are adjusting the valve, some oil will drip onto the exhaust manifold and smoke causing a highly unpleasant working condition. This may be avoided using an extra set of valve covers which can be purchased from a junk yard for only a few dollars. The tops may be cut off the extra covers and they may be temporarily installed on the cylinder heads. The walls of the these covers will keep oil from spilling on the manifolds, while the open tops will allow access to the rocker arm nuts for lash adjustment.

3. If possible, avoid being splashed with hot oil using oil deflector clips. Place one at each oil hole in the rocker arm.

4. Measure between the rocker arm and the valve stem with a flat feeler gauge, then adjust the rocker arm stud nut until clearance agrees with the specification in the chart. If you are using the modified valve covers for oil control, it may be necessary to make additional modifications in the covers to allow access with the feeler gauge.

5. After adjusting all the valves, stop the engine. If you are using the modified valve covers, remove them from the cylinder heads.

6. Clean the gasket surfaces, then install the valve covers using new gaskets.

BREAK-IN PROCEDURE

Start the engine, and allow it to run at low speed for a few minutes, while checking for leaks. Stop the engine, check the oil level, and fill as necessary. Restart the engine, and fill the cooling system to capacity. Check and adjust the ignition timing. Run the engine at low to medium speed (800-2,500 rpm) for approximately ½ hour, and retorque the cylinder head bolts. Road test the vehicle, and check again for leaks.

➡Some gasket manufacturers recommend not retorquing the cylinder head(s) due to the composition of the head gasket. Follow the directions in the gasket set.

TUNE-UP

Spark Plugs

INSTALLATION

1. Inspect the spark plugs and clean or replace, as necessary. Inspect the spark plug boot for tears or damage. If a damaged boot is found, the spark plug wire must be replaced.

2. Using a feeler gauge, check and adjust the spark plug gap to specification. When using a gauge, the proper size should pass between the electrodes with a slight drag. The next larger size should not be able to pass while the next smaller size should pass freely.

✳✳CAUTION

Do not use the spark plug socket to thread the plugs. Always thread the plug by hand to prevent the possibility of cross-threading and damaging the cylinder head bore.

3. Lubricate the spark plug threads with a drop of clean engine oil, then carefully start the spark plugs by hand and tighten a few turns until a socket is needed to continue tightening the spark plug. Do not apply the same amount of force you would use for a bolt; just snug them in. If a torque wrench is available, tighten the plugs to 11-15 ft. lbs. (15-20 Nm).

➡A spark plug threading tool may be made using the end of an old spark plug wire. Cut the wire a few inches from the top of the spark plug boot. The boot may be used to hold the plug while the wire is turned to thread it. Be-

cause the wire is so flexible, it may be turned to bend around difficult angles and, should the plug begin to crossthread, the resistance should be sufficient to bend the wire instead of forcing the plug into the cylinder head, preventing serious thread damage.

4. Apply a small amount of silicone dielectric compound to the end of the spark plug lead or inside the spark plug boot to prevent sticking, then install the boot to the spark plug and push until it clicks into place. The click may be felt or heard, then gently pull back on the boot to assure proper contact.

5. Connect the negative battery cable.

CHECKING AND REPLACING SPARK PLUG WIRES

▸ **See Figures 21 and 22**

Every 15,000 miles, visually inspect the spark plug wires for burns, cuts, or breaks in the insulation. Check the boots and the distributor cap tower connectors. Replace any damaged wiring.

Every 45,000 miles or so, the resistance of the wires should be checked using an ohmmeter. Wires with excessive resistance will cause misfiring and may make the engine difficult to start in damp weather. Generally, the useful life of the cables is 45,000-60,000 miles.

To check resistance, remove the distributor cap, leaving the wires in place. Connect one lead of an ohmmeter to an electrode within the cap; connect the other lead to the corresponding spark plug terminal (remove it from the spark plug for this test). Replace any wire which shows a resistance over 30,000Ω. Generally speaking, it is preferable that resistance be below 25,000Ω, but 30,000Ω must be considered the outer limit of acceptability. It should be remembered that resistance is also a function of length; the longer the wire, the greater the resistance. Thus, if the wires on your car are longer than the factory originals, resistance will be higher, quite possibly outside these limits.

➡**If all of the wires must be disconnected from the spark plugs or from the distributor at the same time, be sure to tag the wires to assure proper reconnection.**

When installing a new set of spark plug wires, replace the wires one at a time so there will be no mix-up. Start by replacing the longest cable first. Install the boot firmly over the spark plug. Route the wire exactly the same as the original. Connect the wire tower connector to the distributor. Repeat the process for each wire. Be sure to apply silicone dielectric compound to the spark plug wire boots and tower connectors prior to installation.

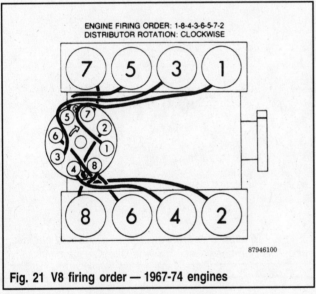

Fig. 21 V8 firing order — 1967-74 engines

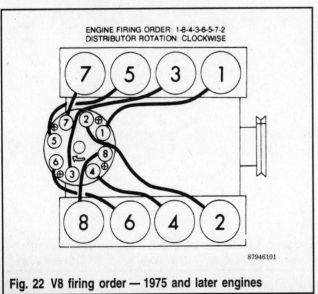

Fig. 22 V8 firing order — 1975 and later engines

Breaker Points and Condenser

➡**A point type ignition was originally installed on all 1964-73 engines covered in this manual. Most 1974 vehicles were also equipped with a point type distributor, though some may be found with the HEI system option. HEI ignition systems are often substituted in repairs or maintenance on these vehicles. If your distributor does not contain points**

The points function as a circuit breaker for the primary circuit of the ignition system. The ignition coil must boost the 12 volts supplied by the vehicle's charging system to as much as 25,000 volts in order to fire the plugs. To accomplish, the coil depends on the points and the condenser to make a clean break in the primary circuit.

The coil has both primary and secondary circuits. When the ignition is turned on, the battery supplies voltage through the coil and to the points. The points are connected to ground, completing the primary circuit. As the current passes through the coil, a magnetic field is created in the iron center core of the coil. When the cam on the distributor shaft turns, the points open, breaking the primary circuit. The magnetic field in the primary circuit of the coil then collapses and cuts through the secondary circuit windings around the iron core. Because of the physical principle called electromagnetic induction, the voltage is increased to a level sufficient to fire the spark plugs.

When the points open, the electrical charge in the primary circuit tries to jump the gap created between the two open contacts of the points. If this electrical charge were not transferred elsewhere, the metal contacts of the points would start to charge rapidly. The function of the condenser is to absorb excessive voltage from the points when they open and thus prevent the points from becoming pitted or burned.

If you have ever wondered why it is necessary to tune-up your engine occasionally, consider the fact that the ignition system must complete the above cycle each time a spark plug fires. On a 4-cylinder, 4-cycle engine, two of the four plugs must fire once for every engine revolution. If the idle speed of you engine is 800 revolutions per minute (800 rpm), the breaker points open and close two times for each revolution. For every minute your engine idles, your points open and close 1,600 times (2 x 800 = 1,600). And that is just at idle. Just think at the work your points are performing at 60 mph and you will begin to realize why periodic engine tuning is so important.

There breaker point gap may be checked in either of 2 ways: with a feeler gauge or with a dwell meter. In both cases setting the points means that you are adjusting the amount of time (in degrees of distributor rotation) that the points will remain open. If you adjust the points with a feeler gauge, you are setting the maximum amount that points will open when the point rubbing block is on a high point of the distributor cam. When you adjust the points with a dwell meter, you are measuring the number of degrees (of distributor cam rotation) that the points will remain closed before they start to open as a high point of the distributor cam approaches the rubbing block of the points.

If you would like a demonstration of how the points function mechanically, take a friend, go outside, and remove the distributor cap from your engine. Make sure the parking brake is set and that the transmission is not in gear, then have your friend operate the starter for a few seconds as you look at the exposed parts of the distributor. Be sure to keep yourself and your clothing away from any moving engine parts for safety reasons. You should see the points open and close as the distributor rotates.

There are two rules that should always be followed when adjusting or replacing points. The points and condenser are normally replaced as a set; when replacing the points, the condenser should also be replaced. If you change the point gap or dwell of the engine, you will affect the ignition timing. Therefore, if you adjust the points, you must also adjust the timing.

REMOVAL & INSTALLATION

▶ **See Figures 23, 24, 25, 26, 27, 28, 29, 30 and 31**

1964-74

The usual procedure is to replace the condenser each time the point set is replaced. Although this is not always necessary, it is easy to do at this time and the cost is negligible. Every time you adjust or replace the breaker points, the ignition timing must be checked and, if necessary, adjusted. No special equipment other than a feeler gauge is required for point replacement or adjustment, but a dwell meter is strongly advised. A magnetic screwdriver is handy to prevent the small points and condenser screws from falling down into the distributor.

Point sets using the push-in type wiring terminal should be used on those distributors equipped with an R.F.I. (Radio Frequency Interference) shield (1970-74). Points using a lock-screw-type terminal may short out when installed in these distributors due to contact between the shield and the screw.

1. Disconnect the negative battery cable. Loosen the distributor cap by either unscrewing the captive retaining screws or by pushing downward and turning on the spring loaded latch screws, as applicable. Remove the distributor cap from the assembly and position aside. You might have to unclip or detach some or all of the plug wires to remove the cap. If so, tag the wires and the cap before disconnecting the wires in order to ease installation.

2. Clean the distributor cap inside and out using a clean rag. Check for cracks and carbon paths. A carbon path shows up as a dark line, usually from one of the cap sockets or inside terminals to a ground. Check the condition of the contact button inside the center of the cap and the inside terminals. If wear, cracks or carbon paths are present, cap replacement is required.

3. Remove the two screws and lift the round V8 rotor from the distributor assembly. There is less danger of losing the screws if you just back them out all the way and lift them off using the rotor. Clean off the metal outer tip if it is burned or corroded, but DO NOT file it. Replace the rotor if it is necessary or if one was supplied with your tune-up kit.

4. Remove the radio frequency interference shield if your distributor has one. Watch out for those little screws! The factory says that the points don't need to be replaced if they are only slightly rough or pitted. However, sad experience shows that it is more economical and reliable in the long run to

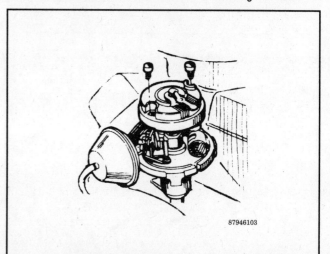

Fig. 24 To remove the rotor on most 8-cylinder engines the 2 rotor retaining screws must first be removed

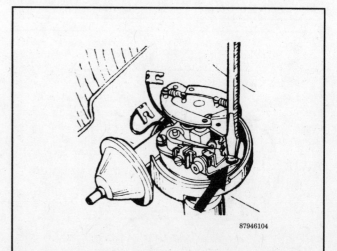

Fig. 25 The points are retained by screws. If possible, use a magnetic screwdriver when removing the screws

Fig. 23 Most 8-cylinder engines utilize a distributor cap which is retained using spring latches with screw-type heads

Fig. 26 The condenser is usually held in place with a screw and a clamp

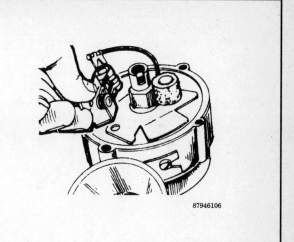

Fig. 27 Position the point set on the breaker plate, then attach the wiring

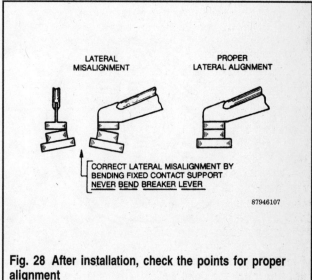

Fig. 28 After installation, check the points for proper alignment

replace the point set while the distributor is open, than to be forced to do this at a later (and possibly more inconvenient) time.

5. Pull one of the two wire terminals from the point assembly. One wire comes from the condenser and the other comes from within the distributor. The terminals are usually held in place by spring tension only. There might be a clamp screw securing the terminals on some older versions. There is also available a one-piece point/condenser assembly for V8s. The radio frequency interference shield isn't needed with this set. Loosen the point set hold-down screw(s). Be very careful not to drop any of these little screws inside the distributor. If this happens, the distributor will probably have to be removed to get at the screw. If the hold-down screw is lost elsewhere, it must be replaced with one that is no longer than the original to avoid interference with the distributor workings. Remove the point set, even if it is to be reused.

6. If the points are to be reused, clean them with a few strokes of a special point file. This is done with the points removed to prevent tiny metal filings from getting into and damaging the distributor. Don't use sandpaper or emery cloth as they are not fine enough and will usually cause rapid point burning.

7. Loosen the condenser hold-down screw and slide the condenser free of the clamp. This will save you a struggle with the clamp, condenser, and the tiny screw when you install the new one. If you have the type of clamp that is permanently fastened to the condenser, remove the screw and the condenser. Again, be careful not to lose the screw.

To install:

8. The distributor cam lubricator should either be switched or replaced at each tune-up. If your distributor is equipped with the round kind, turn it around on its shaft at the first tune-up and replace it at the second. If you have the long kind, switch ends at the first tune-up and replace it at the second.

➡**Don't oil or grease the lubricator. The component's foam is impregnated with a special lubricant.**

If your tune-up kit did not supply a lubricator, your distributor is not equipped with one, or it looks like someone removed the

lubricator, don't worry. Under these circumstances, just rub a match head size dab of grease on the cam lobes.

9. Install the new condenser. If you left the clamp in place, just slide the new condenser into the clamp.

10. Replace the point set and tighten the screw on all V8 engines that are equipped with a hex adjuster bolt. Connect the two wire terminals, making sure that the wires don't interfere with any moving components within the distributor assembly. Some V8 distributors have a ground wire that must go under one of the screws.

11. Check that the contacts meet squarely. If they don't, bend the tab supporting the fixed contact.

➡**If you are installing preset points on a V8, go ahead to Step 16. If they are preset, it will say so on the package. It would be a good idea to make a quick check on point gap, anyway. Sometimes those preset points aren't.**

12. Turn the engine until a high point on the cam which opens the points just contacts the rubbing block on the point arm. You can turn the engine by hand if you can get a wrench

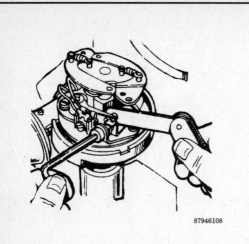

87946108

Fig. 29 You will need a hex wrench to adjust the point gap on most 8-cylinder engines

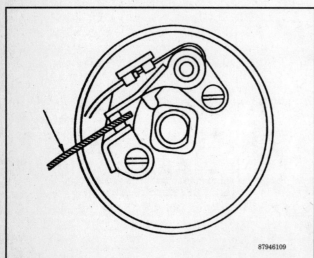

87946109

Fig. 30 The arrow indicates the feeler gauge which is used to check the point gap

on the crankshaft pulley nut, or you can grasp the fan belt and turn the engine by hand if the spark plugs are removed to relieve compression.

✳✳CAUTION

If you try turning the engine by hand, be very careful not to get your fingers pinched in the pulleys.

An alternative is to bump the starter switch or use a remote starter switch. Though using the starter is not a very accurate method and will usually require multiple attempts.

13. On a V8, simply insert a ⅛ in. hex wrench into the adjustment screw and turn. The wrench is sometimes supplied with a tune-up kit.

14. Insert the correct size feeler gauge and adjust the gap until you can push the gauge in and out between the contacts with a slight drag, but without disturbing the point arm. This operation takes a bit of experience to obtain the correct feel. Check by trying the gauges 0.001-0.002 in. larger and smaller than the setting size. The larger one should disturb the point arm, while the smaller one should not drag at all.

15. After all the point adjustments are complete, pull a white index card through (between) the contacts to remove any traces of oil. Oil left on the points will cause rapid contact burning.

16. Replace the radio frequency interference shield, if equipped. You don't need it if you are installing the one-piece point/condenser set. Push the rotor firmly down into place, taking care to make sure it is firmly seated. The rotor will only install one way, but if it is not installed properly it will probably break when the starter is operated. Tighten the rotor screws.

17. Install the distributor cap and connect the negative battery cable.

18. If a dwell meter is available, check the dwell.

1975 and Later

These engines use the breakerless High Energy Ignition (HEI) system. Since there is no mechanical contact, there is no wear or need for periodic service. There is an item in the

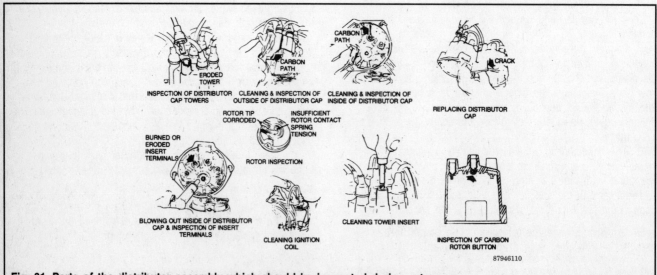

87946110

Fig. 31 Parts of the distributor assembly which should be inspected during a tune-up

distributor that resembles a condenser; it is a radio interference suppression capacitor which requires no service.

Dwell Angle

Dwell angle is the amount of time (measured in degrees of distributor cam rotation) that the contact points remain closed. Initial point gap determines dwell angle. If the points are set too wide they open gradually and dwell angle (the time they remain closed) is small. This wide gap causes excessive arcing at the points and as a result, point burning. A small dwell doesn't give the coil sufficient time to build up maximum energy and so coil output will also suffer. If the points are set too close, the dwell is increased but the points may bounce at higher speed, the idle becomes rough and starting is made harder.

Remember when adjusting the dwell angle that the wider the point opening, the smaller the dwell and the smaller the gap, the larger the dwell. Adjusting the dwell by making the initial point gap setting with a feeler gauge is usually sufficient to get the car started and running, but a finer adjustment should then be made using a dwell meter.

Connect the red lead (positive) wire of the meter to the distributor primary wire connection on the Positive (+) side of the coil, and the black ground (negative) wire of the meter to a good ground on the engine. The dwell angle may be checked either with the engine cranking or running, although the reading will be more accurate if the engine is running. With the engine cranking, the reading will fluctuate between 0° dwell and the maximum figure of that angle. While cranking, the maximum figure is the correct one.

➡Dwell angle is set electronically on HEI distributors, requiring no adjustment or checking.

ADJUSTMENT

1964-74

Dwell can be checked with the engine running or cranking. Decrease dwell by increasing the point gap; increase dwell by decreasing the gap. Dwell angle is simply the number of degrees of distributor shaft rotation during which the points stay closed. Theoretically, if the point gap is correct, the dwell should also be correct, or at least very close. Adjustment with a dwell meter produces more exact and consistent results since it is a dynamic adjustment. If dwell varies more than 3° from idle speed to 1,750 engine rpm, the distributor is worn.

1. An approximate dwell adjustment can be made without a meter on a V8 engine. Turn the adjusting screw clockwise until the engine begins to misfire, then turn the screw outward ½ of a turn.

2. If the engine won't start, check:
  a. That all the spark plug wires are in place.
  b. That the rotor has been installed.
  c. That the two (or three) wires inside the distributor are connected.
  d. That the points open and close when the engine turns.
  e. That the gap is correct and the hold-down screw, if applicable, is tight.

3. After the first 200 miles or so on a new set of points, the point gap often closes up due to initial rubbing block wear. For best performance, recheck the dwell (or gap) at this time. This quick initial wear is the reason the factory recommends 0.003 in. more gap on new points.

4. Since changing the gap affects the ignition timing, the timing should be checked and adjusted as necessary after each point replacement or adjustment.

1975 and Later

The dwell angle on models equipped with the HEI ignition is electronically set and is not adjustable.

High Energy Ignition (HEI) System

The General Motors/Delco-Remy High Energy Ignition (HEI) system is breakerless, pulse-triggered, transistor-controlled, inductive discharge ignition system. It was available as an option in 1974 and was standard all 1975 and later vehicles. The entire HEI system is contained within the distributor cap.

The distributor, in addition to housing the mechanical and vacuum advance mechanisms, contains the ignition coil, the electronic ignition module, and the magnetic pick-up assembly which contains a permanent magnet, a pole piece with internal teeth, and a pick-up coil (not to be confused with the ignition coil).

For 1981 and later an HEI distributor with Electronic Spark Timing is used. This system uses a one piece distributor cap, similar to 1980. All spark timing changes in the 1981 and later distributors are controlled electronically by the Electronic Control Module (ECM) which monitors information from various engine sensors, computes the desired spark timing and then signals the distributor to change the timing accordingly. No vacuum or mechanical advance systems are used whatsoever.

In the HEI system, as in other electronic ignition systems, the breaker points have been replaced with an electronic switch, a transistor, which is located within the ignition module. This switching transistor performs the same function the points did in a conventional ignition system; it simply turns coil primary current on and off at the correct time. Essentially then, electronic and conventional ignition systems operate on the same principle.

The module which houses the switching transistor is controlled (turned on and off) by a magnetically generated impulse induced in the pick-up coil. When the teeth of the rotating timer align with the teeth of the pole piece, the induced voltage in the pick-up coil signals the electronic module to open the coil primary circuit. The primary current then decreases and a high voltage is induced in the ignition coil secondary windings which is then directed through the rotor and high voltage leads (spark plug wires) to fire the spark plugs.

In essence then, the pick-up coil module system simply replaces the conventional breaker points and condenser. The condenser found within the distributor is for radio suppression purposes only and has nothing to do with the ignition process. The module automatically controls the dwell period, increasing it with increasing engine speed. Since dwell is automatically controlled, it cannot be adjusted. The module itself is non-adjustable and non-repairable and must be replaced if found defective.

HEI SYSTEM PRECAUTIONS

Before proceeding with troubleshooting or HEI system service, please note the following precautions:

Timing Light Use

Inductive pick-up timing lights are the best kind of use with the HEI system. Timing lights which connect between the spark plug and the spark plug wire occasionally (not always) give false readings.

Spark Plug Wires

The plug wires used with HEI systems are of a different construction than conventional wires. When replacing them, make sure you get the correct wires, since conventional wires won't carry the voltage. Also, handle them carefully to avoid cracking or splitting them and never pierce them.

Tachometer Use

Not all tachometers will operate or indicate correctly when used on a HEI system. While some tachometers may give a reading, this does not necessarily mean the reading is correct. In addition, some tachometers hook up differently from others. If you can't figure out whether or not your tachometer will work on your car, check with the tachometer manufacturer. Dwell readings, or course, have no significance at all.

Ignition Timing

Ignition timing is the measurement, in degrees of crankshaft rotation, of the point at which the spark plugs fire in each of the cylinders. It is measured in degrees before or after Top Dead Center (TDC) of the compression stroke.

Because it takes a fraction of a second for the spark plug to ignite the mixture in the cylinder, the spark plug must fire a little before the piston reaches TDC. Otherwise, the mixture will not be completely ignited as the piston passes TDC and the full power of the explosion will not be used by the engine.

The timing measurement is given in degrees of crankshaft rotation before the piston reaches TDC (BTDC). If the setting for the ignition timing is 5° BTDC, the spark plug must fire 5° before each piston reaches TDC. This only holds true, however, when the engine is at idle speed.

As the engine speed increases, the pistons go faster. The spark plugs have to ignite the fuel even sooner if it is to be completely ignited when the piston reaches TDC. To do this, most distributors have two means to advance the timing of the spark as the engine speed increases. This is accomplished by centrifugal weights within the distributor, and a vacuum diaphragm mounted on the side of the distributor. Later model vehicles may be equipped with Electronic Spark Timing (EST) in which no vacuum or mechanical advance is used. Instead, the EST system makes all timing changes electronically based on signals from various sensors.

If the ignition is set too far advanced (BTDC), the ignition and expansion of the fuel in the cylinder will occur too soon and tend to force the piston down while it is still traveling up. This causes engine ping. If the ignition spark is set too far retarded, after TDC (ATDC), the piston will have already passed TDC and started on its way down when the fuel is ignited. This will cause the piston to be forced down for only portion of its travel. This will result in poor engine performance and lack of power.

Timing marks consist of a notch on the rim of the crankshaft pulley and a scale of degrees attached to the front of the engine. The notch corresponds to the position of the piston in the number 1 cylinder. A stroboscopic (dynamic) timing light is used, which is hooked into the circuit of the No. 1 cylinder spark plug. Every time the spark plug fires, the timing light flashes. By aiming the timing light at the timing marks while the engine is running, the exact position of the piston within the cylinder can be read, since the stroboscopic flash makes the mark on the pulley appear to be standing still. Proper timing is indicated when the notch is aligned with the correct number on the scale.

There are three basic types of timing lights available. The first is a simple neon bulb with two wire connections (one for the spark plug and one for the plug wire, connecting the light in series). This type of light is quite dim, and must be held closely to the marks to be seen, but it is quite inexpensive. The second type of light operated from the car's battery. Two alligator clips connect to the battery terminals, while a third wire connects to the spark plug with an adapter. This type of light is more expensive, but the xenon bulb provides a nice bright flash which can even be seen in sunlight. The third type replaces the battery source with 110 volt house current, but still attaches to the No. 1 spark plug wire in order to determine when the plug is fired. Some timing lights have other functions built into them, such as dwell meters, tachometers, or remote starting switches. These are convenient, in that they reduce the tangle of wires under the hood, but may duplicate the functions of tools you already have.

➡ **Never pierce a spark plug wire in order to attach a timing light or perform tests. The pierced insulation will eventually lead to an electrical arc and related ignition troubles.**

If your car has electronic ignition, you should use a timing light with an inductive pickup. This pickup simply clamps onto the No. 1 spark plug wire, eliminating the adapter. It is not susceptible to cross-firing or false triggering, which may occur with a conventional light, due to the greater voltages produced by electronic ignition.

CHECKING AND ADJUSTMENT

The vehicle emission label, which is found underhood, will often contain specifications or procedures for checking and adjusting timing that have been updated during production. The information contained on the label should always be used if it differs from these instructions.

The tachometer hookup for cars 1964-74 is the same as that for the dwell meter. On 1975-77 HEI systems, the tachometer connects to the TACH terminal on the distributor and to a ground. For 1978 and later models, all tachometer connections are to the TACH terminal. Some tachometers must connect to the TACH terminal and to the positive battery terminal. Some tachometers won't work at all with HEI. Consult the tachometer manufacturer if the instructions supplied with the unit do not give the proper connection.

1. Set the parking brake and block the drive wheels, warm the engine to normal operating temperature. Shut off the engine and connect the timing light to the No. 1 spark plug (left front). Do not, under any circumstances, pierce a wire to hook up a light.

2. Clean off the timing marks, then label the pulley or damper notch and the timing scale with while chalk or paint for better visibility. If the timing notch on the damper or pulley is not visible from the top, the crankshaft should be bumped around using the starter or turned using a wrench on the front pulley bolt, in order to bring the mark to an accessible position.

3. Disconnect and plug the vacuum advance hose (if equipped) at the distributor, to prevent any distributor advance. The vacuum line is the rubber hose connected to the metal cone-shaped canister on the side of the distributor. A short screw, pencil, or a golf tee can be used to plug the hose.

➡1981 models with Electronic Spark Timing have no vacuum advance, therefore you may skip the previous step, but you must disconnect the four terminal EST connector in order to disable the electronic spark advance before proceeding.

4. Start the engine and adjust the idle speed to specification, refer to the Tune-Up Specifications chart. Some cars require that the timing be set with the transmission in Neutral. You can disconnect the idle solenoid, if any, to get the speed down. Otherwise, adjust the idle speed screw. This is to prevent any centrifugal advance of timing in the distributor.

❄❄WARNING

Never ground the HEI TACH terminal; serious system damage will result, including ignition module burnout.

5. Aim the timing light at the timing marks. Be careful not to touch the fan, which may appear to be standing still. Keep your clothes and hair, and the light's wires clear of the fan, belts and pulleys. If the pulley or damper notch isn't aligned with the proper timing mark (see the Tune-Up Specifications chart), the timing will have to be adjusted.

➡TDC or Top Dead Center corresponds to 0° mark on the scale. Either B, BTDC, or Before Top Dead Center, may be shown as BEFORE on the scale, while A, ATDC or After Top Dead Center, may be shown as AFTER.

6. Loosen the distributor base clamp locknut. You can buy special wrenches which make this task a lot easier. Turn the distributor slowly to adjust the timing, holding it by the body and not the cap. Turn the distributor in the direction of rotor rotation to retard, and against the direction to advance.

7. Once the timing is properly set, hold the distributor to keep it from the turning and tighten the locknut. Check the timing again after finishing with the nut in case the distributor moved as you tightened it.

8. If applicable, remove the plug and connect the distributor vacuum hose.

9. If necessary check and/or adjust the idle speed.

10. Shut off the engine and reconnect the EST wire (if equipped), then disconnect the timing light and tachometer.

Valve Lash

▸ **See Figures 32 and 33**

ADJUSTMENT

Hydraulic valve lifters which are found in most late-model engines rarely require adjustment, and are not adjusted as part of a normal tune-up. Hydraulic valve lifters must be adjusted whenever the rocker arms have been loosened. Proper adjustment will center the pushrods on the lifters and allow the lifters to perform their job of maintaining zero lash.

Solid Lifters (1964-71)

Before adjusting solid lifters, thoroughly warm the engine. The solid lifters are generally found on older vehicles and on certain high-performance engines.

ENGINE RUNNING

1. Set the parking brake and block the drive wheels, then start and run the engine until it reaches normal operating temperature.

2. Remove the valve covers retainers, then remove the covers and gaskets by tapping the end of the cover rearward to break the seal. Do not attempt to pry the cover off.

➡**Until you are thoroughly familiar with the technique, it may take some time to adjust the valves. It is likely that while you are adjusting the valve, some oil will drip onto the exhaust manifold and smoke causing a highly unpleasant working condition. This may be avoided using an extra set of valve covers which can be purchased from a junk yard for only a few dollars. The tops may be cut off the extra covers and they may be temporarily installed on the cylinder heads. The walls of the these covers will keep oil from spilling on the manifolds, while the open tops will allow access to the rocker arm nuts for lash adjustment.**

3. If possible, avoid being splashed with hot oil using oil deflector clips. Place one at each oil hole in the rocker arm.

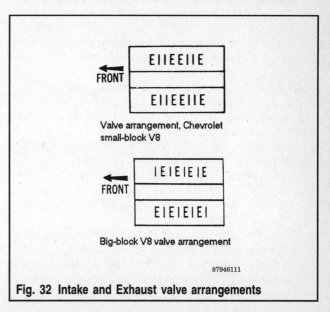

Valve arrangement, Chevrolet small-block V8

Big-block V8 valve arrangement

87946111

Fig. 32 Intake and Exhaust valve arrangements

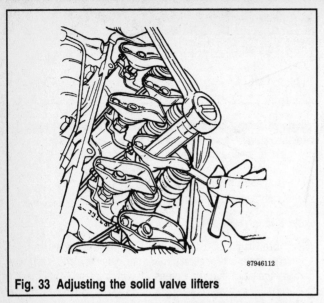

87946112

Fig. 33 Adjusting the solid valve lifters

4. Measure between the rocker arm and the valve stem with a flat feeler gauge, then adjust the rocker arm stud nut until clearance agrees with the specification in the chart. If you are using the modified valve covers for oil control, it may be necessary to make additional modifications in the covers to allow access with the feeler gauge.

5. After adjusting all the valves, stop the engine. If you are using the modified valve covers, remove them from the cylinder heads.

6. Clean the gasket surfaces, then install the valve covers using new gaskets.

ENGINE NOT RUNNING

These are initial adjustments usually required after assembling an engine or performing a valve job. They should be followed up by an adjustment with the engine running as described above.

1. Set the engine to the No. 1 firing position (No. 1 TDC). This can be accomplished by removing the No. 1 spark plug and feeling for compression and the engine is slowly turned or by removing the valve cover and watching the valves for the No. 1 cylinder as the engine is turned. If the valves move while the timing notch approaches the 0 mark on the timing scale, then the engine crankshaft is 360 degrees away from No. 1 TDC. If the valves do not move while the notch approaches the 0 mark, then the No. 1 cylinder is at TDC.

2. Adjust the clearance between the valve stems and the rocker arms using a feeler gauge. Check the chart for the proper clearance. Adjust the following valves in the No. 1 firing position: Intake No. 2, 7, Exhaust No. 4, 8.

3. Turn the crankshaft ½ revolution clockwise. Adjust the following valves: Intake no. 1,8, Exhaust No. 3, 6.

4. Turn the crankshaft ½ revolution clockwise to the top of the No. 1 piston's exhaust stroke (this is TDC for No. 6 cylinder on V8 engines). Adjust the following valves in this position: Intake No. 3, 4, Exhaust No. 5, 7.

5. Turn the crankshaft ½ revolution clockwise. Adjust the following valves: Intake No. 5, 6, Exhaust No. 1, 2.

6. Run the engine until the normal operating temperature is reached. Reset all clearances, using the procedures listed above under Engine Running.

Hydraulic Lifters — 1972 AND LATER

All models, with the exception of those few already discussed, use a hydraulic tappet system with adjustable rocker mounting nuts to obtain zero lash. No periodic adjustment is necessary.

Carburetor

Idle mixture and speed adjustments are critical aspects of exhaust emission control. It is important that all tune-up instructions be carefully followed to ensure satisfactory engine performance and minimum exhaust pollution. The different combinations of emission system applications on the various engines have resulted in a great variety of tune-up specifications. Beginning in 1968, all models should have a decal conspicuously placed in the engine compartment that gives tune-up specifications. Because this label will often contain changes to specification made during production, it's information should always supersede that on the specification chart.

When adjusting a carburetor with two idle mixture screws, adjust them alternately and evenly, unless otherwise stated.

ADJUSTING THE IDLE SPEED AND MIXTURE

In the following adjustment procedures the term lean roll means turning the mixture adjusting screws in (clockwise) from optimum setting to obtain an obvious drop in engine speed (usually 20 rpm).

1964-66

Turn the idle screw(s) slightly in to seat, and then back out 1½ turns (3 when equipped with A.I.R.). Do not turn the idle mixture screws tightly against their seats or you could damage the screws. With the engine idling at operating temperature (air cleaner installed, preheater valve and choke valve wide open), adjust the idle speed to specification (automatic transmission in Drive; manual in Neutral).

Adjust the mixture screw to obtain the highest steady idle speed, then adjust the idle speed screw to the specified rpm. Adjust the mixture screw in to obtain a 20 rpm drop, then back the screw out ¼ turn. Repeat this operation on the second mixture, if so equipped. Readjust the idle speed screw as necessary until the specified rpm is reached.

1967 Without Air

Adjust with the air cleaner removed.

1. Remove the air cleaner.

2. Connect a tachometer and vacuum gauge to the engine, set the parking brake, and place the transmission in Neutral.

3. Turn in the idle mixture screws until they gently seat, then back out 1½ turns.

4. Start the engine and allow it to come to the normal operating temperature. Make sure the choke is fully open, then adjust the idle speed screw to obtain the specified idle speed (automatic in Drive, manual in Neutral).

5. Adjust the idle mixture screw(s) to obtain the highest steady vacuum at the specified idle speed, except for the Rochester BV. For this carburetor, adjust the idle mixture

screw out ¼ turn from lean drop-off (the point where a 20-30 rpm drop is achieved by leaning the mixture).

➡**On carburetors having a hot idle compensator valve (A/C models), hold the brass valve down with a pencil while making the mixture adjustment.**

6. Repeat Steps four and five as necessary.
7. Turn off the engine, remove the gauges, and install the air cleaner.

1967 With Air

Adjust with the air cleaner removed.

➡**During this adjustment, air conditioning should be turned off on 327 and 350 cu. in. engines.**

1. Remove the air cleaner.
2. Connect a tachometer and a vacuum gauge to the engine, set the parking brake, and place the transmission in Neutral.
3. Turn in the idle mixture screw(s) until they gently seat, then back them out three turns.
4. Start the engine and allow it to reach normal operating temperature. Make sure the choke is fully open, then adjust the idle speed screw(s) to obtain the specified idle speed (automatic in Drive, manual in Neutral).
5. Turn the idle mixture screw(s) clockwise (in) to the point where a 20-30 rpm drop in the speed is achieved; this is the lean drop off point. Back out the screws ¼ turn from this point.
6. Repeat Steps four and five if necessary.
7. Turn off the engine, remove the gauges, and install the air cleaner.

1968-69

Adjust with the air cleaner installed.

➡**Turn off the air conditioner.**

1. Turn in the idle mixture screws until they seat gently, then back them out three turns.
2. Start the engine and allow it to reach operating temperature. Make sure the choke is fully open and the preheater valve is open, then adjust the idle speed screw to obtain the specified idle speed (automatic in Drive, manual in Neutral).
3. Adjust the idle mixture screw(s) to obtain the highest steady idle speed, then readjust the idle speed screw to obtain the specified speed. On cars with an idle stop solenoid adjust as follows:
   a. Adjust the idle speed to 600 rpm by turning the hex on the solenoid plunger.
   b. Disconnect the wire at the solenoid. This allows the throttle lever to seat against the idle screw.
   c. Adjust the idle screw to obtain 400 rpm.
4. Adjust one mixture screw to obtain a 20 rpm drop in idle speed, and back out the screw ¼ turn from this point.
5. Repeat Steps three and four for the second mixture screw (if so equipped).
6. Readjust the idle speed to obtain the specified idle speed.

1970 Initial Adjustments

Adjust with the air cleaner installed.

1. Disconnect the fuel tank line from the vapor canister (EEC).
2. Connect a tachometer to the engine, start the engine and allow it to reach operating temperature. Make sure the choke and preheater valves are fully open.
3. Turn off the air conditioner and set the parking brake. Disconnect and plug the distributor vacuum line.
4. Make the following adjustments:

V8-307 & 400 ENGINES

1. Turn in the mixture screws until they seat gently, then back them out four turns.
2. Adjust the carburetor idle speed screw to obtain 800 rpm for manual transmissions (in Neutral), or adjust the solenoid screw to obtain 630 rpm for automatic transmissions (in Drive).
3. Adjust both mixture screws equally inward to obtain 700 rpm for manual transmissions, 600 rpm for automatic transmissions (in Drive).
4. On cars with automatic transmissions, disconnect the solenoid wire, set the carburetor idle screw to obtain 450 rpm and reconnect the solenoid.
5. Reconnect the distributor vacuum line.

V8-350 (250 HP) ENGINE

1. Turn in the mixture screws until they gently seat, then back them out four turns.
2. Adjust the solenoid screw to obtain 830 rpm for manual transmissions (in Neutral), or 630 rpm for automatic transmissions (in Drive).
3. Adjust both mixture screw equally inward to obtain 750 rpm for manual transmissions or 600 rpm for automatics (in Drive).
4. Disconnect the solenoid wire, set the carburetor idle screw to obtain 450 rpm, and reconnect the solenoid.
5. Reconnect the distributor vacuum line.

V8-350 (300 HP) & 402 (330 HP) ENGINES

1. Turn in both mixture screws until they gently seat, then back them out four turns.
2. Adjust the carburetor idle screw to obtain 775 rpm for manual transmission, 630 rpm for automatics (in Drive).
3. Adjust the mixture screw equally to obtain 700 rpm for manual transmission, 600 rpm for automatics (in Drive).
4. Reconnect the distributor vacuum line.

V8-402 (350 HP) & 454 ENGINES

1. Turn in both mixture screws until they gently seat, then back them out four turns.
2. Adjust the carburetor idle screw to obtain 700 rpm for manual transmission or 630 rpm for automatics (in Drive).
3. For cars with automatic transmission: adjust the mixture screws equally to obtain 600 rpm with the transmission in Drive.
4. For cars with manual transmissions: Turn in one mixture screw until the speed drops to 400 rpm, then adjust the carburetor idle screw to obtain 700 rpm. Turn in the other mixture screw until the speed drops 400 rpm, then regain 700 rpm by adjusting the carburetor idle screw.
5. Reconnect the distributor vacuum line.

1971-72 Initial Adjustments

Adjust with air cleaner installed. The following initial idle adjustments are part of the normal engine tune-up. There should be a tune-up decal placed conspicuously in the engine compartment outlining the specific procedure and settings for each engine application. Follow all of the instructions when adjusting the idle. These tuning procedures are necessary to obtain the delicate balance of variables for the maintenance of both reliable engine performance and efficient exhaust emission control.

➡ **All engines have limiter caps on the mixture adjusting screws. The idle mixture is preset and the limiter caps installed at the factory in order to meet emission control standards. Do not remove these limiter caps unless all other possible causes of poor idle condition have been thoroughly checked out. The solenoid used on 1971 carburetors is different from the one used on earlier models. The Combination Emission Control System (C.E.C.) solenoid valve regulates distributor vacuum as a function of transmission gear position. The C.E.C solenoid is adjusted only after: 1) replacement of the solenoid, 2) major carburetor overhaul, or 3) after the throttle body is removed or replaced.**

All initial adjustments described below are made:
1. With the engine warmed up and running.
2. With the choke fully open.
3. With the fuel tank line disconnected from the Evaporative Emission canister on all models.
4. With the vacuum hose disconnected at the distributor and plugged.

Be sure to reconnect the distributor vacuum hose and to connect the fuel tank-to-evaporative emission canister line or install the gas cap when idle adjustments are complete.

V8-307 & 350 (2-BBL) ENGINES

1. On 1971 models, adjust the carburetor idle speed screw to obtain 600 rpm for manual transmission (in Neutral) with the air conditioning turned off, or 550 rpm for automatic transmissions (in Drive) with the air conditioning turned on. Do not adjust the solenoid screw. On 1972 models, turn the air conditioning off and adjust the idle stop solenoid screw to obtain 900 rpm for manual transmissions (in Neutral) or 600 rpm for automatics (in Drive). Place the transmission in Park or Neutral and adjust the fast idle cam screw to get 1,850 rpm on 307 engines and 2,200 rpm on 350 engines.
2. Reconnect the vapor line and distributor vacuum advance line.

V8-350 (4-BBL) ENGINE

1. On 1971 models, adjust the carburetor idle speed screw to obtain 600 rpm for manual transmissions (in Neutral) with the air conditioning turned off, or 550 rpm for automatics (in Drive) with the air conditioning turned on. Do not adjust the solenoid screw. On 1972 models, turn the air conditioning off and adjust the idle stop solenoid screw to get 800 rpm for manual transmissions (in Neutral) or 600 rpm for automatic transmissions (in Drive).
2. For both 1971 and 1972 models, place the fast idle cam follower on the second step of the fast idle cam, turn the air conditioning off and adjust the fast idle to 1,350 rpm for manual transmissions (in Neutral) or 1,500 rpm for automatics (in Park).
3. Reconnect the vapor line and the distributor vacuum advance line on all models.

V8-402 & 454 ENGINES

1. On 1971 models, turn off the air conditioner and adjust the carburetor idle speed screw to obtain 600 rpm with manual transmissions in Neutral and automatics in Drive. Do not adjust the solenoid screw. On 1972 cars, turn off the air conditioning and adjust the idle stop solenoid screw to 800 rpm (in Neutral) for manual transmissions and 600 rpm (in Drive) for automatics.
2. On both 1971 and 1972 cars, place the fast idle cam follower on the second stop of the fast idle cam, turn off the air conditioner and adjust the fast idle to 1,350 rpm for manual transmissions (in Neutral) or 1,500 rpm for automatics (in Park).
3. Reconnect the vapor line and the distributor vacuum line on 1971 and 1972 cars.

1973

INITIAL ADJUSTMENTS

All models are equipped with idle limiter caps and idle solenoids. Disconnect the fuel tank line from the evaporative canister. The engine must be running at operating temperature, choke off, parking brake on, and rear wheels blocked. Disconnect the distributor vacuum hose and plug it. After adjustment, reconnect the vacuum and evaporative hoses.

V8-307, 350 & 400 (2-BBL) ENGINES

1. With the air conditioning Off, adjust the idle stop solenoid screw for a speed of 900 rpm on manual models; 600 rpm for automatics in Drive.
2. Disconnect the idle stop solenoid electrical connector and adjust the idle speed screw (screw resting on lower stop of the cam) for 450 rpm on all 307 cu. in. engines, 400 rpm on 350 and 400 engines with automatic transmissions, or 500 rpm or 350 and 400 cu. in engine with manual transmissions.

V8-350 & 400 (4-BBL) ENGINES

1. Adjust the idle stop solenoid screw to 900 rpm (manual), 600 rpm (automatic in Drive).
2. Connect the distributor vacuum hose and position the fast idle cam follower on the top step of the fast idle cam (turn air conditioning off) and adjust the fast idle to 1,300 rpm on manual transmission 350 engines; 1,600 rpm for all automatics in Park.

V8-454 ENGINE

1. With the air conditioning off, adjust the idle stop solenoid screw to 900 rpm for the manual transmission; 700 rpm with the automatic transmission in Drive.
2. Connect the distributor vacuum hose and place fast idle cam follower on the top step of the fast idle cam. Adjust the fast idle to 1,300 rpm for manual transmission; and 1,600 rpm for automatic transmissions (in Park).

1974

INITIAL ADJUSTMENTS

All models are equipped with idle limiter caps and idle sole-noids. Disconnect the fuel tank line from the evaporative canis-ter. The engine must be running at operating temperature, choke off, parking brake on, and rear wheels blocked. Discon-nect the distributor vacuum hose and plug it. After adjustment, reconnect the vacuum and evaporative hoses.

V8-350 & 400 (2-BBL) ENGINES

1. Turn the air conditioning off. Adjust the idle stop sole-noid screw for 900 rpm on manual; 600 rpm on automatic (in Drive).
2. De-energize the solenoid and adjust the carburetor idle cam screw (on low step of cam) for 400 rpm on automatic models (in Drive); 500 rpm on 350 engines with manual transmission.

V8-350 & 400 (4-BBL) ENGINES

1. Turn the air conditioning off. Adjust the idle stop sole-noid screw for 900 rpm on manual transmission models; 600 rpm on automatic (in Drive).
2. Connect the distributor vacuum hose. Position the fast idle cam follower on the top step of the fast idle cam and adjust the fast idle speed to 1,300 rpm on manual; 1,600 on automatic (in Park).

V8-454 ENGINE

1. With the air conditioning off, adjust the idle stop solenoid screw for 800 rpm with the manual transmission; 600 with the automatic transmission in Drive.
2. Reconnect the distributor vacuum advance hose and place the fast idle cam follower on the top step of the fast idle cam. With the air conditioning off, adjust the fast idle to 1,600 rpm for manual transmissions; 1,500 rpm for all automatics in Park.

1975-76

V8-350 (2-BBL) ENGINE

1. Idle speed is adjusted with the engine at normal operat-ing temperature, air cleaner on, choke open, and air condition-ing off. Hook up a tachometer to the engine.
2. Block the rear wheels and apply the parking brake.
3. Disconnect the fuel tank hose from the evaporative canister.
4. Disconnect and plug the distributor vacuum advance hose.
5. Start the engine and check the ignition timing. Adjust if necessary, then reconnect the vacuum hose.
6. Adjust the idle speed screw to the specified rpm. If the figures given in the Tune-Up Specifications chart differ from those on the tune-up decal, those on the decal take prece-dence. Automatic transmissions should be in Drive, manual transmissions should be in Neutral.

✳✳CAUTION

Make doubly sure that the rear wheels are blocked and that the parking brake is applied.

7. Adjust the idle speed to the higher of the two figures on the tune-up decal. Back out the two mixture screws equally until the highest idle is reached. Reset the speed if necessary to the higher one on the tune-up decal. Next, turn the screws in equally until the lower of the two figures on the decal is obtained.
8. Shut off the engine, reconnect hose to evaporative can-ister, and remove blocks from wheels.

V8-350, 400 & 454 ENGINES

1975 4-barrel carburetors are equipped with idle stop sole-noids. There are two idle speeds, one with the solenoid ener-gized and second with the solenoid de-energized. Both are set using the solenoid. The slower speed (solenoid de-energized) is necessary to prevent dieseling by allowing the throttle plate to close further than at a normal idle speed.

1. Idle speed is set with the engine at normal operating temperature, air cleaner on, choke open, and air conditioning off. Hook up a tachometer to the engine.
2. Block the rear wheels and apply the parking brake.
3. Disconnect the fuel tank hose from the evaporative canister.
4. Disconnect and plug the distributor vacuum advance hose.
5. Start the engine and check the ignition timing. Adjust if necessary, then reconnect the vacuum hose.

➡**For 1976, the idle solenoid has been dropped. To adjust the idle, follow Steps 1-5, skip Steps 6, 7, and 8, then follow Steps 9 and 10, using the idle speed screw.**

6. Disengage the electrical connector at the idle solenoid.
7. Set the transmission in Drive, then adjust the low idle speed screw for the lower of the two figures given for idle speed.

✳✳CAUTION

Make sure that the drive wheels are blocked and the park-ing brake is applied.

8. Reconnect the idle solenoid and open the throttle slightly to extend the solenoid plunger.
9. Turn the solenoid plunger screw in or out to obtain the higher of the two idle speed figures (this is normal curb-idle)
10. To adjust the mixture, break off the limiter caps. Make sure that the idle is at the higher of the two speeds listed on the decal. Turn the mixture screws out equally to obtain the highest idle. Reset the idle speed with the plunger screw if necessary. Turn the mixture screw in until the lower of the two figures on the decal is obtained.
11. Shut off the engine, remove blocks from drive wheels, and reconnect hose to evaporative canister.

1977

▶ **See Figures 34 and 35**

1. First satisfy all the following requirements:
   a. Set parking brake and block drive wheels.
   b. Bring the engine to operating temperature.
   c. Remove the air cleaner for access, but make sure all hoses stay connected.

d. Consult the Emission Control Information label under the hood, and disconnect and plug hoses as required by the instructions there.

e. Connect an accurate tach to the engine.

2. Set ignition timing as described above.

3. Remove the cap(s) from the idle mixture screw(s). Remove caps carefully, to prevent bending these screws.

4. Turn in the screw(s) till they seat very lightly, then back screw(s) out just far enough to permit the engine to run.

5. Put automatic transmission in Drive.

6. Back out screw(s) ⅛ turn at a time, going alternately from screw to screw after each ⅛ turn where there are two screws, until the highest possible idle speed is achieved. Then, set the idle speed as follows: with manual transmission - 650; with automatic - 550; standard 350 V8 with automatic - 550; 350 V8 used at high altitudes - 650.

7. After setting the idle speed, repeat the mixture adjustment to ensure that mixture is at the point where highest idle speed is obtained. Then, if idle speed has increased, repeat idle speed adjustment of Step 6.

8. Now, turn screw(s) in, going evenly in ⅛ turn increments where there are two, until the following idle speed are obtained: 305 V8 with manual transmission - 600; with automatic - 500; standard 350 V8, manual transmission - 700; standard 350 V8 with automatic - 500; 350 V8 used at high altitudes - 600.

9. Reset idle speed to the value shown on the engine compartment sticker, if that differs from the final setting in the step above.

10. Check and adjust fast idle as described on the engine compartment sticker.

11. Reconnect any vacuum hoses that were disconnect for the procedure, and install the air cleaner.

12. If idle speed has changed, reset according to the engine compartment sticker. Disconnect tach.

1978-80

These models have sealed idle mixture screws; in most cases these are concealed under staked-in plugs. Idle mixture is adjustable only during carburetor overhaul, and requires the addition of propane as an artificial mixture enrichener.

See the emission control label in the engine compartment for procedures and specifications not supplied here. Prepare the car for adjustment (engine warm, choke open, fast idle screw off the fast idle cam) as per the label instructions.

2-BBL AND 4-BBL (EXCEPT V8-350 ENGINE)

▶ **See Figures 36, 37, 38, 39, 40 and 41**

1. Run the engine to normal operating temperature.

2. Make sure that the choke is fully opened, turn the A/C off, set the parking brake, block the drive wheels and connect a tachometer to the engine according to the manufacturer's instructions.

3. Disconnect and plug the vacuum hoses at the EGR valve and the vapor canister.

4. If equipped with an automatic transmission, place the transmission in Park. If equipped with a manual transmission, place transmission in Neutral.

5. Disconnect and plug the vacuum advance hose at the distributor. Check and adjust the timing.

6. Connect the distributor vacuum line.

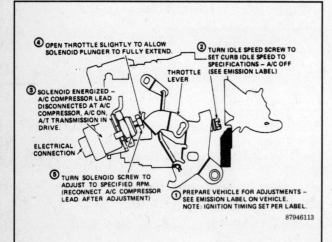

Fig. 34 Idle speed adjustment on a 4BBL, V8 engine with solenoid — 1977

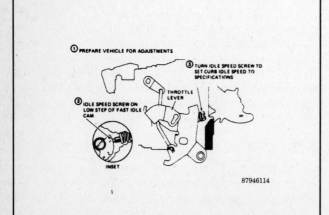

Fig. 35 Idle speed adjustment on a 4BBL, V8 engine without solenoid — 1977

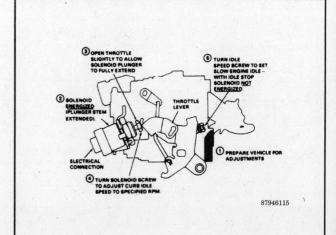

Fig. 36 Idle speed adjustment on a 2BBL, with solenoid — 1978-79

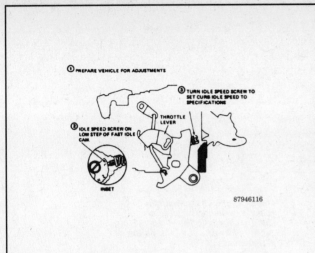

Fig. 37 Idle speed adjustment on a 2BBL, without solenoid — 1978-79

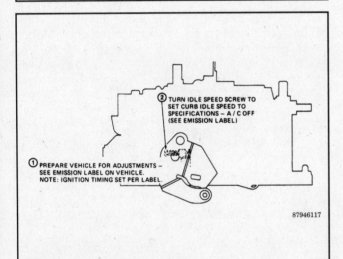

Fig. 38 Idle speed adjustment on a 4BBL, without solenoid — 1979 and later vehicles

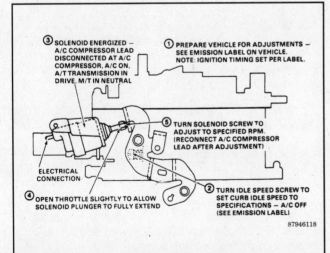

Fig. 39 Idle speed adjustment on a 4BBL, with solenoid — 1979 and later vehicles

7. Manual transmission cars without A/C and without solenoid: place the idle speed screw on the low step of the fast idle cam and turn the screw to achieve the specified idle speed.

8. If equipped with A/C: set the idle speed screw to the specified rpm. Disconnect the compressor clutch wire and turn the A/C on. Open the throttle momentarily to extend the solenoid plunger. Turn the solenoid screw to obtain the specified rpm. Finally, adjust the fast idle speed using the choke screw on the opposite side of the carburetor assembly.

9. Automatic transmission cars without A/C: manual transmission cars without A/C, solenoid-equipped carburetor: momentarily open the throttle to extend the solenoid plunger. Turn the solenoid screw to obtain the specified rpm. Disconnect the solenoid wire and turn the idle speed screw to obtain the slow engine idle speed.

V8-350 ENGINE

1. Run the engine to normal operating temperature.
2. Set the parking brake and block the drive wheels.
3. Connect a tachometer to the engine according to the manufacturer's instructions.
4. Disconnect and plug the purge hose at the vapor canister, then disconnect and plug the EGR vacuum hose at the EGR valve.
5. Turn the A/C off.
6. Place the transmission in Park (Automatic) or Neutral (Manual).
7. Disconnect and plug the vacuum advance line at the distributor. Check and adjust the timing.
8. Connect the vacuum advance line. Place the automatic transmission in Drive.
9. Manual transmission cars without A/C: adjust the idle stop screw to obtain the specified rpm. If equipped with A/C: with the A/C Off, adjust the idle stop screw to obtain the specified rpm. Disconnect the compressor clutch wire and turn the A/C On. Open the throttle slightly to allow the solenoid plunger to extend. Turn the solenoid screw to obtain the solenoid rpm listed on the underhood emission sticker.
10. Connect all hoses and remove the tachometer.

1981-82
▶ **See Figure 42**

Most of the E2ME (two barrel) and E4ME (four barrel) carburetors used on these models are equipped with an Idle Speed Control (ISC) assembly, monitored by the ECM, which controls which controls engine idle speed. The curb idle is programmed into the ECM and is not adjustable. Some models with A/C may be equipped with an Idle Speed Solenoid (ISS), if so, refer to the 1978-80 procedure.

1983-88
▶ **See Figure 43**

The E2ME (two barrel) and the E4ME (four barrel) carburetors used on these models all are equipped with an Idle Speed Control (ISC) assembly, monitored by the ECM, which controls engine idle speed. The curb idle is programmed into the ECM and is not adjustable.

On the E4MC models, an Idle Load Compensator (ILC) mounted on the float bowl is used to control curb idle speeds.

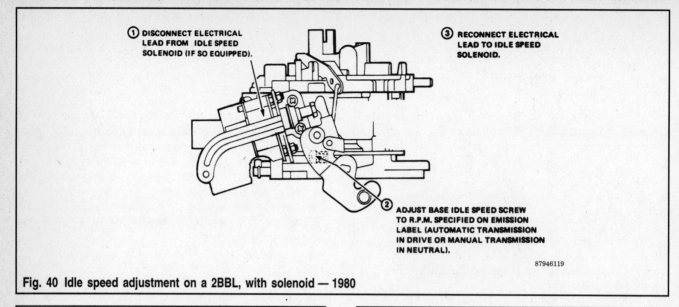

① DISCONNECT ELECTRICAL LEAD FROM IDLE SPEED SOLENOID (IF SO EQUIPPED).

③ RECONNECT ELECTRICAL LEAD TO IDLE SPEED SOLENOID.

② ADJUST BASE IDLE SPEED SCREW TO R.P.M. SPECIFIED ON EMISSION LABEL (AUTOMATIC TRANSMISSION IN DRIVE OR MANUAL TRANSMISSION IN NEUTRAL).

87946119

Fig. 40 Idle speed adjustment on a 2BBL, with solenoid — 1980

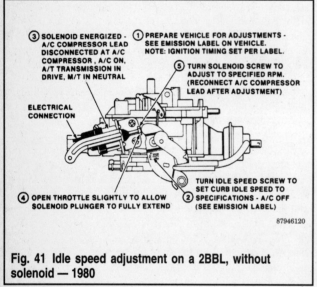

③ SOLENOID ENERGIZED - A/C COMPRESSOR LEAD DISCONNECTED AT A/C COMPRESSOR , A/C ON, A/T TRANSMISSION IN DRIVE, M/T IN NEUTRAL

① PREPARE VEHICLE FOR ADJUSTMENTS - SEE EMISSION LABEL ON VEHICLE. NOTE: IGNITION TIMING SET PER LABEL.

⑤ TURN SOLENOID SCREW TO ADJUST TO SPECIFIED RPM. (RECONNECT A/C COMPRESSOR LEAD AFTER ADJUSTMENT)

ELECTRICAL CONNECTION

④ OPEN THROTTLE SLIGHTLY TO ALLOW SOLENOID PLUNGER TO FULLY EXTEND

② TURN IDLE SPEED SCREW TO SET CURB IDLE SPEED TO SPECIFICATIONS - A/C OFF (SEE EMISSION LABEL)

87946120

Fig. 41 Idle speed adjustment on a 2BBL, without solenoid — 1980

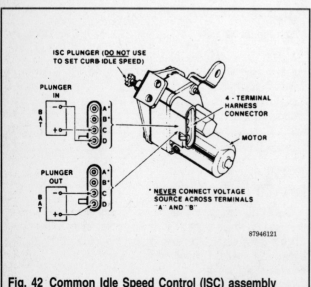

ISC PLUNGER (DO NOT USE TO SET CURB IDLE SPEED)

PLUNGER IN

B A T

4 - TERMINAL HARNESS CONNECTOR

MOTOR

PLUNGER OUT

B A T

* NEVER CONNECT VOLTAGE SOURCE ACROSS TERMINALS "A" AND "B"

87946121

Fig. 42 Common Idle Speed Control (ISC) assembly

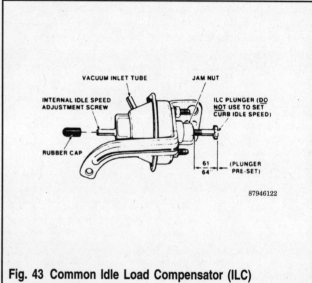

VACUUM INLET TUBE   JAM NUT

INTERNAL IDLE SPEED ADJUSTMENT SCREW

ILC PLUNGER (DO NOT USE TO SET CURB IDLE SPEED)

RUBBER CAP

61 / 64   (PLUNGER PRE-SET)

87946122

Fig. 43 Common Idle Load Compensator (ILC)

No attempt should be made to adjust this since it is controlled by the ECM.

On vehicles that do not include an ISC or ILC but are equipped with air conditioning, an Idle Speed Solenoid (ISS) is used to maintain curb idle speed any time the air conditioner compressor clutch is engaged. If so refer to the 1978-80 procedures.

Throttle Body Injection (TBI)

MINIMUM IDLE SPEED ADJUSTMENT

Beginning in 1985, some engines were available with a throttle body fuel injection system. All throttle body injected vehicles are controlled by a computer which regulates idle speeds and supplies the correct amount of fuel during all engine operating conditions. No periodic adjustments are necessary. However, if throttle body is replaced and a proper idle speed cannot be obtained, there is an adjustment which may be made. An idle stop screw is set at the factory and then covered to discourage tampering. If all other components of the fuel system are working properly and there is still a problem with the idle speed, the screw may be adjusted.

➡**Incorrectly adjusting the minimum idle speed stop screw will result in the IAC valve pintle to constantly bottom on its seat leading to an early valve failure.**

1. Set the parking brake and block the drive wheels.
2. Start and run the engine until it reaches normal operating temperature. Make sure all accessories are turned OFF.
3. Stop the engine, then disconnect and plug any vacuum lines, as required.
4. Using an awl, pierce the idle stop screw cap and carefully pry the cap from the throttle body. The cap and screw can be found on the opposite side of the throttle body from the Idle Air Control (IAC) valve and Throttle Position (TP) sensor.
5. Connect a tachometer to the engine.
6. Ground the diagnostic terminal of the Assembly Line Data Link (ALDL) connector by using a jumper wire to connect the terminal to the Electronic Control Module (ECM) system ground terminal. The diagnostic and ground terminals are the 2 top right terminals on the ALDL connector which is found under the dash, near the steering column.
7. Turn the ignition **ON**, but DO NOT start the engine. Wait at least 45 seconds for the IAC valve pintle to extend and seat in the throttle body.
8. With the ignition **ON** and the ALDL test terminal still grounded, unplug the IAC valve connector. This will keep the pintle extended throughout the procedure and prevent the ECM from adjusting idle speed using the valve.

9. Remove the ground from the ALDL terminal, then disengage the distributor set timing connector in order to prevent the possibility of engine speed changing during the procedure due to timing changes.
10. Place the transmission in Neutral, then start the engine and allow it to idle.

➡**If equipped, double check to make sure that the cruise control cables do not hold the throttle open.**

11. Wait until the idle stabilizes, then check and adjust the idle speed as necessary:
    a. For 1985 vehicles, set the idle screw to obtain 500-600 rpm.
    b. For 1986 vehicles, have an assistant place the transmission in Drive and apply the brake pedal, then set the idle speed to 400-450 rpm.
    c. For 1987-88 vehicles, set the idle screw to obtain 400-450 rpm.
12. Turn the ignition **OFF**, then reconnect the IAC valve and distributor timing wiring.
13. For 1985 vehicles, turn the ignition **ON**, but do not start the engine, then adjust the TP sensor using a digital voltmeter to backprobe terminals A and B of the TP sensor connector. If necessary loosen the sensor retainers and pivot the switch in order to achieve an output of 0.525-0.075 volts, then tighten the retainers to secure the switch. Make sure the switch does not move when tightening the retainers or adjustment will be lost.
14. Use silicone sealant to cover the idle stop screw, then reconnect and vacuum lines which were plugged for the procedure.
15. Start the engine and check for proper idle operation.

TUNE-UP SPECIFICATIONS
1964 - 71 All Models

YEAR	MODEL	SPARK PLUGS Type	Gap (In.)	DISTRIBUTOR Point Dwell (Deg.)	Point Gap (In.)	IGNITION TIMING (Deg.) ▲	CRANKING COMP. PRESSURE (Psi)	VALVES Tappet (Hot) Clearance (In.) Intake	Exhaust	Intake Opens (Deg.)	FUEL PUMP PRESSURE (Psi)	IDLE SPEED (Rpm) *
1964	6 cyl.—230 Cu. In.	46N	.035	32°	.019	4B	130	■	■	34B	4	500
	V8—283 Cu. In.	45	.035	30°	.019	4B	150	■	■	32½B	6	500
	V8—327 Cu. In. Std.	44	.035	30°	.019	4B	160	■	■	32½B	6	500
	V8—327 Cu. In. Hi. Perf.	44	.035	30°	.019	8B	160	.030	.030	32½B	6	500
	V8—409 Cu. In. Std.	43N	.035	30°	.019	6B	150	■	■	38½B	6	700
	V8—409 Cu. In. Hi. Perf.	43N	.035	30°	.019	12B	150	.012	.020	49½B	8	700
1965	6 cyl.—230 Cu. In.	46N	.035	32°	.019	4B	130	■	■	62B	4	500
	V8—283 Cu. In.	45	.035	30°	.019	4B	150	■	■	32½B	6	500
	V8—327 Cu. In. Std.	44	.035	30°	.019	4B	160	■	■	32½B	6	500
	V8—327 Cu. In. (300 H.P.)	44	.035	30°	.019	8B	160	■	■	32½B	6	500
	V8—327 Cu. In. (350 H.P.)	44	.035	30°	.019	12B	150	■	■	54B	6	800
	V8—327 Cu. In. (365 H.P.)	44	.035	30°	.019	10B	150	.030	.030	54B	6	800
	V8—327 Cu. In. (Fuel Inj.)	44	.035	30°	.019	12B	150	.030	.030	54B	6	800
	V8—396 Cu. In. Std.	43N	.035	30°	.019	4-6B	150	■	■	N.A.	5½	800
	V8—396 Cu. In. Hi. Perf.	43N	.035	30°	.019	10B	150	.020	.024	N.A.	7½	800
	V8—409 Cu. In. Std.	43N	.035	30°	.019	6B	150	■	■	38½B	8	500
	V8—409 Cu. In. Opt.	43N	.035	30°	.019	12B	150	.018	.030	50¾B	8	700
1966	6 Cyl.—250 Cu. In.	46N	.035	34°	.019	6B	130	■	■	62B	4	500
	V8—283 Cu. In.	45	.035	30°	.019	4B	150	■	■	32½B	6	500
	V8—327 Cu. In. Std.	44	.035	30°	.019	③	160	■	■	32½B	6	500
	V8—327 Cu. In. (350 H.P.)	44	.035	30°	.019	10B	160	■	■	54B	6	700
	V8—396 Cu. In.	43N	.035	30°	.019	4B	150	■	■	40B	6	500
	V8—427 Cu. In.	43N	.035	30°	.019	4B	150	■	■	58B	6	600
	V8—427 Cu. In. (425 H.P.)	43N	.035	30°	.019	8B	150	.020	.024	54B	6	800
1967	6 cyl.—250 Cu. In.	46N	.035	32°	.019	4B	130	■	■	62B	4	500
	V8—283 Cu. In. (195 H.P.)	45	.035	30°	.019	4B	150	■	■	36B	6	500
	V8—327 Cu. In. (275 H.P.)	44	.035	30°	.019	8B ⑥	160	■	■	38B	6	500
	V8—327 Cu. In. (300 H.P.)	44	.035	30°	.019	6B ⑥	160	■	■	38B	6	500
	V8—327 Cu. In. (350 H.P.)	44	.035	30°	.019	10B	150	■	■	54B	6	700
	V8—396 Cu. In. (325 H.P.)	43N	.035	30°	.019	4B	160	■	■	40B	6	500
	V8—427 Cu. In. (385 H.P.)	43N	.035	30°	.019	4B	160	■	■	56B	6	550
	V8—427 Cu. In. (390 H.P.)	43N	.035	30°	.019	4B	160	■	■	56B	6	550
	V8—427 Cu. In. (400 H.P.)	43N	.035	30°	.019	4B	160	■	■	56B	6	550
	V8—427 Cu. In. (425 H.P.)	43N	.035	30°	.019	10B	150	.022	.024	44B	6	1000
	V8—427 Cu. In. (435 H.P.)	43N	.035	30°	.019	5B	150	.024	.028	44B	6	750
1968	6 Cyl.—250 Cu. In.	46N	.035	32°	.019	TDC⑦	130	■	■	16B	4	700①
	V8—307 Cu. In. (200 H.P.)	45	.035	30°	.019	2B	150	■	■	28B	6	700①
	V8—327 Cu. In. (250 H.P.)	45	.035	30°	.019	4B	150	■	■	28B	6	700①
	V8—327 Cu. In. (275 H.P.)	44	.035	30°	.019	TDC⑦	160	■	■	28B	6	700①
	V8—327 Cu. In. (300 H.P.)	44	.035	30°	.019	4B	160	■	■	28B	6	700①
	V8—327 Cu. In. (350 H.P.)	44	.035	30°	.019	4B	160	■	■	40B	6	750
	V8—396 Cu. In. (325 H.P.)	43N	.035	30°	.019	4B	160	■	■	28B	6	700①
	V8—427 Cu. In. (385 H.P.)	43N	.035	30°	.019	4B	160	■	■	40B	8	700①
	V8—427 Cu. In. (390 H.P.)	43N	.035	30°	.019	4B	160	■	■	40B	8	700①
	V8—427 Cu. In. (400 H.P.)	43N	.035	30°	.019	4B	160	■	■	40B	8	750①
	V8—427 Cu. In. (435 H.P.)	43N	.035	30°	.019	4B	150	.024	.028	44B	8	750
1969	6 Cyl.—250 Cu. In.	46N	.035	32°	.019	TDC⑤	130	■	■	16B	4	700⑦
	V8—327 Cu. In. (235 H.P.)	45S	.035	30°	.019	2A⑥	150	■	■	28B	6	700①

TUNE-UP SPECIFICATIONS
1964 - 71 All Models (Cont.)

| YEAR | MODEL | SPARK PLUGS | | DISTRIBUTOR | | IGNITION TIMING (Deg.) ▲ | CRANKING COMP. PRESSURE (Psi) | VALVES | | INTAKE OPENS (Deg.) | FUEL PUMP PRESSURE (Psi) | IDLE SPEED (Rpm) ★ |
| | | Type | Gap (In.) | Point Dwell (Deg.) | Point Gap (In.) | | | Tappet (Hot) Clearance (In.) | | | | |
								Intake	Exhaust			
	V8—350 Cu. In. (255 H.P.)	44S	.035	30°	.019	TDC⑤	160	■	■	28B	6	700①
	V8—350 Cu. In. (300 H.P.)	44S	.035	30°	.019	TDC⑤	160	■	■	28B	6	700①
	V8—350 Cu. In. (350 H.P.)	44	.035	30°	.019	8B	160	■	■	52B	6	750
	V8—396 Cu. In. (265 H.P.)	44N	.035	30°	.019	TDC⑤	160	■	■	28B	6	700①
	V8—427 Cu. In. (335 H.P.)	43N	.035	30°	.019	4B	160	■	■	28B	8	800①
	V8—427 Cu. In. (390 H.P.)	43N	.035	30°	.019	4B	160	■	■	56B	8	800①
	V8—427 Cu. In. (400 H.P.)	43N	.035	30°	.019	4B	160	■	■	56B	8	800①
	V8—427 Cu. In. (435 H.P.)	43LX	.035	Transistor	Ign.	4B	160	■	■	44B	8	750
1970	6 Cyl.—250 Cu. In.	R46T	.035	31–34	.019	TDC⑤	130	■	■	16B	4	750①
	V8—350 Cu. In. (250 H.P.)	R44	.035	29–31	.019	TDC⑤	160	■	■	28B	8	750①
	V8—350 Cu. In. (300 H.P.)	R44	.035	29–31	.019	TDC⑤	160	■	■	28B	8	750①
	V8—350 Cu. In. (350 H.P.)	R44	.035	29–31	.019	8B	160	■	■	52B	8	750
	V8—350 Cu. In. (370 H.P.)	R43	.035	Transistor Ign.		8B	160	.030	.030	43B	8	900
	V8—400 Cu. In. (265 H.P.)	R44	.035	29–31	.019	4B⑦	160	■	■	34B	8	700①
	V8—454 Cu. In. (345 H.P.)	R44T	.035	28–30	.019	6B	160	■	■	30B	8	600
	V8—454 Cu. In. (390 H.P.)	R43T	.035	28–30	.019	6B	160	■	■	56B	8	700①
	V8—454 Cu. In. (450 H.P.)	R43XL	.035	Transistor Ign.		8B	160	.024	.028	62B	8	700①
1971	6 Cyl.—250 Cu. In.	R46T	.035	31–34	.019	①	130	■	■	16B	4	750①
	V8—350 Cu. In. (250 H.P.)	R44	.035	29–31	.019	①	160	■	■	28B	8	750①
	V8—350 Cu. In. (300 H.P.)	R44	.035	29–31	.019	①	160	■	■	28B	8	750①
	V8—350 Cu. In. (350 H.P.)	R44	.035	29–31	.019	①	160	■	■	52B	8	750
	V8—350 Cu. In. (370 H.P.)	R43	.035	Transistor Ign.		①	160	.030	.030	43B	8	900
	V8—400 Cu. In. (265 H.P.)	R44	.035	29–31	.019	①	160	■	■	34B	8	700①
	V8—454 Cu. In. (345 H.P.)	R44T	.035	28–30	.019	①	160	■	■	30B	8	600
	V8—454 Cu. In. (390 H.P.)	R43T	.035	28–30	.019	①	160	■	■	56B	8	700①
	V8—454 Cu. In. (450 H.P.)	R43XL	.035	Transistor Ign.		①	160	.024	.028	62B	8	700①

★—with manual transmission in N and automatic in D. Add 50 rpm if equipped with air conditioning

▲—with vacuum advance disconnected. NOTE: These settings are only approximate. Engine design, altitude, temperature, fuel octane rating and the condition of the individual engine are all factors which can influence timing. The limiting advance factor must, therefore, be the "knock point" of the individual engine.

■—1 turn tighter than zero lash.

①—N.A. @ publication, see decal under hood for data.

②—if exhaust emission equipped:
.283 Cu. In., w/M.T.—TDC

②—w/A.T.—4B

③—V8—327, Dist. No. 1111152—8° B.
　　Dist. No. 1111116—2° A.
　　Dist. No. 1111153—6° B.
　　Dist. No. 1111117—4° A.

④—6 Cyl. w/A.T.—Idle 500 rpm.

⑤—w/Auto. Trans.—4° B.

⑥—w/Auto. Trans.—2° B.

⑦—w/Auto. Trans.—500 rpm.

⑧—w/Auto. Trans.—600 rpm

⑨—w/Auto. Trans.—8° B.

A—After top dead center.

B—Before top dead center.

TDC—Top dead center.

87946c04

TUNE-UP SPECIFICATIONS
1961 - 71 Truck

CU. IN. DISPLACE-MENT	YEAR	SPARK PLUG GAP	DISTRIBUTOR POINT DWELL	POINT GAP	IGNITION TIMING DEGREES	CRANKCASE COMP. PRESSURE	VALVE CLEARANCE IN LOT EXTEN.	GOV. R.P.M. NO LOAD	FUEL PUMP PRESS	IDLE SPEED STD.	AUTO.
FOUR CYLINDER											
153	1963-65	.035	31-34	.019	4B	130	0+1 Turn	—	3½-4½	500	—
SIX CYLINDER											
194	1964-65	.035	31-34	.019	8B	130	0+1 Turn	—	3½-4½	500	—
	1966-67	.035	31-34	.019	8B[1]	130	0+1 Turn	—	3-4½	700●	600●
230	1963-65	.035	31-34	.019	4B	130	0+1 Turn	—	3½-4½	500	450
	1966	.035	31-34	.019	6B[2]	130	0+1 Turn	—	3½-4½	700●	600●
	1967	.035	31-34	.019	4B	130	0+1 Turn	—	3-4½	700●	500●
	1968-69	.035	31-34	.019	4B[3]	130	0+1 Turn	—	3½-4½	700●	550●
235	1961-62	.035	28-33	.019	5B	130	.006H-.018H	—	3½-4½	500	●
250	1966	.035	31-34	.019	6B	150	0+1 Turn	4000	3-4½	700●	600●
	1967	.035	31-34	.019	4B	130	0+1 Turn	—	3-4½	700●	500●
	1968-71	.035	31-34	.019	4B[3]	130	0+1 Turn	4000	3-4½	700	500
261	1961-62	.035	28-33	.019	TDC	130	.006H-.018H	—	3½-4½	500	450
292	1963-65	.035	31-34	.019	4B	130	0+1 Turn	—	3½-4½	500	450
	1966	.035	31-34	.019	4B[4]	140	0+1 Turn	3900	3-4½	700●	600●
	1967	.035	31-34	.019	4B[5]	130	0+1 Turn	3900	3-4½	700●	600●
	1968	.035	31-34	.019	4B[3]	130	0+1 Turn	3900	3-4½	700●	600●
	1969-71	.035	31-34	.019	TDC[6]	130	0+1 Turn	3900	3-4½	700	550
401 (V6)	1966-68	.035	31-34	.019	5B	130	.012H-.018H	3700	5-6½	500	—
478 (V6)	1966-68	.035	31-34	.019	2½B	130	.012H-.018H	3400	5-6½	500	—
EIGHT CYLINDER											
283	1961	.035	28-32	.019	4B	150	0+¾ Turn	3700	5¼-6½	500	●
	1962	.035	28-32	.019	4B	150	0+1 Turn	3700	5½-6½	500	●
	1963-66	.035	28-32	.019	4B	160	0+1 Turn	4000	5-6½	500	●
	1967	.035	28-32	.019	4B[7]	150	0+1 Turn	4000	5-6½	700●	600●
307	1968-69	.035	28-32	.019	2B	150	0+1 Turn	4000	5-6½	700●	600●
	1970-71	.035	28-32	.019	2B[8]	150	0+1 Turn	4000	5-6½	700	600
327	1962-65	.035	28-32	.019	8B	150	0+1 Turn	4000	5-6½	500	●
	1966	.035	28-32	.019	2B[9]	150	0+1 Turn	4000	5-6½	700●	600
185 H.P.	1967	.035	28-32	.019	8B	150	0+1 Turn	4000	5-6½	500	●
220 H.P.	1967	.035	28-32	.019	2B[10]	150	0+1 Turn	4000	5-6½	700●	600●
348	1961-62	.035	28-32	.019	4B	125	0+1 Turn	3700	5¼-6½	500	●
	1963-65	.035	28-32	.019	8B	140	0+1 Turn	4000	5¼-6½	500	●
350 215 H.P.	1969-71	.035	28-32	.019	4B	150	0+1 Turn	4000	5-6½	500	500
255 H.P.	1969-71	.035	28-32	.019	TDC[6]	150	0+1 Turn	4000	5-6½	700	600
366	1966-71	.035	29-31	.019	6B	130	0+1 Turn	4000	5-6½	500	500
396	1968-69	.035	29-31	.019	4B	150	0+1 Turn	4000	5-6½	700	600
409	1962-65	.035	28-32	.019	4B	140	0+1 Turn	4000	5-6½	500	●
427	1968-71	.035	28-32	.019	6B	150	0+1 Turn	4000	5-6½	500	500

WITH AIR INJECTION REACTOR SYSTEM

1—Std. Trans. 3° BTC.
2—Std. Auto. Trans. 4° BTC.
3—Std. TDC.
4—Std. 1° BTC.
5—Std. 2° BTC.
6—Auto. 4° BTC.
7—Std. 6° ATC.
8—Auto. 8° BTC.
9—Std. 8° BTC.
10—All TDC.

●—w/out A.I.R. Std. Trans. 500, Auto. Trans. Set As Low As Possible To Obtain A Good Idle.

87946c16

TUNE-UP SPECIFICATIONS
1972 - 79 Camaro
When analyzing compression test results, look for uniformity among cylinders rather than specific pressures.

Year	ENGINE No. Cyl. Displacement (cu in.)	hp	Orig. Type	Gap (in.)	Point Dwell (deg)	Point Gap (in.)	IGNITION TIMING (deg) ▲ ● Man Trans	Auto Trans	VALVES Intake Opens ■ (deg) ●	Fuel Pump Pressure (psi)	IDLE SPEED (rpm) ▲ * Trans Man ●	Trans Auto
'72	6-250	110	R-46T	.035	31-34	.019	4B	4B	16	3½-4½	700	600
	8-307	130	R-44T	.035	29-31	.019	4B	8B	28	5-6½	900	600
	8-350	165	R-44T	.035	29-31	.019	6B	6B	28(44)	7-8½	900	600
	8-350	200	R-44T	.035	29-31	.019	4B	8B	28(44)	7-8½	800	600
	8-350	255	R-44T	.035	29-31	.019	8B	12B	43	7-8½	900	700
	8-402	240	R-44TS	.035	28-30	.019	8B	8B	28	7-8½	800	600
'73	6-250	100	R-46T	.035	31-34	.019	6B	6B	16	3½-4½	700/450	600/450
	8-307	115	R-44T	.035	29-31	.019	4B	8B	28	5-6½	900/450	600/450
	8-350	145	R-44T	.035	29-31	.019	8B	8B	28	7½-8½	900/450	600/450
	8-350	175	R-44T	.035	29-31	.019	8B	12B	28	7½-8½	900/450	600/450
	8-350	245	R-44T	.035	29-31	.019	8B	12B	52	7½-8½	900/450	700/450
'74	6-250	100	R-46T	.035	31-34	.019	6B	6B	16	4-5	800/450	600/450
	8-350	145	R-44T	.035	29-31	.019	4B	8B	28	7½-9	900/450	600/450
	8-350	160	R-44T	.035	29-31	.019	4B	8B	44	7½-9	900/450	600/450
	8-350	185	R-44T	.035	29-31	.019	4B	8B	28	7½-9	900/450	600/450
	8-350	245	R-44T	.035	29-31	.019	8B	8B	52	7½-9	900/450	700/450
'75	6-250	105	R-46TX	.060	Electronic		10B	10B	16	4-5	800/425	550/425① (600/425)
	8-350	145	R-44TX	.060	Electronic		6B	6B	28	7½-9	800	600
	8-350	155	R-44TX	.060	Electronic		6B	8B(6B)	28	7½-9	800	600
'76	6-250	105	R-46TS	.035	Electronic		6B	6B	16	4-5	850	550②(600)
	8-305	140	R-45TS	.045	Electronic		6B	8B(TDC)	28	7½-9	800	600
	8-350	165	R-45TS	.045	Electronic		8B(6B)	8B(6B)	28	7½-9	800	600
'77	6-250	All	R-46TS	.035	Electronic		6B	8B(6B)③	16	4-5	④	550(600)
	8-305	All	R-45TS	.045	Electronic		8B	8B(6B)	28	7½-9	600	500
	8-350	All	R-45TS	.045	Electronic		8B	8B	28	7½-9	700	500

87946c05

TUNE-UP SPECIFICATIONS
1972 - 79 Camaro (Cont.)

When analyzing compression test results, look for uniformity among cylinders rather than specific pressures.

Year	Engine No. Cyl. Displacement (cu in.)	hp	Orig. Type	Gap (in.)	Point Dwell (deg)	Point Gap (in.)	Man Trans	Auto Trans	Valves Intake Opens ■ (deg) ●	Fuel Pump Pressure (psi)	Trans Man	Trans Auto
'78	6-250 Chev.	All	R-46TS	.035	Electronic		6B	②	16	4-5	800/425	550(600)/425(400)
	8-305 Chev.	All	R-45TS	.045	Electronic		4B	4B	28	7.5-9	600	500
	8-350 Chev.	All	R-45TS	.045	Electronic		6B	⑤	28	7.5-9	700	500
'79	6-250 Chev.	All	R-46TS	.035	Electronic		8B	10B(6B)	16	4.5-6.0	800	550
	8-305 Chev.	All	R-45TS	.045	Electronic		4B	4B	28	7.5-9.0	600	500
	8-350 Chev.	All	R-45TS	.045	Electronic		6B	6B(8B)	28	7.5-9.0	700	500

▲ See text for procedure.
● Figure in parentheses indicates California engine
■ All figures Before Top Dead Center
* When two idle speed figures are separated by a slash, the lower figure is with the idle speed solenoid disconnected.
① Without intake manifold integral with head—600/450
② Non A/C; Non Calif: 10B
with A/C, except Calif: 8B
Calif.: 6B
③ 6B for Calif. engines exc. engine code CCC which is 8B
10B for high altitude engines
④ 750 w/o AC
800 w/AC
⑤ AT, except Calif. and High Altitude: 6B
Calif: 8B
High Alt. w/o A/C: 6B
High Alt. with A/C: 8B
A After Top Dead Center
B Before Top Dead Center
TDC Top Dead Center
— Not applicable

MECHANICAL VALVE LIFTER CLEARANCE

Year	Engine	Intake (Hot) In.	Exhaust (Hot) In.
1972	V8-350 255 hp	.024	.030

NOTE: The underhood specifications sticker often reflects tune-up specification changes made in production. Sticker figures must be used if they disagree with those in this chart.

87946c06

TUNE-UP SPECIFICATIONS
1972 - 79 Chevelle, Malibu, Monte Carlo

When analyzing compression test results, look for uniformity among cylinders rather than specific pressures.

Year	Engine No. Cyl. Displacement (cu in.)	hp	Orig. Type	Gap (in.)	Point Dwell (deg)	Point Gap (in.)	Man Trans	Auto Trans	Valves Intake Opens ■ (deg) ●	Fuel Pump Pressure (psi)	Trans Man	Trans Auto
'72	6-250	110	R-46TS	.035	31-34	.019	4B	4B	16	3½-4½	700	600
	8-307	130	R-44T	.035	29-31	.019	4B	8B	28	5-6½	900	600
	8-350	165	R-44T	.035	29-31	.019	6B	6B	28	7-8½	900	600
	8-350	175	R-44T	.035	29-31	.019	4B	8B	28	7-8½	800	600
	8-402	240	R-44T	.035	29-31	.019	8B	8B	30	7-8½	750	600
	8-454	270	R-44T	.035	29-31	.019	8B	8B	56	7-8½	750	600
'73	6-250	100	R-46T	.035	31-34	.019	6B	6B	16	3½-4½	700/450	600/450
	8-307	115	R-44T	.035	29-31	.019	4B	8B	28	5-6½	900/450	600/450
	8-350	145	R-44T	.035	29-31	.019	8B	8B	28	7-8½	900/450	600/450
	8-350	175	R-44T	.035	29-31	.019	8B	12B	28	7-8½	900/450	600/450
	8-454	245	R-44T	.035	29-31	.019	10B	10B	55	7-8½	900/450	600/450

87946c07

TUNE-UP SPECIFICATIONS
1972 - 79 Chevelle, Malibu, Monte Carlo (Cont.)

When analyzing compression test results, look for uniformity among cylinders rather than specific pressures.

Year	ENGINE No. Cyl. Displacement (cu in.)	hp	SPARK PLUGS Orig. Type	Gap (in.)	DISTRIBUTOR Point Dwell (deg)	Point Gap (in.)	IGNITION TIMING (deg) ▲ ● Man Trans	Auto Trans	VALVES Intake Opens ■ (deg) ●	Fuel Pump Pressure (psi)	IDLE SPEED (rpm) ▲ * Trans Man	● Trans Auto
'74	6-250	100	R-46T	.035	31-34	.019	6B	6B	16	4-5	800/450	600/450
	8-350	145	R-44T	.035	29-31	.019	4B	8B	28	7½-9	900/450	600/450
	8-350	160	R-44T	.035	29-31	.019	4B	8B	44	7½-9	900/450	600/450
	8-400	150	R-44T	.035	29-31	.019	—	8B	28	7½-9	—	600/450
	8-400	180	R-44T	.035	29-31	.019	—	8B	44	7½-9	—	600/450
	8-454	235	R-44T	.035	29-31	.019	10B	10B	55	7½-9	800/450	600/450
'75	6-250	105	R-46TX	.060	Electronic		10B	10B	16	4-5	850/425	550/425 (600/425)
	8-350	145	R-44TX	.060	Electronic		6B	6B	28	7½-9	—	600
	8-350	155	R-44TX	.060	Electronic		—	6B	28	7½-9	800	600
	8-400	175	R-44TX	.060	Electronic		—	8B	28	7½-9	—	600
	8-454	215	R-44TX	.060	Electronic		—	16B	55	7½-9	—	600/500
'76	6-250	105	R-46TS	.035	Electronic		6B	6B	16	3½-4½	850	550(600)
	8-305	140	R-45TS	.045	Electronic		—	8B(TDC)	28	7-8½	—	600
	8-350	145	R-45TS	.045	Electronic		—	6B	28	7-8½	—	600
	8-350	165	R-45TS	.045	Electronic		—	8B(6B)	28	7-8½	—	600
	8-400	175	R-45TS	.045	Electronic		—	8B	28	7-8½	—	600
'77	6-250	All	R-46TS	.035	Electronic		6B	8B(6B)①	16	4-5	②	550(600)
	8-305	All	R-45TS	.045	Electronic		8B	8B(6B)	28	7½-9	600	500
	8-350	All	R-45TS	.045	Electronic		8B	8B	28	7½-9	700	500
'78	6-200 Chev.	95	R-45TS	.045	Electronic		8B	8B	28	7.5-9	700	600
	6-231 Buick	105	R-46TSX	.060	Electronic		15B	15B	17	6-7	600	500
	8-305 Chev.	145	R-45TS	.045	Electronic		4B	③	28	7.5-9	600	500④
	8-350 Chev.	170	R-45TS	.045	Electronic		—	8B	28	7.5-9	—	500
'79	6-200 Chev.	All	R-45TS	.045	Electronic		8B	14B	34	4.5-6.0	700	600
	6-231 Buick	All	R-46TSX	.060	Electronic		15B	15B	16	4.25-5.75	600	500
	8-267 Chev.	All	R-45TS	.045	Electronic		4B	10B	28	7.5-9.0	600	500
	8-305 Chev.	All	R-45TS	.045	Electronic		4B	4B	28	7.5-9.0	600	500
	8-350 Chev.	All	R-43TS	.045	Electronic		—	8B	28	7.5-9.0	—	500

NOTE: The underhood specifications sticker often reflects tune-up specification changes made in production. Sticker figures must be used if they disagree with those in this chart.
  ▲ See text for procedure
  ● Figure in parentheses indicates California engine
  ■ All gures Before Top Dead Center
  * When two idle speed figures are separated by a slash, the lower figure is with the idle speed solenoid disconnected
  ① 6B for Calif. engines except engine code CCC which is 8B 10 B for high altitude engines

② 750 w/o AC
   800 w/AC
③ 49 states: 4B
   Calif.: 6B
   High Altitude: 8B
④ High Altitude: 600
A After Top Dead Center
B Before Top Dead Center
TDC Top Dead Center
— Not applicable

87946c08

TUNE-UP SPECIFICATIONS
1972 - 79 Nova

When analyzing compression test results, look for uniformity among cylinders rather than specific pressures.

Year	ENGINE No. Cyl. Displacement (cu in.)	hp	SPARK PLUGS Orig. Type	Gap (in.)	DISTRIBUTOR Point Dwell (deg)	Point Gap (in.)	IGNITION TIMING (deg) ▲ • Man Trans	Auto Trans	VALVES Intake Opens ■ (deg) •	Fuel Pump Pressure (psi)	IDLE SPEED (rpm) ▲ * Trans Man •	Trans Auto
'72	6-250	110	R-46T	.035	31-34	.019	4B	4B	16	4-5	700	600
	8-307	130	R-44T	.035	29-31	.019	4B	8B	28	5½-7½	900	600
	8-350	165	R-44T	.035	29-31	.019	6B	6B	28(44)	7½-9	900	600
	8-350	200	R-44T	.035	29-31	.019	4B	8B	28(44)	7½-9	800	600
'73	6-250	100	R-46T	.035	31-34	.019	6B	6B	16	3½-4½	700/450	600/450
	8-307	115	R-44T	.035	29-31	.019	4B	8B	28	5-6½	900/450	600/450
	8-350	145	R-44T	.035	29-31	.019	8B	8B	28	7-8½	900/450	600/450
	8-350	175	R-44T	.035	29-31	.019	8B	12B	28	7-8½	900/450	600/450
'74	6-250	100	R-46T	.035	31-34	.019	6B	6B	16	4-5	800/450	600/450
	8-350	145	R-44T	.035	29-31	.019	4B	8B	28	7½-9	900/450	600/450
	8-350	160	R-44T	.035	29-31	.019	4B	8B	44	7½-9	900/450	600/450
	8-350	185	R-44T	.035	29-31	.019	4B	8B	28	7½-9	900/450	600/450
'75	6-250	105	R46TX	.060	Electronic		10B	10B	16	4-5	800/425	550/425③ (600/425)
	8-262	110	R-44TX	.060	Electronic		8B	8B	26	7½-9	800	600
	8-350	145	R-44TX	.060	Electronic		6B	6B	28	7½-9	800	600
	8-350	155	R-44TX	.060	Electronic		6B	8B(6B)	28	7½-9	800	600
'76	6-250	105	R-46TS	.035	Electronic		6B	6B	16	3½-4½	850	550(600)
	6-250①	105	R-46TS	.035	Electronic		6B	8B	16	3½-4½	850	600
	8-305	140	R-45TS	.045	Electronic		6B	8B(TDC)	28	7-8½	800	600
	8-350	165	R-45TS	.045	Electronic		8B(6B)	8B(6B)	28	7-8½	800	600
'77	6-250	All	R-46TS	.035	Electronic		6B	8B(6B)④	16	4-5	⑤	550(600)
	8-305	All	R-45TS	.045	Electronic		8B	8B(6B)	28	7½-9	600	500
	8-350	All	R-45TS	.045	Electronic		8B	8B	28	7½-9	700	500
'78	6-250 Chev.	All	R-46TS	.035	Electronic		6B	②	16	4-5	800/425	500(600)/ 425(400)
	8-305 Chev.	All	R-45TS	.045	Electronic		4B	4B(6B)	28	7.5-9	600	500
	8-350 Chev.	All	R-45TS	.045	Electronic		——	8B	28	7.5-9	——	500
'79	6-250 Chev.	All	R-46TS	.035	Electronic		8B	10B(6B)	16	4.5-6.0	800	500
	8-305 Chev.	All	R-45TS	.045	Electronic		4B	4B	28	7.5-9.0	600	500
	8-350 Chev.	All	R-45TS	.045	Electronic		—	8B	28	7.5-9.0	——	500

NOTE: The underhood specifications sticker often reflects tune-up specification changes made in production. Sticker figures must be used if they disagree with those in this chart.

▲ See text for procedure
• Figure in parentheses indicates California engine
■ All figures before top dead center
* When two idle speed figures are separated by a slash, the lower figure is with the idle speed solenoid disconnected.
① not used
② 49 states without A/C: 10B
　49 states with A/C: 8B
　Calif.: 6B

③ Without intake manifold integral with head—600/450
④ 6B for Calif. engines except engine code CCC which is 8B
　10B for high altitude engines
⑤ 750 w/o AC; 800 w/AC
A After Top Dead Center
B Before Top Dead Center
TDC Top Dead Center
— Not applicable

87946c09

TUNE-UP SPECIFICATIONS
1972 - 79 Full-Sized Chevrolet
When analyzing compression test results, look for uniformity among cylinders rather than specific pressures.

Year	ENGINE No. Cyl Displacement	hp (cu in.)	SPARK PLUGS Orig. Type	Gap (in.)	DISTRIBUTOR Point Dwell (deg)	Point Gap (in.)	IGNITION TIMING (deg) ▲ Man Trans	● Auto Trans	VALVES Intake Opens ■ (deg) ●	Fuel Pump Pressure (psi)	IDLE SPEED (rpm) ▲ ● Man Trans	Auto Trans
'72	6-250	.110	R46T	.035	31-34	.019	4B	4B	16	4-5	700	600
	8-350	165	R44T	.035	29-31	.019	6B	6B	28(44)	7½-9	900	600
	8-400	170	R44T	.035	29-31	.019	2B	6B	28(44)	7½-9	900	600
	8-402	210	R44T	.035	29-31	.019	8B	8B	30(44)	7½-9	750	600
	8-454	270	R44T	.035	29-31	.019	8B	8B	56	7½-9	750	600
'73	6-250	100	R46T	.035	31-34	.019	6B	—	16	3½-4½	700/450②	—
	8-350	145	R44T	.035	29-31	.019	—	8B	28	7½-9	—	600/450②
	8-350	175	R44T	.035	29-31	.019	—	12B	28	7½-9	—	600/450②
	8-400	140	R44T	.035	29-31	.019	—	8B	28	7½-9	—	600/450②
	8-454	245	R44T	.035	29-31	.019	—	10B	55	7½-9	—	600/450②
'74	8-350	145	R44T	.035	29-31	.019	—	8B	28(44)	7½-9	—	600
	8-350	160	R44T	.035	29-31	.019	—	12B(8B)	28(44)	7½-9	—	600
	8-400	150	R44T	.035	29-31	.019	—	8B	28(44)	7½-9	—	600
	8-400	180	R44T	.035	29-31	.019	—	8B	28(44)	7½-9	—	600
	8-454	235	R44T	.035	29-31	.019	—	10B	55	7½-9	—	600
'75	8-350	145	R-44TX	.060	Electronic		—	6B	28	7½-9	—	600
	8-350	155	R-44TX	.060	Electronic		—	6B	28	7½-9	—	600
	8-400	175	R-44TX	.060	Electronic		—	8B	28	7½-9	—	600
	8-454	215	R-44TX	.060	Electronic		—	16B	55	7½-9	—	650
'76	8-350	145	R-45TS	.045	Electronic		—	6B	28	7½-9	—	600
	8-350	165	R-45TS	.045	Electronic		—	8B (6B)	28	7½-9	—	600
	8-400	175	R-45TS	.045	Electronic		—	8B	28	7½-9	—	600
	8-454	225	R-45TS	.045	Electronic		—	12B	55	7½-9	—	550
'77	6-250	All	R-46TS	.035	Electronic		—	8B(6B)③	16	4-5	—	550/600④
	8-305	All	R-45TS	.045	Electronic		—	8B(6B)	28	7½-9	—	500
	8-350	All	R-45TS	.045	Electronic		—	8B	28	7½-9	—	500/600④
'78	6-250	110	R-46TS	.035	Electronic		—	①	16	4-5	—	550(600)
	8-305	145	R-45TS	.045	Electronic		—	4B(6B)	28	7-9	—	500
	8-350	170	R-45TS	.045	Electronic		—	6B(8B)	28	7-9	—	500
'79	6-250	110	R-46TS	.035	Electronic		—	10B(6B)	16	4.5-6.0	⑥	⑥
	8-305	145	R-45TS	.045	Electronic		—	4B	28	7.5-9.0	⑥	⑥
	8-350	170	R-45TS	.045	Electronic		—	6B(8B)	28	7.5-9.0	⑥	⑥

▲ See text for procedure
● Figure in parentheses indicates California engine
■ All figures Before Top Dead Center
① Non-California, non-air conditioning: 10B
  Non-California, with air conditioning: 8B
  California: 6B
② Lower figure with Idle Solenoid disconnected

③ High altitude—10B
④ High figure with A/C
⑤ See underhood specifications sticker
⑥ See Underhood Sticker
B Before Top Dead Center
TDC Top Dead Center
— Not applicable

87946c10

TUNE-UP SPECIFICATIONS
1972 - 79 Corvette
When analyzing compression test results, look for uniformity among cylinders rather than specific pressures.

Year	ENGINE No. Cyl Displacement (cu in.)	hp	SPARK PLUGS Orig. Type	Gap (in.)	DISTRIBUTOR Point Dwell (deg)	Point Gap (in.)	IGNITION TIMING (deg) ▲ Man Trans •	Auto Trans	VALVES Intake Opens ■ (deg)	Fuel Pump Pressure (psi)	IDLE SPEED • (rpm) ▲ Man Trans	Auto Trans
'72	8-350	200	R44T	.035	29-31	.019	8B	8B	28(44)	7½-9	800	600
	8-350	255	R44T	.035	29-31	.019	4B	8B	42½	7½-9	900	700
	8-454	270	R44T	.035	29-31	.019	8B	8B	56	7½-9	800	600
'73	8-350	190	R44T	.035	29-31	.019	12B	12B	28	7½-9	900/450①	600/450
	8-350	250	R44T	.035	29-31	.019	8B	8B	52	7½-9	900/450①	700/450
	8-454	275	R44T	.035	29-31	.019	10B	10B	55	7½-9	900/450①	600/450
'74	8-350	195	R44T	.035	29-31	.019	8B(4B)	8B	28(44)	7½-9	900	600
	8-350	250	R44T	.035	29-31	.019	8B	8B	52	7½-9	900	700
	8-454	270	R44T	.035	29-31.	.019	10B	10B	55	7½-9	800	600
'75	8-350	165	R-44TX	.060	Electronic		6B	6B	28	7½-9	800	600
	8-350	205	R-44TX	.060	Electronic		12B	12B	52	7½-9	900	700
76	8-350	180	R-45TS	.045	Electronic		8B	8B(6B)	28	7½-9	800	600
	8-350	210	R-45TS	.045	Electronic		12B	12B	52	7½-9	1000	700
'77	8-350	180	R-45TS	.045	Electronic		8B	8B	28	7½-9	700	500/600②
	8-350	210	R-45TS	.045	Electronic		12B	12B	52	7½-9	800	500/600②
'78	8-350	185	R-45TS	.045	Electronic		6B	6B(8B)	28	7-9	700	500③
	8-350	220	R-45TS	.045	Electronic		12B	12B	52	7-9	900	700
'79	8-350	185	R-45TS	.045	Electronic		6B	④	28	7.5-9.0	⑤	⑤
	8-350	220	R-45TS	.045	Electronic		12B	12B	52	7.5-9.0	⑤	⑤

▲ See text for procedure
● Figure in parentheses iindicates California engine
■ All figures Before Top Dead Center
① Lower figure with Idle Solenoid disconnected
② Higher figure with A/C
③ High Altitude: 600
④ Except Calif. and High Altitude: 6B
  Calif. and High Altitude: 8B
⑤ See Underhood Sticker
B Before Top Dead Center
— Not applicable

MECHANICAL VALVE LIFTER CLEARANCE

Year	Engine	Intake (Hot) In.	Exhaust (Hot) In.
1972	V8-350 255 hp	.024	.030

87946c11

TUNE-UP SPECIFICATIONS
1972 - 78 Truck

CU. IN. DISPLACEMENT (cu. in.)	YEAR	SPARK PLUG GAP (in.)	DISTRIBUTOR POINT DWELL (deg.)	POINT GAP (in.)	IGNITION TIMING (DEGREES)	CRANKCASE COMP. PRESSURE	VALVE CLEARANCE Int. Exh.	NO LOAD GOV. RPM (rpm)	PUMP FUEL PRESS (psi)	IDLE SPEED* (rpm) STD.	AUTO.
					**SIX CYLINDER**						
250	1971	0.035	31-34	0.019	4B	130	Hyd.		3.5-4.5	550	500
	1972	0.035	31-34	0.019	4B②	130	Hyd.		3.5-4.5	700	600
	1973	0.035	31-34	0.019	6B③	130	Hyd.		3.5-4.5	700	600④
	1974	0.035	31-34	0.019	8B⑩	130	Hyd.		3.5-4.5	850⑤	600
	1975-78	0.035	Elec.	Elec.	10B	130	Hyd.		3.5-4.5	900N	550DR
292	1971	0.035	31-34	0.019	4B	130	Hyd.		3.5-4.5	550	500
	1972	0.035	31-34	0.019	4B	130	Hyd.		3.5-4.5	700	700
	1973	0.035	31-34	0.019	4B⑧	130	Hyd.		3.5-4.5	700⑨	700⑨
	1974	0.035	31-34	0.019	8B	130	Hyd.		3.5-4.5	700	700
	1975-78	0.035	Elec.	Elec.	8B	130	Hyd.		3.5-4.5	600	600
305C (V6)	1973	0.040	31-34	0.019	7-½B	125	0.012-0.018	3600	5.0-7.0	550	550
	1974	0.035	31-34	0.019	7-½B	125	0.012-0.018	3600	5.0-7.0	600	600
379 (V6)	1973	0.035	31-34	0.019	8B	125	0.012-0.018	4000	5.0-7.0	550	550
	1974	0.035	31-34	0.019	6B	125	0.012-0.018	4000	5.0-7.0	575	575
432 (V6)	1973	0.035	31-34	0.019	8B	125		3200	5.0-7.0	525	525
	1974	0.035	31-34	0.019	6B	125	0.012-0.018	3200	5.0-7.0	525	525
					**EIGHT CYLINDER**						
307	1971 (200hp)	0.035	28-32	0.019	4B⑫	150	Hyd.		5.0-6.5	600	550
	1971 (215hp)	0.035	28-32	0.019	4B	150	Hyd.		5.0-6.5	550	500
	1972	0.035	28-32	0.019	4B⑬	150	Hyd.		5.0-6.5	900⑭	600
	1973	0.035	29-31	0.019	4B⑮	150	Hyd.		5.0-6.5	900⑯	600
350	1971	0.035	28-32	0.019	4B⑳	150	Hyd.		5.0-6.5	600	550
	1972	0.035	29-31	0.019	4B⑳	150	Hyd.		5.0-6.5	750	600
	1973	0.035	29-31	0.019	㉑	150	Hyd.		5.0-6.5	900㉒	600㉒
	1974	0.035	29-31	0.019	㉓	150	Hyd.		5.0-6.5	900㉔	600㉔
	1975 (2bbl)	0.060	Elec.	Elec.	6B	150	Hyd.		5.0-6.5	——	600
	1975	0.060	Elec.	Elec.	6B	150	Hyd.		5.0-6.5	700	600
	1975-78 (Calif.)	0.060	Elec.	Elec.	2B	150	Hyd.		5.0-6.5	700	600
366	1971	0.035	28-32	0.019	8B	150	Hyd.		5.0-6.5	500	500
	1972	0.035	28-32	0.019	8B	150	Hyd.		5.0-6.5	550	550
	1973	0.035	28-32	0.019	8B	150	Hyd.		5.0-6.5	550㉕	550㉕
	1974	0.035	28-32	0.019	8B	150	Hyd.		5.0-6.5	600	600
	1975 (Fed.)	0.035	28-32	0.019	8B	150	Hyd.		5.0-6.5	700	700
	1975 (w/AT-475)	0.035	28-32	0.019	8B	150	Hyd.	3600	5.0-6.5	700	700
	1975-76 (Calif.)	0.060	Elec.	Elec.	8B	150	Hyd.		5.0-6.5	700	700
400	1975-78 (fed.)	0.045	Elec.	Elec.	4B	150	Hyd.		5.0-6.5	700	700
	1975-78 (Calif.)	0.045	Elec.	Elec.	2B	150	Hyd.		5.0-6.5	700	700
402	1971	0.035	28-32	0.019	8B	150	Hyd.		7.0-8.5	600	600
	1972	0.035	28-32	0.019	8B	150	Hyd.		7.0-8.5	750	600

87946c17

TUNE-UP SPECIFICATIONS
1972 - 78 Truck (Cont.)

CU. IN. DISPLACE-MENT (cu. in.)	YEAR	SPARK PLUG GAP (in.)	DISTRIBUTOR POINT DWELL (deg.)	POINT GAP (in.)	IGNITION TIMING (DEGREES)	CRANKCASE COMP. PRESSURE	VALVE CLEARANCE Int. Exh.	NO LOAD GOV. RPM (rpm)	PUMP FUEL PRESS (psi)	IDLE SPEED* (rpm) STD.	AUTO.
EIGHT CYLINDER										
427	1971	0.035	28-32	0.019	8B	150	Hyd.		7.0-8.5	500	500
	1972	0.035	28-32	0.019	8B	150	Hyd.		7.0-8.5	550	550
	1973	0.035	28-32	0.019	8B	150	Hyd.		7.0-8.5	550㉓	550㉓
	1974	0.035	28-32	0.019	8B	150	Hyd.		7.0-8.5	600	600
	1975-76 (Calif.)	0.060	Elec.	Elec.	8B	150	Hyd.		7.0-8.5	700	700
	1975-76 (Fed.)	0.035	28-32	0.019	8B	150	Hyd.		7.0-8.5	700	700
454	1973 (Fed.)	0.035	28-32	0.019	10B	150	Hyd.		7.0-8.5	900④	600④
	1973 (Calif.)	0.035	28-32	0.019	㉘	150	Hyd.		7.0-8.5	900④	600④
	1974	0.035	29-31	0.019	10B㉙	150	Hyd.		7.0-8.5	800④	600④
	1975-76 (Fed.)	0.045	Elec.	Elec.	16B㉙	150	Hyd.		7.0-8.5	—	650④
	1975-78 (Calif.)	0.045	Elec.	Elec.	8B	150	Hyd.		7.0-8.5	700	700

—— Not Applicable
Elec.—Electronic Ignition
Hyd.—Hydraulic valve lifters
N—Neutral
DR—Drive
B—BTDC

①—Not used
②—TDC on K-20 Suburban California only
③—4B All C-K 20 except Suburban; all C-P 30 series and all G-30 except Sportvan
④—700 rpm All C-K 20 except Suburban; all C-P 30 series and all G-30 except Sportvan
⑤—600 rpm All C-K 20 except Suburban; all C-P 30 series and all G-30 except Sportvan
⑥—Not used
⑦—Not used
⑧—8B California
⑨—600 rpm California
⑩—68 All C-K 20 series except Suburban; all C-P 30 series and all G-30 except Sportvan
⑪—Not used
⑫—8B w/automatic transmission
⑬—8B 10 series w/automatic transmission only
⑭—950 rpm California
⑮—8B All 10 series, C-K 20 Suburban, G-20 & 30 Sportvans w/auto transmission TDC All others
⑯—600 rpm All C-K 20 except Suburban; all C-P 30 series and all G-30 except Sportvan
⑰—Not used

⑱—Not used
⑲—Not used
⑳—8B w/automatic transmission
㉑—C-20 Suburban 2B
All 10 series, K-20 Suburban, G-20, and G-30 Sportvan:
  w/manual transmission 8B
  w/automatic transmission 12B
All others 4B
㉒—All C-K 20 except Suburban; all C-P 30 series and all G-20 & 30 except Sportvan 700 rpm
㉓—Federal except C-K 10 & 20 Suburban and G-20 & 30 Sportvan 8B
Federal C-K 10 & 20 Suburban and G-20 & 30 Sportvan:
  w/automatic transmission 12B
  w/automatic transmission (except Suburban) 8B
  Suburban (w/manual transmission) 6B
California:
  w/automatic transmission 8B
  Suburban (w/manual transmission) 6B
  w/manual transmission 4B
㉔—All C-K 20 except Suburban, all C-P 30 series and all G-20 & 30 except Sportvan 600 rpm
㉕—750 rpm California
㉖—Not used
㉗—Not used
㉘—All 10 series, C-K 20 Suburban, G-20 and G-30 Sportvan 10 B
All C-K 20 except Suburban, all C-P 30 Series and all G-30 except Sportvan:
  w/manual transmission 5B
  w/automatic transmission 8B
㉙—All C-K 20 except Suburban, all C-P 30 series and all G-30 except Sportvan 8B

87946c18

TUNE-UP SPECIFICATIONS
1979 - 86 Pick-Ups and Suburban

Year	Engine Displacement (cu in.)	Spark Plugs Type	Gap (in.)	Distributor	Ignition Timing (deg) MT	AT	Fuel Pump Pressure (psi)	Compression Pressure (psi) ●	Idle Speed (rpm)* MT	AT
'79	6-250 (LD Fed)	R46TS	0.035	Electronic	10B	10B	4.5-6.0	130	750	600
	6-250 ③	R46TS	0.035	Electronic	6B	8B	4.5-6.0	130	750	600
	6-292	R44T	0.035	Electronic	8B	8B	4.5-6.0	130	700	700
	8-305	R45TS	0.045	Electronic	6B	6B	7.5-9.0	150	600	500
	8-350 (LD)	R45TS	0.045	Electronic	8B	8B	7.5-9.0	150	700	500
	8-350 (HD)	R44T	0.045	Electronic	4B	4B	7.5-9.0	150	700	700(N)
	8-400	R45TS	0.045	Electronic	—	4B	7.5-9.0	150	—	500
	8-454 (LD)	R45TS	0.045	Electronic	8B	8B	7.5-9.0 ②	150	700	500
	8-454 (HD)	R44T	0.045	Electronic	—	4B	7.5-9.0 ②	150	—	700(N)

87946c19

TUNE-UP SPECIFICATIONS
1979 - 86 Pick-Ups and Suburban (Cont.)

Year	Engine Displacement (cu in.)	Spark Plugs Type	Spark Plugs Gap (in.)	Distributor	Ignition Timing (deg) MT	Ignition Timing (deg) AT	Fuel Pump Pressure (psi)	Compression Pressure (psi) ●	Idle Speed (rpm)* MT	Idle Speed (rpm)* AT
'80	6-250 (LD Fed)	R46TS	0.035	Electronic	10B	10B	4.5–6.0	130	750	650
	6-250 (LD Calif)	R46TS	0.035	Electronic	10B	10B	4.5–6.0	130	750	600
	6-250 [3]	R46TS	0.035	Electronic	—	8B	4.5–6.0	130	—	600
	6-292	R44T	0.035	Electronic	8B	8B	4.5–6.0	130	700	700(N)
	8-305	R45TS	0.045	Electronic	8B	8B	7.5–9.0	150	600	500
	8-350 (LD)	R45TS	0.045	Electronic	8B	8B	7.5–9.0	150	700	500
	8-350 (HD Fed)	R44T	0.045	Electronic	4B	4B	7.5–9.0	150	700	700(N)
	8-350 (HD Calif)	R44T	0.045	Electronic	6B	6B	7.5–9.0	150	700	700(N)
	8-400 (HD Fed)	R44T	0.045	Electronic	—	4B	7.5–9.0	150	—	700(N)
	8-400 (HD Calif)	R44T	0.045	Electronic	—	6B	7.5–9.0	150	—	700(N)
	8-454	R44T	0.045	Electronic	4B	4B	7.5–9.0 [2]	150	700	700(N)
'81	6-250 (Fed)	R45TS	0.035	Electronic	10B	10B	4.5–6.0	130	750	650(D)
	6-250 (Calif)	R46TS	0.035	Electronic	10B	10B	4.5–6.0	130	750	650(D)
	6-292	R44T	0.035	Electronic	8B	8B	4.5–6.0	130	700	700(N)
	8-305 2 bbl	R45TS	0.045	Electronic	8B	8B	7.5–9.0	150	600	500(D)
	8-305 4 bbl	R45TS	0.045	Electronic	4B	4B [4]	7.5–9.0	150	700	500(D)
	8-350 (LD)	R45TS	0.045	Electronic	8B	8B [5]	7.5–9.0	150	700	500(D)
	8-350 (HD Fed)	R44T	0.045	Electronic	4B	4B	7.5–9.0	150	700	700(N)
	8-350 (HD Calif)	R44T	0.045	Electronic	6B	6B	7.5–9.0	150	700	700(N)
	8-350 Diesel	—	—	Electronic	—	8B [6]		450	—	575(D) [7]
	8-454	R44T	0.045	Electronic	4B	4B	7.5–9.0	150	700	700(N)
'82	6-250	R45TS	[8]	Electronic	[8]	[8]	4.5–6	—	[8]	[8]
	6-292	R44T	.035	Electronic	8	8	4–5	—	700	700
	8-305	R45TS	.045	Electronic	[8]	[8]	[8]	—	[8]	[8]
	8-350 LD	R45TS	.045	Electronic	[8]	[8]	[8]	—	[8]	[8]
	8-350 HD	R44T	.045	Electronic	[8]	[8]	[8]	—	[8]	[8]
	8-379	Diesel	—	—	[8]	[8]	[8]	—	[8]	[8]
	8-454	R44T	.045	Electronic	[8]	[8]	[8]	—	[8]	[8]
'83	6-250	R45TS	[8]	Electronic	[8]	[8]	4.5–6	—	[8]	[8]
	6-292	R44T	.035	Electronic	8	8	4–6	—	700	700
	8-305	R45TS	.045	Electronic	[8]	[8]	[8]	—	[8]	[8]
	8-350 LD	R45TS	.045	Electronic	[8]	[8]	[8]	—	[8]	[8]
	8-350 HD	R44T	.045	Electronic	[8]	[8]	[8]	—	[8]	[8]
	8-379	Diesel	—	—	[8]	[8]	[8]	—	[8]	[8]
	8-454	R44T	.045	Electronic	[8]	[8]	[8]	—	[8]	[8]
'84	6-250	R45TS	[8]	Electronic	[8]	[8]	4.5–6	—	[8]	[8]
	6-292	R44T	.035	Electronic	8	8	4.5–6	—	700	700
	8-305	R45TS	.045	Electronic	[8]	[8]	[8]	—	[8]	[8]
	8-350 LD	R45TS	.045	Distributor	[8]	[8]	[8]	—	[8]	[8]
	8-350 HD	R44T	.045	Electronic	[8]	[8]	[8]	—	[8]	[8]
	8-379	Diesel	—	—	[8]	[8]	[8]	—	[8]	[8]
	8-454	R44T	.045	Electronic	[8]	[8]	[8]	—	[8]	[8]
'85–'86	6-292	R43CTS	[8]	Electronic	[8]	[8]	4–6.5	—	[8]	[8]
	6-292	R44T	[8]	Electronic	[8]	[8]	4–6.5	—	[8]	[8]
	8-305	R45TS	[8]	Electronic	[8]	[8]	4–6.5	—	[8]	[8]
	8-350	R45TS	[8]	Electronic	[8]	[8]	4–6.5	—	[8]	[8]
	8-454	R44T	[8]	Electronic	[8]	[8]	4–6.5	—	[8]	[8]

NOTE: All engines use hydraulic valve lifters
NOTE: Part numbers in this chart are not recommendations by Chilton for any product by brand name.
NOTE: The underhood sticker often reflects tune-up changes made in production. Sticker figures must be used if they disagree with those in this chart.
● Maximum variation among cylinders—20 psi
B Before Top Dead Center
LD Light-duty
HD Heavy-duty

87946c20

TUNE-UP SPECIFICATIONS
1979 - 86 Full-Sized Vans

When analyzing compression results, look for uniformity among cylinders rather than specific pressures.

Year	Engine Cu In. Displacement	Spark Plugs Orig Type	Gap (in.)	Distributor	Ignition Timing (deg)▲ MT	AT	Fuel Pump Pressure (psi)	Curb Idle Speed (rpm)● MT	AT
'79	6-250	R46TS	.035	Electronic	10B⑤	10B⑦	4.5-6	750	600
	8-305	R45TS	.045	Electronic	6B	6B	7.5-9	700	600
	8-350⑧	R45TS	.045	Electronic	8B	8B	7.5-9	700	500
	8-400⑧	R45TS	.045	Electronic	—	4B	7.5-9	—	500
'80-'81	6-250	R46TS	.035	Electronic	10B	8B⑨	4-6	750	650(D)
	8-305 (2-bbl)	R45TS	.045	Electronic	8B	8B	7-9	700	600(D)
	8-305 (4-bbl)	R45TS	.045	Electronic	6B	4B	7-9	700	500(D)
	8-350	R45TS	.045	Electronic	8B⑩	8B⑪	7-9	700	500(D)⑫
'82	6-250	R45TS	.045	Electronic	①	①	4-6	①	①
	8-305	R45TS	.045	Electronic	①	①	7-9	①	①
	8-350	R45TS	.045	Electronic	①	①	7-9	①	①
'83	6-250	R45TS	.045	Electronic	①	①	4-6	①	①
	8-305	R45TS	.045	Electronic	①	①	7-9	①	①
	8-350	R45TS	.045	Electronic	①	①	7-9	①	①
	8-379	Diesel	—	—	①	①	—	①	①
'84	6-250	R45TS	.045	Electronic	①	①	4-6	①	①
	8-305	R45TS	.045	Electronic	①	①	7-9	①	①
	8-350	R45TS	.045	Electronic	①	①	7-9	①	①
	8-379	Diesel	—	—	①	①	—	①	①
'85-'86	6-252	R43CTS	①	Electronic	①	①	4-6.5	③	③
	8-305	R45TS	①	Electronic	①	①	4-6.5	③	③
	8-350	R45TS	②	Electronic	①	①	4-6.5	③	③
	8-379	—	—	Diesel	—	—	6.5-9	650	650④

NOTE: The underhood specifications sticker often reflects tune-up changes made in production. Sticker figures must be used if they disagree with those in this chart.

NOTE: Part numbers in this chart are not recommendations by Chilton for any product by brand name.

NOTE: All engines use hydraulic valve lifters.

● Figures in parentheses are for California, and are given only if they differ from the 49 state specification. Automatic transmission idle speeds are set in Drive, unless specified otherwise.

▲ At idle speed with vacuum advance hose disconnected and plugged, unless specified otherwise in the text.

N—Transmission in Neutral
D—Transmission in Drive
HD Heavy Duty
LD Light Duty

① See the underhood specifications sticker
② Vehicles w/HD emissions use R44T
③ If equipped w/ECM, no adjustment required
④ Adjust w/AT in Park
⑤ California only
⑥ G-20, G-30, 2500, 3500 series in Calif.—6B
⑦ G-20, G-30, 2500, 3500 series in Calif.—8B

⑧ Some G-30/3500 series vans differ. Check the underhood emission sticker.
⑨ High Alt.—10B
⑩ Fed 1 ton models—4B Calif 3/4 and 1 ton models—6B
⑪ 1 ton models—6B
⑫ 1 ton models—700(N) Calif. 1/2 and 1/3 ton models—550 (D)

TUNE-UP SPECIFICATIONS
1979 - 86 Blazer/Jimmy

When analyzing compression test results, look for uniformity among cylinders rather than specific pressures.

Year	Engine No. Cyl Displacement	Spark Plugs Orig Type	Gap (in.)	Distributor	Ignition Timing (deg) Man Trans	Auto Trans	Fuel Pump Pressure (psi)	Idle Speed (rpm) Man Trans	Auto Trans ▲
'79	6-250	R46TS	.035	Electronic	10B	10B	4½-6	750	600
	8-305	R45TS	.045	Electronic	6B	6B	7-9	600	500
	8-350	R45TS	.045	Electronic	8B	8B	7-9	700	500
	8-400	R45TS	.060	Electronic	—	4B	7-9	—	500
'80-'81	6-250	R46TS	.035	Electronic	10B	10B	3.5-4.5	750	650(D)
	8-305	R45TS	.045	Electronic	4B	2B	7.0-8.5	700	500(D)
	8-350	R45TS	.045	Electronic	8B	8B	7.0-8.5	700	500(D)
'82	6-250	R45TS	.045	Electronic	①	①	4-6	①	①
	8-305	R45TS	.045	Electronic	①	①	7-9	①	①
	8-350	R45TS	.045	Electronic	①	①	7-9	①	①
	8-379	Diesel	—	—	①	①	—	①	①
'83	6-250	R45TS	.045	Electronic	①	①	4-6	①	①
	8-305	R45TS	.045	Electronic	①	①	7-9	①	①
	8-350	R45TS	.045	Electronic	①	①	7-9	①	①
	8-379	Diesel	—	—	①	①	—	①	①
	8-454	R44T	.045	Electronic	①	①	—	①	①
'84	6-250	R45TS	.045	Electronic	①	①	4-6	①	①
	8-305	R45TS	.045	Electronic	①	①	7-9	①	①
	8-350	R45TS	.045	Electronic	①	①	7-9	①	①
	8-379	Diesel	—	—	①	①	—	①	①
	8-454	R44T	.045	Electronic	①	①	—	①	①
'85-'86	8-305	R45TS	①	Electronic	①	①	4-6.5	①②	①②
	8-350 LD	R45TS	①	Electronic	①	①	4-6.5	①②	①②
	8-350 HD	R45TS	①	Electronic	①	①	4-6.5	①②	①②
	8-379	—	—	Diesel	—	—	6.5-9	①	①
	8-454	R44T	①	Electronic	①	①	4-6.5	①②	①②

NOTE: The underhood specifications sticker often reflects tuneup specification changes made in production. Sticker figures must be used if they disagree with those in this chart. Part numbers in this chart are not recommendations by Chilton for any product name.

NOTE: All engines use hydraulic valve lifters.

● Figures in parentheses are for California, and are given only when they differ from the 49 State models. When two idle speeds separated by a slash are given, the lower figure is with the solenoid disconnected.

▲ Automatic transmission idle speed set in Drive unless otherwise indicated

B Before Top Dead Center
N Neutral
TDC Top Dead Center
2WD Two wheel drive
4WD 4 wheel drive
① See under hood sticker
② Computer controlled on some models

87946c23

TUNE-UP SPECIFICATIONS
1980 - 86 Corvette
(When analyzing compression test results, look for uniformity among cylinders rather than specific pressures.)

Year	Engine No. of Cyl. Displacement (cu. in.)	VIN Code	Option Code	hp	Spark Plugs Type (A.C.)	Gap (in.)	Ignition Timing (deg.)④ Man. Trans.	Auto. Trans.	Valves Intake Opens ⑤(deg.)	Fuel Pump Pressure (psi)	Idle Speed (rpm)④ Man. Trans.	Auto. Trans.
'80	8-305	H	LG4	180	R45TS	0.045	4B	4B	28	7½–9	②	②
	8-350	8	L48	190	R45TS	0.045	6B③	6B	28	7½–9	②	②
	8-350	6	L82	230	R45TS	0.045	12B	12B	52	7½–9	②	②
'81	8-350	6	L81	190	R45TS	0.045	6B	6B	38	7½–9	②	②
'82	8-350	8	L83	200	R45TS	0.045	①	②	32	9–13	①	②
'84	8-350	8	L83	205	R45TS	0.045	②	②	32	9–13	②	②
'85–'86	8-350	8	L98	230	R45TS	0.045	②	②	NA	NA	②	②
'87	See Underhood Specifications Sticker											

NOTE: All models use electronic ignition systems. No adjustments are necessary. The underhood specifications sticker often reflects tuneup specification changes made in production. Sticker figures must be used if they disagree with those in this chart. Part numbers in this chart are not recommendations by Chilton for any product by brand name.

B—Before Top Dead Center
① Manual transmission not available
② See Underhood Sticker
③ Except Calif. and High Altitude: 6B Calif. and
   High Altitude: 8B
④ See text for procedure
⑤ All figures Before Top Dead Center

87946c12

TUNE-UP SPECIFICATIONS
1980 - 86 Full-Sized Chevrolet
(When analyzing compression test results, look for uniformity among cylinders rather then specific pressures.)

Year	V.I.N. Code	Eng. No. Cyl. Displ. Cu. In.	Eng. Mfg.	Spark Plugs Orig Type	Gap (in.)	Ignition Timing (deg)▲● Man. Trans	Ignition Timing (deg)▲● Auto. Trans	Intake Valve Opens ■(deg)●	Fuel Pump Pressure (psi)	Idle Speed (rpm)▲* Man.● Trans	Idle Speed (rpm)▲* Auto. Trans
'80–'81	K	6-229	Chev.	R-45TS	0.045	8B	12B	42	4.5–6.0	700	600
	A	6-231	Buick	R-45TSX	0.060	①	15B	16	4.25–5.75	①	560(600)
	3	6-231	Buick	R-45TSX	0.060	①	15B	16	4.25–5.75	①	550(600)
	J	8-267	Chev.	R-45TS	0.045	①	4B	28	7.5–9.0	①	500
	H	8-305	Chev.	R-45TS	0.045	4B	4B	28	7.5–9.0	700	500(550)
	N	8-350	Olds. Diesel	—	—	①	①	16	5.5–6.5	①	①
'82	K	6-229	Chev.	R-45TS	0.045	—	6B	42	4.5–6.0	—	600
'82–'83	A	6-231	Buick	R-45TS	0.045	—	15B	16	4.25–5.75	—	500
	V	6-263	Olds. Diesel	—	—		①	16	5.5–6.5	—	①
'82	J	8-267	Chev.	R-45TS	0.045	—	6B	44	5.5–7.0	—	500
'82–'83	H	8-305	Chev.	R-45TS	0.045	—	6B	44	5.5–7.0	—	500
'82–'84	N	8-350	Olds. Diesel	—	—		①	16	5.5–6.5	—	①
'83–'84	9	6-229	Chev.	R-45TS	0.045	—	6B	42	4.5–6.0	—	600
'84	A	6-231	Buick	R-45TS	0.045	—	①	16	4.25–5.75	—	①
'84–'86	G	8-305	Chev.	R-45TS③	0.045③	—	①	—	7.5–9.0	—	①
	H	8-305	Chev.	R-45TS③	0.045③	—	①	44	5.5–7.0	—	①
'86–'87	Z	6-262	Chev.	R-43CTS②	0.035	—	①	—	—	—	①
'86	Y	8-307	Olds.	FR3LS6	0.060	—	①	—	6–7.5	—	①
'87	All			See Underhood Specifications Sticker							

NOTE: The underhood specifications sticker often reflects tune-up specifications changes made in production. Sticker figures must be used if they disagree with those in this chart.

▲ See text for procedure
● Figure in parentheses indicates California engine
■ All figures Before Top Dead Center
* When two idle speed figures are spearated by a slash, the lower figure is with the idle speed solenoid disconnected

B Before Top Dead Center
TDC Top Dead Center
— Not available
① Refer to underhood specifications sticker
② '86 Monte Carlo: R-43TS w/.035 gap
③ '86 Caprice: R-44TS w/.035 gap

87946c13

TUNE-UP SPECIFICATIONS
1980 - 86 Camaro

Year	Engine VIN Code	Engine No. of Cyl. Displacement (cu. in.)	Engine Manufac- turer	Spark Plugs Type	Gap (in.)	Ignition Timing (deg)①② Man. Trans.	Ignition Timing (deg)①② Auto. Trans.	Intake Valve Opens (deg)③	Fuel Pump Pressure (psi)	Idle Speed (rpm)①② Man. Trans.	Idle Speed (rpm)①② Auto. Trans.
'80	K	6-229	Chev.	R-45TS⑤	0.045	8B	12B	42	4½–6	700	600
	A	6-231	Buick	R-45TSX	0.060	—	15B	16	4¼–5¾	—	600
	J	8-267	Chev.	R-45TS	0.045	—	4B	28	7½–9	—	500
	H	8-305	Chev.	R-45TS	0.045	4B	4B	28	7½–9	700	500(550)
	L	8-350	Chev.	R-45TS	0.045	6B	6B	28	7½–9	700	500
'81	K	6-229	Chev.	R-45TS	0.045	6B	6B	42	4½–6	700⑥	600⑥
	A	6-231	Buick	R-45TS8	0.080	—	15B	16	4¼–5¾	—	500⑥
	J	8-267	Chev.	R-45TS	0.045	—	6B	44	7½–9	—	500⑥
	H	8-305	Chev.	R-45TS	0.045	6B	6B	44	7½–9	700	500
	L	8-350	Chev.	R-45TS	0.045	—	6B	38	7½–9	—	500⑥

87946c14

TUNE-UP SPECIFICATIONS
1980 - 86 Camaro (Cont.)

Year	Engine VIN Code	Engine No. of Cyl. Displacement (cu. in.)	Engine Manufacturer	Spark Plugs Type	Gap (in.)	Ignition Timing (deg)① ② Man. Trans.	Auto. Trans.	Intake Valve Opens (deg)③	Fuel Pump Pressure (psi)	Idle Speed (rpm)① ② Man. Trans.	Auto. Trans.
'82	2	4-151	Pont.	R-44TSX	0.060	⑦	⑦	—	9–13	⑦	⑦
	1	6-173	Chev.	R-43TS	0.045	⑦	⑦	—	5½–6½	⑦	⑦
	H	8-305	Chev.	R-45TS	0.045	⑦	⑦	—	5½–6½	⑦	⑦
	7	8-305	Chev.	R-45TS④	0.045	⑦	⑦	—	9–13	⑦	⑦
'83	2	4-151	Pont.	R-44TSX	0.060	⑦	⑦	—	9–13	⑦	⑦
	1	6-173	Chev.	R-43CTS	0.045	⑦	⑦	—	5½–6½	⑦	⑦
	H	8-305	Chev.	R-45TS	0.045	⑦	⑦	—	5½–6½	⑦	⑦
	S	8-305	Chev.	R-45TS	0.045	⑦	⑦	—	9–13	⑦	⑦
'84	2	4-151	Pont.	R-44TSX	0.060	⑦	⑦	—	9–13	⑦	⑦
	1	6-173	Chev.	R-43CTS	0.045	⑦	⑦	—	5½–6½	⑦	⑦
	H	8-305	Chev.	R-45TS	0.045	⑦	⑦	—	5½–6½	⑦	⑦
	G	8-305	Chev.	R-45TS	0.045	⑦	⑦	—	9–13	⑦	⑦
'85	2	4-151	Pont.	R-43TSX	0.060	⑦	⑦	—	9–13	⑦	⑦
	S	6-173	Chev.	R-42CTS	0.045	⑦	⑦	—	40.5–47	⑦	⑦
	F	8-305	Chev.	R-43CTS	0.045	⑦	⑦	—	40.5–47	⑦	⑦
	H	8-305	Chev.	R-45TS	0.045	⑦	⑦	—	5½–6½	⑦	⑦
	G	8-305	Chev.	R-44TS	0.045	⑦	⑦	—	9–13	⑦	⑦
'86	2	4-151	Pont.	R-43CTS6	0.060	⑦	⑦	—	9–13	⑦	⑦
	S	6-173	Chev.	R-42CTS	0.045	⑦	⑦	—	40½–47	⑦	⑦
	F	8-305	Chev.	R-43TS	0.035	⑦	⑦	—	40½–47	⑦	⑦
	H	8-305	Chev.	R-45TS	0.045	⑦	⑦	—	5½–6½	⑦	⑦
	G	8-305	Chev.	R-43TS	0.035	⑦	⑦	—	9–13	⑦	⑦
'87	ALL			See Underhood Specifications Sticker							

NOTE: The underhood specifications sticker often reflects tune-up specification changes made during the production run. Sticker figures must always be used if they disagree with those in this chart. Part numbers in this chart are not recommendations by Chilton for any product by brand name.
All models use electronic ignition systems.
B Before Top Dead Center
TDC Top Dead Center
—Not applicable
① See text for procedure
② Figure in parenthesis indicates California engine
③ All figures Before Top Dead Center (BTDC)
④ R-44TS if a colder plug is needed
⑤ With automatic trans.—R-45TS

⑥ Equipped with Idle Speed Control (I.S.C.)
⑦ These functions are controlled by the emissions computer. In rare instances when adjustment is necessary, refer to the underhood emissions sticker for specifications.

87946c15

TUNE-UP SPECIFICATIONS
1987 - 93 All Car and Truck Models

Year	Engine ID/VIN	Engine Displacement cu. in. (liter)	Spa Plugs Gap (in.)	Ignition Timing (deg.) MT	AT	Fuel Pump (psi)	Idle Speed (rpm) MT	AT	Valve Clearance In.	Ex.
1987-88	Z	6-262 (4.3)	0.040	0	0	9-13③	①	①	Hyd.	Hyd.
	T	6-292 (4.8)	0.035	8	8	5.0	700	700	Hyd.	Hyd.
	H	8-305 (5.0)	0.045	4	4	9-13③	700	700	Hyd.	Hyd.
	M	8-350 (5.7)	0.045	4	4	5.0	700	700	Hyd.	Hyd.
	K	8-350 (5.7)	0.045	4	4	9-13③	700	700	Hyd.	Hyd.
	N	8-454 (7.4)	0.045	4	4	9-13③	700	700	Hyd.	Hyd.
	W	8-454 (7.4)	0.045	4	4	5.0	700	700	Hyd.	Hyd.
1989	Z	6-262 (4.3)	0.045	②	②	9-13③	②	②	Hyd.	Hyd.
	T	6-292 (4.8)	0.035	8	8	5.0	700	700	Hyd.	Hyd.
	H	8-305 (5.0)	0.045	②	②	9-13③	②	②	Hyd.	Hyd.
	K	8-350 (5.7)	0.045	②	②	9-13③	②	②	Hyd.	Hyd.
	N	8-454 (7.4)	0.045	②	②	9-13③	②	②	Hyd.	Hyd.
	W	8-454 (7.4)	0.045	②	②	5.0③	②	②	Hyd.	Hyd.
1990	Z	6-262 (4.3)	0.045	②	②	9-13③	②	②	Hyd.	Hyd.
	H	8-305 (5.0)	0.045	②	②	9-13③	②	②	Hyd.	Hyd.
	K	8-350 (5.7)	0.045	②	②	9-13③	②	②	Hyd.	Hyd.
	N	8-454 (7.4)	0.045	②	②	9-13③	②	②	Hyd.	Hyd.
1991	Z	6-262 (4.3)	0.045	②	②	9-13③	②	②	Hyd.	Hyd.
	H	8-305 (5.0)	0.045	②	②	9-13③	②	②	Hyd.	Hyd.
	K	8-350 (5.7)	0.045	②	②	9-13③	②	②	Hyd.	Hyd.
	N	8-454 (7.4)	0.045	②	②	9-13③	②	②	Hyd.	Hyd.
1992	Z	6-262 (4.3)	0.045	②	②	9-13③	②	②	Hyd.	Hyd.
	H	8-305 (5.0)	0.035	②	②	9-13③	②	②	Hyd.	Hyd.
	K	8-350 (5.7)	0.035	②	②	9-13③	②	②	Hyd.	Hyd.
	N	8-454 (7.4)	0.035	②	②	9-13③	②	②	Hyd.	Hyd.
1993	Z	6-262 (4.3)	0.045	②	②	9-13③	②	②	Hyd.	Hyd.
	H	8-305 (5.0)	0.035	②	②	9-13③	②	②	Hyd.	Hyd.
	K	8-350 (5.7)	0.035	②	②	9-13③	②	②	Hyd.	Hyd.
	N	8-454 (7.4)	0.035	②	②	9-13③	②	②	Hyd.	Hyd.

Hyd. —Hydraulic
① Controlled by ECM
② See Underhood Sticker
③ Fuel injected

87946c22

GLOSSARY

AIR/FUEL RATIO: The ratio of air-to-gasoline by weight in the fuel mixture drawn into the engine.

AIR INJECTION: One method of reducing harmful exhaust emissions by injecting air into each of the exhaust ports of an engine. The fresh air entering the hot exhaust manifold causes any remaining fuel to be burned before it can exit the tailpipe.

ALTERNATOR: A device used for converting mechanical energy into electrical energy.

AMMETER: An instrument, calibrated in amperes, used to measure the flow of an electrical current in a circuit. Ammeters are always connected in series with the circuit being tested.

AMPERE: The rate of flow of electrical current present when one volt of electrical pressure is applied against one ohm of electrical resistance.

ANALOG COMPUTER: Any microprocessor that uses similar (analogous) electrical signals to make its calculations.

ARMATURE: A laminated, soft iron core wrapped by a wire that converts electrical energy to mechanical energy as in a motor or relay. When rotated in a magnetic field, it changes mechanical energy into electrical energy as in a generator.

ATMOSPHERIC PRESSURE: The pressure on the Earth's surface caused by the weight of the air in the atmosphere. At sea level, this pressure is 14.7 psi at 32°F (101 kPa at 0°C).

ATOMIZATION: The breaking down of a liquid into a fine mist that can be suspended in air.

AXIAL PLAY: Movement parallel to a shaft or bearing bore.

BACKFIRE: The sudden combustion of gases in the intake or exhaust system that results in a loud explosion.

BACKLASH: The clearance or play between two parts, such as meshed gears.

BACKPRESSURE: Restrictions in the exhaust system that slow the exit of exhaust gases from the combustion chamber.

BAKELITE: A heat resistant, plastic insulator material commonly used in printed circuit boards and transistorized components.

BALL BEARING: A bearing made up of hardened inner and outer races between which hardened steel balls roll.

BALLAST RESISTOR: A resistor in the primary ignition circuit that lowers voltage after the engine is started to reduce wear on ignition components.

BEARING: A friction reducing, supportive device usually located between a stationary part and a moving part.

BIMETAL TEMPERATURE SENSOR: Any sensor or switch made of two dissimilar types of metal that bend when heated or cooled due to the different expansion rates of the alloys. These types of sensors usually function as an on/off switch.

BLOWBY: Combustion gases, composed of water vapor and unburned fuel, that leak past the piston rings into the crankcase during normal engine operation. These gases are removed by the PCV system to prevent the buildup of harmful acids in the crankcase.

BRAKE PAD: A brake shoe and lining assembly used with disc brakes.

BRAKE SHOE: The backing for the brake lining. The term is, however, usually applied to the assembly of the brake backing and lining.

BUSHING: A liner, usually removable, for a bearing; an anti-friction liner used in place of a bearing.

CALIPER: A hydraulically activated device in a disc brake system, which is mounted straddling the brake rotor (disc). The caliper contains at least one piston and two brake pads. Hydraulic pressure on the piston(s) forces the pads against the rotor.

CAMSHAFT: A shaft in the engine on which are the lobes (cams) which operate the valves. The camshaft is driven by the crankshaft, via a belt, chain or gears, at one half the crankshaft speed.

CAPACITOR: A device which stores an electrical charge.

CARBON MONOXIDE (CO): A colorless, odorless gas given off as a normal byproduct of combustion. It is poisonous and extremely dangerous in confined areas, building up slowly to toxic levels without warning if adequate ventilation is not available.

CARBURETOR: A device, usually mounted on the intake manifold of an engine, which mixes the air and fuel in the proper proportion to allow even combustion.

CATALYTIC CONVERTER: A device installed in the exhaust system, like a muffler, that converts harmful byproducts of combustion into carbon dioxide and water vapor by means of a heat-producing chemical reaction.

CENTRIFUGAL ADVANCE: A mechanical method of advancing the spark timing by using flyweights in the distributor that react to centrifugal force generated by the distributor shaft rotation.

CHECK VALVE: Any one-way valve installed to permit the flow of air, fuel or vacuum in one direction only.

CHOKE: A device, usually a moveable valve, placed in the intake path of a carburetor to restrict the flow of air.

CIRCUIT: Any unbroken path through which an electrical current can flow. Also used to describe fuel flow in some instances.

CIRCUIT BREAKER: A switch which protects an electrical circuit from overload by opening the circuit when the current flow exceeds a predetermined level. Some circuit breakers must be reset manually, while most reset automatically.

COIL (IGNITION): A transformer in the ignition circuit which steps up the voltage provided to the spark plugs.

COMBINATION MANIFOLD: An assembly which includes both the intake and exhaust manifolds in one casting.

COMBINATION VALVE: A device used in some fuel systems that routes fuel vapors to a charcoal storage canister instead of venting them into the atmosphere. The valve relieves fuel tank pressure and allows fresh air into the tank as the fuel level drops to prevent a vapor lock situation.

COMPRESSION RATIO: The comparison of the total volume of the cylinder and combustion chamber with the piston at BDC and the piston at TDC.

CONDENSER: 1. An electrical device which acts to store an electrical charge, preventing voltage surges. 2. A radiator-like device in the air conditioning system in which refrigerant gas condenses into a liquid, giving off heat.

CONDUCTOR: Any material through which an electrical current can be transmitted easily.

CONTINUITY: Continuous or complete circuit. Can be checked with an ohmmeter.

COUNTERSHAFT: An intermediate shaft which is rotated by a mainshaft and transmits, in turn, that rotation to a working part.

CRANKCASE: The lower part of an engine in which the crankshaft and related parts operate.

CRANKSHAFT: The main driving shaft of an engine which receives reciprocating motion from the pistons and converts it to rotary motion.

CYLINDER: In an engine, the round hole in the engine block in which the piston(s) ride.

CYLINDER BLOCK: The main structural member of an engine in which is found the cylinders, crankshaft and other principal parts.

CYLINDER HEAD: The detachable portion of the engine, usually fastened to the top of the cylinder block and containing all or most of the combustion chambers. On overhead valve engines, it contains the valves and their operating parts. On overhead cam engines, it contains the camshaft as well.

DEAD CENTER: The extreme top or bottom of the piston stroke.

DETONATION: An unwanted explosion of the air/fuel mixture in the combustion chamber caused by excess heat and compression, advanced timing, or an overly lean mixture. Also referred to as "ping".

DIAPHRAGM: A thin, flexible wall separating two cavities, such as in a vacuum advance unit.

DIESELING: A condition in which hot spots in the combustion chamber cause the engine to run on after the key is turned off.

DIFFERENTIAL: A geared assembly which allows the transmission of motion between drive axles, giving one axle the ability to turn faster than the other.

DIODE: An electrical device that will allow current to flow in one direction only.

DISC BRAKE: A hydraulic braking assembly consisting of a brake disc, or rotor, mounted on an axle, and a caliper assembly containing, usually two brake pads which are activated by hydraulic pressure. The pads are forced against the sides of the disc, creating friction which slows the vehicle.

DISTRIBUTOR: A mechanically driven device on an engine which is responsible for electrically firing the spark plug at a predetermined point of the piston stroke.

DOWEL PIN: A pin, inserted in mating holes in two different parts allowing those parts to maintain a fixed relationship.

DRUM BRAKE: A braking system which consists of two brake shoes and one or two wheel cylinders, mounted on a fixed backing plate, and a brake drum, mounted on an axle, which revolves around the assembly.

DWELL: The rate, measured in degrees of shaft rotation, at which an electrical circuit cycles on and off.

ELECTRONIC CONTROL UNIT (ECU): Ignition module, module, amplifier or igniter. See Module for definition.

ELECTRONIC IGNITION: A system in which the timing and firing of the spark plugs is controlled by an electronic control unit, usually called a module. These systems have no points or condenser.

END-PLAY: The measured amount of axial movement in a shaft.

ENGINE: A device that converts heat into mechanical energy.

EXHAUST MANIFOLD: A set of cast passages or pipes which conduct exhaust gases from the engine.

FEELER GAUGE: A blade, usually metal, of precisely predetermined thickness, used to measure the clearance between two parts.

FIRING ORDER: The order in which combustion occurs in the cylinders of an engine. Also the order in which spark is distributed to the plugs by the distributor.

FLOODING: The presence of too much fuel in the intake manifold and combustion chamber which prevents the air/fuel mixture from firing, thereby causing a no-start situation.

FLYWHEEL: A disc shaped part bolted to the rear end of the crankshaft. Around the outer perimeter is affixed the ring gear. The starter drive engages the ring gear, turning the flywheel, which rotates the crankshaft, imparting the initial starting motion to the engine.

FOOT POUND (ft. lbs. or sometimes, ft.lb.): The amount of energy or work needed to raise an item weighing one pound, a distance of one foot.

FUSE: A protective device in a circuit which prevents circuit overload by breaking the circuit when a specific amperage is present. The device is constructed around a strip or wire of a lower amperage rating than the circuit it is designed to protect. When an amperage higher than that stamped on the fuse is present in the circuit, the strip or wire melts, opening the circuit.

GEAR RATIO: The ratio between the number of teeth on meshing gears.

GENERATOR: A device which converts mechanical energy into electrical energy.

HEAT RANGE: The measure of a spark plug's ability to dissipate heat from its firing end. The higher the heat range, the hotter the plug fires.

HUB: The center part of a wheel or gear.

HYDROCARBON (HC): Any chemical compound made up of hydrogen and carbon. A major pollutant formed by the engine as a byproduct of combustion.

HYDROMETER: An instrument used to measure the specific gravity of a solution.

INCH POUND (inch lbs.; sometimes in.lb. or in. lbs.): One twelfth of a foot pound.

INDUCTION: A means of transferring electrical energy in the form of a magnetic field. Principle used in the ignition coil to increase voltage.

INJECTOR: A device which receives metered fuel under relatively low pressure and is activated to inject the fuel into the engine under relatively high pressure at a predetermined time.

INPUT SHAFT: The shaft to which torque is applied, usually carrying the driving gear or gears.

INTAKE MANIFOLD: A casting of passages or pipes used to conduct air or a fuel/air mixture to the cylinders.

JOURNAL: The bearing surface within which a shaft operates.

KEY: A small block usually fitted in a notch between a shaft and a hub to prevent slippage of the two parts.

MANIFOLD: A casting of passages or set of pipes which connect the cylinders to an inlet or outlet source.

MANIFOLD VACUUM: Low pressure in an engine intake manifold formed just below the throttle plates. Manifold vacuum is highest at idle and drops under acceleration.

MASTER CYLINDER: The primary fluid pressurizing device in a hydraulic system. In automotive use, it is found in brake and hydraulic clutch systems and is pedal activated, either directly or, in a power brake system, through the power booster.

MODULE: Electronic control unit, amplifier or igniter of solid state or integrated design which controls the current flow in the ignition primary circuit based on input from the pick-up coil. When the module opens the primary circuit, high secondary voltage is induced in the coil.

NEEDLE BEARING: A bearing which consists of a number (usually a large number) of long, thin rollers.

OHM:(Ω) The unit used to measure the resistance of conductor-to-electrical flow. One ohm is the amount of resistance that limits current flow to one ampere in a circuit with one volt of pressure.

OHMMETER: An instrument used for measuring the resistance, in ohms, in an electrical circuit.

OUTPUT SHAFT: The shaft which transmits torque from a device, such as a transmission.

OVERDRIVE: A gear assembly which produces more shaft revolutions than that transmitted to it.

OVERHEAD CAMSHAFT (OHC): An engine configuration in which the camshaft is mounted on top of the cylinder head and operates the valve either directly or by means of rocker arms.

OVERHEAD VALVE (OHV): An engine configuration in which all of the valves are located in the cylinder head and the camshaft is located in the cylinder block. The camshaft operates the valves via lifters and pushrods.

OXIDES OF NITROGEN (NOx): Chemical compounds of nitrogen produced as a byproduct of combustion. They combine with hydrocarbons to produce smog.

OXYGEN SENSOR: Used with the feedback system to sense the presence of oxygen in the exhaust gas and signal the computer which can reference the voltage signal to an air/fuel ratio.

PINION: The smaller of two meshing gears.

PISTON RING: An open-ended ring which fits into a groove on the outer diameter of the piston. Its chief function is to form a seal between the piston and cylinder wall. Most automotive pistons have three rings: two for compression sealing; one for oil sealing.

PRELOAD: A predetermined load placed on a bearing during assembly or by adjustment.

PRIMARY CIRCUIT: The low voltage side of the ignition system which consists of the ignition switch, ballast resistor or resistance wire, bypass, coil, electronic control unit and pick-up coil as well as the connecting wires and harnesses.

PRESS FIT: The mating of two parts under pressure, due to the inner diameter of one being smaller than the outer diameter of the other, or vice versa; an interference fit.

RACE: The surface on the inner or outer ring of a bearing on which the balls, needles or rollers move.

REGULATOR: A device which maintains the amperage and/or voltage levels of a circuit at predetermined values.

RELAY: A switch which automatically opens and/or closes a circuit.

RESISTANCE: The opposition to the flow of current through a circuit or electrical device, and is measured in ohms. Resistance is equal to the voltage divided by the amperage.

RESISTOR: A device, usually made of wire, which offers a preset amount of resistance in an electrical circuit.

RING GEAR: The name given to a ring-shaped gear attached to a differential case, or affixed to a flywheel or as part of a planetary gear set.

ROLLER BEARING: A bearing made up of hardened inner and outer races between which hardened steel rollers move.

ROTOR: 1. The disc-shaped part of a disc brake assembly, upon which the brake pads bear; also called, brake disc. 2. The device mounted atop the distributor shaft, which passes current to the distributor cap tower contacts.

SECONDARY CIRCUIT: The high voltage side of the ignition system, usually above 20,000 volts. The secondary includes the ignition coil, coil wire, distributor cap and rotor, spark plug wires and spark plugs.

SENDING UNIT: A mechanical, electrical, hydraulic or electromagnetic device which transmits information to a gauge.

SENSOR: Any device designed to measure engine operating conditions or ambient pressures and temperatures. Usually electronic in nature and designed to send a voltage signal to an on-board computer, some sensors may operate as a simple on/off switch or they may provide a variable voltage signal (like a potentiometer) as conditions or measured parameters change.

SHIM: Spacers of precise, predetermined thickness used between parts to establish a proper working relationship.

SLAVE CYLINDER: In automotive use, a device in the hydraulic clutch system which is activated by hydraulic force, disengaging the clutch.

SOLENOID: A coil used to produce a magnetic field, the effect of which is to produce work.

SPARK PLUG: A device screwed into the combustion chamber of a spark ignition engine. The basic construction is a conductive core inside of a ceramic insulator, mounted in an outer conductive base. An electrical charge from the spark plug wire travels along the conductive core and jumps a preset air gap to a grounding point or points at the end of the conductive base. The resultant spark ignites the fuel/air mixture in the combustion chamber.

SPLINES: Ridges machined or cast onto the outer diameter of a shaft or inner diameter of a bore to enable parts to mate without rotation.

TACHOMETER: A device used to measure the rotary speed of an engine, shaft, gear, etc., usually in rotations per minute.

THERMOSTAT: A valve, located in the cooling system of an engine, which is closed when cold and opens gradually in response to engine heating, controlling the temperature of the coolant and rate of coolant flow.

TOP DEAD CENTER (TDC): The point at which the piston reaches the top of its travel on the compression stroke.

TORQUE: The twisting force applied to an object.

TORQUE CONVERTER: A turbine used to transmit power from a driving member to a driven member via hydraulic action, providing changes in drive ratio and torque. In automotive use, it links the driveplate at the rear of the engine to the automatic transmission.

TRANSDUCER: A device used to change a force into an electrical signal.

TRANSISTOR: A semi-conductor component which can be actuated by a small voltage to perform an electrical switching function.

TUNE-UP: A regular maintenance function, usually associated with the replacement and adjustment of parts and components in the electrical and fuel systems of a vehicle for the purpose of attaining optimum performance.

TURBOCHARGER: An exhaust driven pump which compresses intake air and forces it into the combustion chambers at higher than atmospheric pressures. The increased air pressure allows more fuel to be burned and results in increased horsepower being produced.

VACUUM ADVANCE: A device which advances the ignition timing in response to increased engine vacuum.

VACUUM GAUGE: An instrument used to measure the presence of vacuum in a chamber.

VALVE: A device which control the pressure, direction of flow or rate of flow of a liquid or gas.

VALVE CLEARANCE: The measured gap between the end of the valve stem and the rocker arm, cam lobe or follower that activates the valve.

VISCOSITY: The rating of a liquid's internal resistance to flow.

VOLTMETER: An instrument used for measuring electrical force in units called volts. Voltmeters are always connected parallel with the circuit being tested.

WHEEL CYLINDER: Found in the automotive drum brake assembly, it is a device, actuated by hydraulic pressure, which, through internal pistons, pushes the brake shoes outward against the drums.

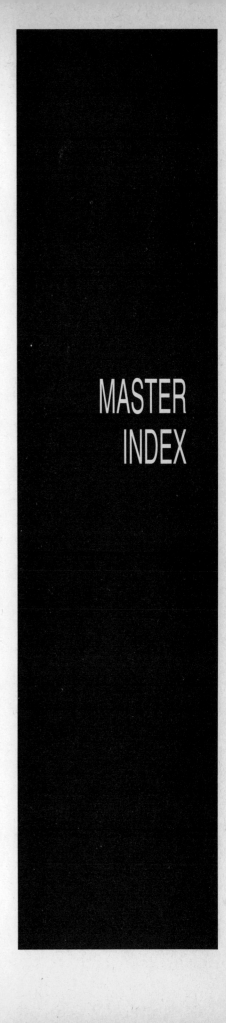

MASTER INDEX